St Helena
Ascension • Tristan da Cunha

THE BRADT TRAVEL GUIDE

THE BRADT STORY

The first Bradt travel guide was written by Hilary and George Bradt in 1974 on a river barge floating down a tributary of the Amazon in Bolivia. From their base in Boston, Massachusetts, they went on to write and publish four other backpacking guides to the Americas and one to Africa.

In the 1980s Hilary continued to develop the Bradt list in England, and also established herself as a travel writer and tour leader. The company's publishing emphasis evolved towards broader-based guides to new destinations – usually the first to be published on those countries – complemented by hiking, rail and wildlife guides.

Since winning *The Sunday Times* Small Publisher of the Year Award in 1997, we have continued to fill the demand for detailed, well-written guides to unusual destinations, while maintaining the company's original ethos of low-impact travel.

Travel guides are by their nature continuously evolving. If you experience anything which you would like to share with us, or if you have any amendments to make to this guide, please write; all your letters are read and passed on to the author. Most importantly, do remember to travel with an open mind and to respect the customs of your hosts – it will add immeasurably to your enjoyment.

Happy travelling!

Hilary Bradt

Hilary Bradt

19 High Street, Chalfont St Peter, Bucks SL9 9QE, England
Tel: 01753 893444 Fax: 01753 892333
Email: info@bradt-travelguides.com
Web: www.bradt-travelguides.com

St Helena

Ascension • Tristan da Cunha

THE BRADT TRAVEL GUIDE

Sue Steiner

Bradt Travel Guides Ltd, UK
The Globe Pequot Press Inc, USA

First published in 2002 by Bradt Travel Guides Ltd,
19 High Street, Chalfont St Peter, Bucks SL9 9QE, England
Published in the USA by The Globe Pequot Press Inc,
246 Goose Lane, PO Box 480, Guilford, Connecticut 06437-0480

British Library Cataloguing in Publication Data
A catalogue record for this book is available from the British Library
ISBN 1 84162 050 5

Library of Congress Cataloging-in-Publication Data applied for

Photographs
Front cover Ebony *Trochetiopsis ebenus* (W Stuppy/Royal Botanical Gardens, Kew)
Text Hans Mühlematter (HM), Neil Rusch (NR), Urs Steiner (US)

Illustrations Hedvika Fraser
Maps Steve Munns

Typeset from the author's disc by Wakewing, High Wycombe
Printed and bound in Italy by Legoprint SpA, Trento

Author

Sue Steiner is co-founder and part-owner of the Swiss-based tour operator, Xanadu Travel. She wrote and published a St Helena guide booklet in 1998.

Sue grew up in the northeast of the USA. After completing her education, she travelled across North America, Europe and northern Africa. Thousands of bus, train and cargoship miles later, she settled down in Switzerland. Becoming a mother of two beautiful daughters curtailed her travel activities to shorter and less out-of-the-way places.

A new opportunity for a long and exciting trip came in the second half of the 1990s. Sue's husband had amassed so much overtime that he could take leave from his work for nearly five months. Along with the children, who had not yet started school, they filled a 60-year-old steamer trunk, travelled up to Cardiff and boarded the *RMS St Helena* for a three-month stay on the island of St Helena.

That's when Sue fell in love with the people and the island of St Helena, at last understanding why her husband wanted to come back to this isolated place he had discovered during a brief visit in 1985.

Contents

LIST OF MAPS

Acknowledgements

A big thank you goes to my family and friends, without whose love, immense moral support and patience, I would not have been able to complete this book.

Other people who have helped me tremendously are as follows: Pamela Young and her staff at the St Helena Tourism Office for keeping me updated. Barbara George who gave me a lot of insight into life on St Helena. Julie Anthony and Geoffrey Fairhurst on Ascension Island for their co-operation and for answering all my queries at the last minute. Ian Mathieson, from Miles Apart, who helped me compile the list of books for further reading. Adam Kossowski, Stephen Fowler, John Ekwall, and Hans and Brigitte Mühlematter who kindly allowed me to use their photos and maps. Trevor Hearl for his helpful comments on the history of St Helena. These are just a few of the many who gave me their time, assistance and understanding.

I also don't want to forget to acknowledge Guy Marriott and Bradt Travel Guides for believing in me and making this guide possible.

DEDICATION

Dedicated to the people and the island of St Helena
who inspired me to share my unforgettable experience
on this magical island.

Introduction

In 1985, my husband made a ship's journey from Avonmouth in the UK to St Helena, stopping briefly at Tristan da Cunha, before continuing on to the final destination of Cape Town, South Africa. Over the years he talked about the island of St Helena and what a magical place it is. Many times he told me of his desire to return one day, and he wanted me to accompany him. Finally, in 1997, along with our two young children, we were able to make this much dreamed-about trip. A lot of planning went into what was not going to be just a normal holiday. We had saved up enough money and my husband had accumulated enough overtime from his job that we could spend three months on St Helena.

With much anticipation we made all the necessary preparations and arrangements to make this dream possible. My husband's enthusiasm was contagious and, even though I had little knowledge of the place where I was going to be living for a quarter of a year, I was very much looking forward to this family adventure.

Like most other people, what I knew of the island was quite limited. I knew that St Helena was the location of Napoleon Bonaparte's exile. Other than that, I was only familiar with the island though the many pictures, slides and stories my husband had shared with me. So what is so special about this isolated piece of land in the middle of nowhere, that would make people want to take the time and trouble to visit, and leave them with the desire to return again one day?

I realised there was something unique about St Helena the moment we anchored at James Bay and I saw the large number of people gathered at the wharf to welcome the ship and its passengers. Clearly, a good deal of them were there to greet family and loved ones. There are, however, those who stop what they are doing to go down to the bay just to get a glimpse of the ship and the people she has brought with her. It is only after spending some time on the island that you learn what a happy event it is to see the ship again, for St Helena is virtually 'in the middle of nowhere'. Only the *RMS St Helena* has a regularly scheduled service to the island, so when she makes her voyage to the UK four times a year, there is a period of at least six weeks in which no new people and no new supplies reach the island, unless the occasional cruise ship or yacht drops anchor.

Soon after arriving at the island, I got my first taste of the magic of this special place. Visitors are welcomed warmly by the Saints and, as in any small town, sometimes people know who you are before they actually meet you. We were frequently greeted with, 'Hello, you must be the Swiss family.' Before long we were being invited to tea or to parties. Quite often while we were walking someone would stop and offer us a ride to where we wanted to go. Having lived in a city for many years, I was a bit wary at first of so much 'friendliness', but what the people of this island do and say is genuine: they really do want to get to know you.

The island and the islanders taught me the concept of time. On St Helena, there is no reason to hurry. The islanders themselves are relaxed and, in time, you learn that you *can* put things off until tomorrow. It feels like another world, a slower-moving one, and it is good to stop for a friendly chat with someone. Somehow, what is happening elsewhere doesn't seem so grave or important.

This book deals mostly with St Helena and Ascension Island, two relatively unknown tourist destinations in the South Atlantic Ocean. It also covers the tiny island of Tristan da Cunha, with only 300 inhabitants, and four days' journey from St Helena by ship. All are unique in their own ways; all deserve to be more widely known.

For all its diverse attractions, St Helena is not the typical island paradise you would imagine. There are no luxurious sandy beaches with palm trees for shade. It is quite difficult to get to, accessible at present only by sea. Still, visitors come for many reasons. Some have family and friends they haven't met before or haven't seen for many years. Others have employment contracts with the UK government to fulfill. Still others have an intense interest in history, or see the unique flora and fauna as the big attraction. Then there are those who come to the island quite simply because it is there. I went with my own ideas of what things would be like, but the impression and memories I came back with were totally unexpected.

Personally, I have never been strongly interested in history. I knew very little about Napoleon's stay and I couldn't imagine what would be so fascinating about it. Yet after visiting Longwood House and spending some time in the interior of the island, I started to sense the loneliness and desperation Napoleon must have felt being kept captive here. Yes, the area where he lived is interesting and attractive, but he lacked the freedom to enjoy any of it. It gave me a whole new view on Napoleon as a person and how harsh a punishment his exile was for him.

During the time we lived on St Helena we developed a deep affection for the people. As with anything about which you have strong feelings, there are things that disturb you, that you want to change for the better. I was determined that somehow I would find a way to contribute something to the island, in order that more people could be made aware of this little-known place that has fascinated all who have found their way here. This is my way of giving something back to this island whose natural beauty was once compared to that rare jewel, an emerald set in bronze.

Part One

St Helena

ST HELENA AT A GLANCE

Location South Atlantic Ocean, 1,200 miles (1,950km) west of Angola and 1,800 miles (2,900km) from the east coast of Brazil

Size 47 square miles (122km²)

Highest point 2,685ft (818m)

Status British Overseas Dependent Territory

Dependencies Ascension, Tristan da Cunha

Capital Jamestown

Gross national product *Total* £10,530,000 (1994/95) *Per capita* £2,062 (1994/95)

Currency St Helena pound (= £1 sterling)

Population 5,157 (1998)

Population growth rate 0.76% (2000 estimate)

Birth rate per 1,000 population 11.3 (2000)

Death rate per 1,000 population 8.5 (2000)

Infant mortality per 1,000 live births 3.6 (2000)

Life expectancy at birth 75.0 (male 70.8, female 77.2)

Language English

Religion Predominantly Christian

Flag Blue with the flag of the UK in the upper quadrant and the St Helena shield centred on the outer half of the flag; the shield features a rocky coastline and a three-masted sailing ship, with the wirebird at the top.

National anthem 'God save the Queen'

National flower Arum lily

National bird Wirebird

National tree Gumwood tree

Time GMT

Electricity 240V, 50Hz. The standard electrical socket is the 13-amp flat pin used in the UK.

International dialling code + 290

Background Information

GEOGRAPHY AND CLIMATE

St Helena is situated 5° 43' west, and 15° 56' south. The nearest land is Ascension Island, located 703 miles (1,200km) to the northwest. The nearest mainland is the west coast of Angola, about 1,200 miles (1,950km) away. To the west, about 1,800 miles (2,900km) away, is the east coast of Brazil. The territorial sea measures 12 nautical miles. The exclusive fishing zone is 200 nautical miles.

Since the island is of volcanic origin, the terrain is steep and rocky, with small, scattered plateaux and plains. Rising dramatically from the ocean, the island has sheer barren cliffs that are intersected with deep valleys, or 'guts' as they are called locally, which slope steeply from the central ridges. There is very little flat land. Access to the sea by car is only possible in three places: Jamestown, Rupert's Bay and Sandy Bay. The island has no sandy beaches. The highest point on St Helena is Diana's Peak at 2,685ft (818m). On the higher central ground, bush and semi-tropical vegetation is plentiful. This changes to grassland and pastures before the terrain becomes drier and semi-barren below 1,640ft (500m) and down to the sea. There are a very few small mountain streams, which occasionally dry up in the summer months.

In spite of the fact that St Helena is located in the tropics, her climate is kept mild, equable and healthy by the southeast tradewinds. On the whole, summers are warm and sunny, and winters are cool and mild, with moderate rain. There are noticeable climatical differences between Jamestown, located on the northern coast, and the interior of the island. Jamestown can be sunny and humid, while at the same time in Longwood, they would be experiencing cool mists and a higher amount of rainfall.

In the past ten years annual rainfall has averaged ten inches (259mm) in Jamestown and about 32 to 43 inches (800–1,100mm) below the peaks of the central hills. As with many isolated places, St Helena has its share of water shortages. During these times, a water restriction is put into effect on certain parts of the island, and water may be used only at certain times of the day.

Temperatures vary at different points around the island. The interior, which is at a higher elevation, is cooler than in the capital. In Jamestown, the warmest area on the island, the temperature averages 68–86°F (20–30°C), while inland the temperatures are considerably cooler with an average of 57–72°F (14–22°C). Humidity varies between 75% and 94%. The windiest area of the island is Bottom Woods, whilst Scotland is the area with the least wind and the least sunshine per month.

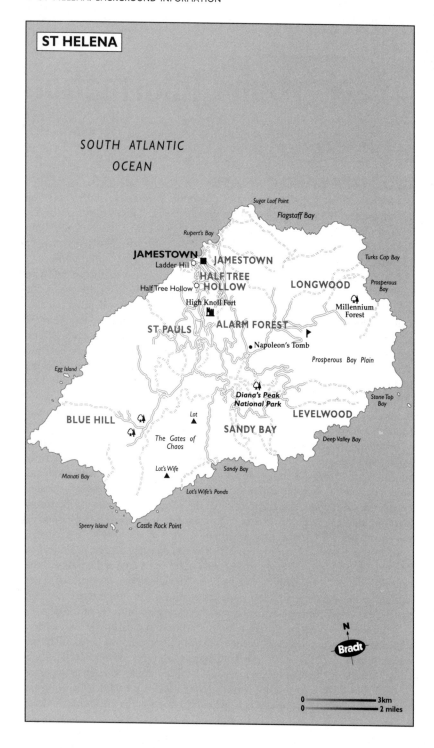

NATURAL HISTORY AND CONSERVATION
Flora
David Sayers

More than any other of the world's isolated oceanic islands, St Helena is most famously associated with rare and endemic plants, thanks to well-documented conservation work by the Wildlife Fund for Nature (WWF), the Royal Botanic Gardens, Kew and other organisations. Plant species have been pulled back from the very brink of extinction, and the island is a showcase for the international conservation role of botanic gardens. That said, most of the original vegetation has been almost totally destroyed and some 60% of the island is now bare, eroded rock, colonised in places by a few tough alien plant species. Over two thirds of the island is classified as barren Crown Wastes. Although much of the interior of the island remains green, this is due to the imported exotic vegetation.

History

Approaching the island and seeing today's bare rocky cliffs ascending from the sea one can only conjecture as to how these impressive cliffs appeared to the first Portuguese who landed here in the early 1500s. There are no contemporary descriptions of the native vegetation, and almost as soon as the island was discovered destruction of the forests began. It was not until 1771, when Captain James Cook's *Endeavour* called at the island on the way back from Australia, that the discovery of St Helena's botany really took off. On board were the great naturalists, Banks and Solander, who collected many specimens and brought them back to Europe.

Most of the native forests had already been well cleared earlier in the 18th century, before their visit, so there are no scientific accounts of the flora as it was originally. By carefully looking at historical references in various sources, allied with knowledge of the distribution of the indigenous flora from the few remaining locations, botanists today have been able to picture what the island might have been like. The now barren rocks down to sea level would have been covered with scrubwood scrub, *Commidendrum rugosum*, and ebony, *Trochetiopsis ebenus*. Above these, from about 400m to 600m, a low forest of gumwood, *Commidendrum robustum*, with a canopy height of about 6m, would have covered the island with other associated species. Between 600m and 750m one would have had to ascend through a woodland of cabbage trees – the now almost extinct false gumwood, *Commidendrum spurium*, the she cabbage, *Lachanodes arborea*, now with just two tiny populations left in the wild, whitewood, *Petrobium arboreum*, redwood, *Trochetiopsis eryhtroxylon*, now extinct in the wild, and finally the he cabbage tree, *Pladaroxylon leucadendron* – before emerging into a landscape dominated by the endemic tree fern, *Dicksonia arborescens*, between 700m and 800m. We know the species that have become extinct since scientific records began; what we cannot know is how many more species became extinct before this.

Today, in spite of the ravages caused by humans and their animals, there remain extant in tiny, isolated and often almost inaccessible refugia, 49

GEOLOGY OF ST HELENA, ASCENSION AND TRISTAN DA CUNHA

Tim Ireland

Perhaps surprisingly, the islands of the South Atlantic Ocean are not randomly located. They are all of volcanic origin, and relate directly to locations of highly anomalous heat-flow from the Earth. Some 120 million years ago, extreme heat-flow in the same locations caused an ancient supercontinent to rift apart, separating the modern Africa and South American continental blocks. Yes, the continents move.

St Helena, Ascension and Tristan da Cunha are isolated, broadly conical volcanic edifices that each rise more than 3,000m above the ocean floor, and actually cause the oceanic crust to subside beneath their weight. They are located on the flanks of the Mid-Atlantic Ridge (MAR), a continuous volcanic ridge that runs the entire length of the Atlantic Ocean, but rather than being a result of the MAR, they are part of its cause. There are hundreds of similar volcanoes, but the vast majority are concealed beneath the water. The islands themselves are the tip of the proverbial iceberg; only 1% of the total volume of Ascension is exposed above water.

Formation

The islands are geologically very young; volcanism on St Helena ceased only 8 million years ago, and on Ascension only 500,000 years ago; Tristan da Cunha has formed entirely in the last 210,000 years. (By comparison, humans evolved about 2 million years ago, the dinosaurs died out 63 million years ago, and the Earth formed over 3.6 billion years ago.) Tristan da Cunha erupted in 1961, and is likely to erupt again. That would truly be worth seeing – volcanism in the South Atlantic has been exciting compared to that in other famous volcanic archipelagos such as Hawaii. In addition to lava flows indicative of effusive eruption, these South Atlantic islands are also composed of a roughly equal proportion of fire-fragment (pyroclastic) rocks. Deep underground, molten rock contains significant amounts of dissolved gases. Eruption at the surface causes dramatic release of the confining pressure, and the contained gases expand and explode inside the lava, tearing it into tiny fragments that are propelled into the air as a cloud of scalding ash. Lava is erupted at temperatures around 1,000°C, and because there is abundant water in the oceanic environment, eruptions on volcanic islands are often augmented by steam explosions caused by instantaneous boiling of seawater upon contact with lava or ash.

Each island consists of many – possibly several hundred – overlapping volcanic cones and fissures from which lava and/or ash has erupted. On Tristan da Cunha there is a clear distinction between a main, repeatedly active central crater zone, and a peripheral zone of multiple, small-scale, single-event explosive cones. Volcanism began on the sea floor, and each eruption has built on to the edifice, so that today the formation breaches sea level.

The rocks generated by volcanism on the South Atlantic islands have a distinctive and diverse chemistry that tell us about the interior of our planet. At any one time, there are up to 20 spots around the world where heat is channelled from the Earth's interior toward the surface. High heat-flow causes dramatically increased melting of the Earth's mantle, and a plume of ascending molten material causes volcanoes at the surface. The lavas of Ascension, St Helena and Tristan da Cunha are indisputably of mantle origin; they tend to contain no quartz, unusually high concentrations of sodium and potassium, and have characteristic patterns of radioactive and trace element abundance. The chemistry of these lavas suggests that they are the result of selective partial melting of the most easily mobilised components of the original mantle.

Seamounts

Undersea volcanoes (called 'seamounts') occur along parallel linear ridges in the South Atlantic that lead northeast to mainland Africa – from Tristan da Cunha to Namibia and from St Helena to Cameroon/Nigeria – becoming progressively older as they approach the continent. The rocks of each seamount chain share a subtle geochemical 'fingerprint' that is characteristic of a particular mantle plume. Ascension is not part of a seamount chain, and is considered to be caused by a weak and intermittent plume.

The upwelling plumes of molten material are evidence of convection in the upper part of the mantle. The Earth's crust consists of numerous discrete plates, and these are pushed around by convective currents in the mantle like buoyant rafts. When the dinosaurs were at their prime, Africa and South America were part of the same continent, Gondwanaland. At that time, several new plumes, including those under St Helena and Tristan da Cunha, emerged under Gondwanaland, and split the supercontinent along a zig-zag line connecting the plumes. As the continents have continued to rift apart along the MAR, the African plate has slid over the stationary plume sites, which continue to cause volcanism. Broadly, as a volcano forms on the sea floor, the continent drifts slowly past the plume, and the molten rock finds a new conduit to the surface, thus forming a new volcano. In this way, seamount chains are formed.

There are other, less well-defined seamount chains in the western Atlantic, that trace back to volcanic rocks in Brazil. Realisation of continuous sequential age progression, from continental volcanic rocks out along the seamount chains to the volcanic islands near the MAR, is one of a handful of strong arguments for the widely accepted 'Continental Drift' theory.

endemic species (including six genera) of ferns and flowering plants that occur naturally only on St Helena and nowhere else in the world. Some of them have grown on St Helena for over eight million years, surviving while their relatives on distant land masses became extinct through climate change.

So, how could St Helena, with an unspoiled environment, so quickly change by human incursion into one of the world's most spectacularly eroded islands?

For voyagers into largely unknown seas and facing numerous hazards, this island was understandably viewed as a source of supplies on a very long voyage. The Portuguese kept their island a secret and, although they did not establish any permanent settlement, they planted large numbers of fruit trees, especially lemons, limes and oranges, and introduced pigs and, significantly, goats. These animals are the curse of botanists the world over, for their appetites are voracious; they bred well and quickly and at one time were said to be in their thousands. Culinary herbs and vegetables were also brought, such as parsley, fennel, mint and purslane, melon and pumpkin that thrived and spread, alongside the various weeds unwittingly introduced. It must have seemed a paradise garden to the sailors, a mid-ocean supply of fresh fruit and herbs, and abundant meat for the shooting. Indeed, as sea traffic increased with the development of trade it later became the equivalent of a motorway café on the run between the East Indies, the Cape and Europe.

In 1588 the British discovered the island and with the ascendance of Dutch and British naval power these two nations continued where the Portuguese left off, except that they took what was there and ceased to care for the plantations. As a consequence produce and pigs declined and the Dutch came to prefer their new Cape of Good Hope settlement, established in 1652.

When the East India Company annexed the island in 1659 they promptly encouraged settlement and change accelerated as the remaining forests were felled for fuel or tan bark, or cleared for pasture. They also introduced seeds of plants, such as various grasses, English oak, and gorse, *Ulex europaeus*, for fuel wood and hedging.

Early houses were of simple design made of roughly dressed volcanic rock, usually bound with a mud or lime mortar mixed with the cut leaves of hair grass, *Eragrostis saxatalis*; this is now one of St Helena's rare endemics, found only on inaccessible cliffs and rocky places, but must have once been widespread. The roof was thatched with indigenous *Scirpus nodosus*, a sedge relative. Native timbers known to have been used in house construction included redwood, *Trochetiopsis erythroxylon*, she cabbage, *Lachanodes arborea*, he cabbage, *Pladaroxylon leucadendron*, black cabbage, *Melanodendron integrifolium*, and gumwood *Commiodendrum robustum*, all endemic species.

By 1700 a serious timber shortage had been created by the overuse of the native forests, but another 50 years had to pass before the introduction of the first successful timber-producing species, *Pinus pinaster*, a native of the Mediterranean region which today may be seen planted in many parts of the world. When Joseph Banks returned to London he influenced the establishment of a small botanic garden on the island, located on a site below the present hospital in Jamestown; the large Indian fig trees are its most obvious legacy. This was simply another link in what became an empire-wide chain of gardens designed to facilitate the import and exchange of useful plants. New introductions came from the Calcutta botanic gardens, Cape Town, from Kew, and from other colonies, and included grapefruit, coffee, quinine, *Cinchona succirubra*, sugar and many others. Either by accident or by intent, other species were introduced that escaped and became dreadful weeds, such as Madagascar's attractive endemic *Buddleja madagascariensis* and the South American *Solanum mauritianum*, now seemingly in every corner of the world. From a legacy of plant introduction during the past 500 years there are now some 270 species firmly naturalised on the island. These have not only created new vegetation types on the lands previously cleared of the native forest, but they also seriously compete with what little remains of the native flora and further threaten its survival. The goats that at one time were numbered in their thousands were, after many attempts, finally controlled in the 1960s, so at last allowing the vegetation to begin to regenerate.

The present vegetation cover

Again, beginning at sea level with those bare and eroded hillsides, one may find the Hottentot fig, *Carpobrotus edulis*, an evergreen succulent ground creeper from South Africa that can form extensive patches with large, quite spectacular, flowers. Also to be found is its Cape relative, *Mesembryanthemum crystallinum*, another succulent but with tiny pink flowers, and the pretty Madagascan endemic periwinkle, *Catharanthus rosea*, all now pan-tropical weeds. At higher elevation, but before one reaches the good agricultural land, there is a scrub zone dominated in different places by different species; perhaps prickly pear, *Opuntia* spp. or elsewhere Brazilian mastic, *Schinus terebinthifolius*, with its showy holly-like berries, or that dreadful weed curse of the tropics, *Lantana camara* from Mexico, much loved by gardeners with conservatories in cold countries. Other common species include *Nicotiana glauca*, *Pittosporum undulatum*, *Olea africana* and more. The cultivated landscape includes grasslands of introduced species, mostly kikuyu grass, *Pennisetum clandestinum*, in the moister areas, while the woodlands are of pine species. Unmissable are the extensive areas of pure New Zealand flax, *Phormium tenax*; its successful naturalisation and aggression probably identifies it as the greatest plant killer of what was left of the indigenous flora. During the late 19th and into the following century it was widely planted on the central ridge for cordage and sacking, and was the island's main industry until the 1960s. Finally, and above 2,300ft (700m) or so, are the few hectares of what remains of the tree-fern thicket, the vegetation that covered the high central ridge and particularly Diana's Peak and High Peak. Here one finds endemic dogwood, *Nesohedyotis arborea*, black cabbage, *Melanodendron integrifolium*, and whitewood, *Petrobium arborea*. Even here New Zealand flax threatens, along with other invaders, including *Fuchsia coccinea*. For details of the individual plants, see *Appendix 1, Endemic Flora of St Helena*, page 145.

Where to find these endemic plants

It is the places inaccessible to humans and goats that still support many of the rarities, so that any cliff vegetation is always well worth scanning carefully to see what one might recognise or see in flower. Peak Gut waterfall is a good location. Content yourself with binoculars, however, since attempts at closer inspection can be hazardous. For other habitats, it is a long walk to higher altitudes. Cabbage trees may be seen at High Peak and, via Cabbage Tree Road, Cuckhold's Point, while the woodland of Peak Dale gumwood via Thompson Wood Hill is a good place to see dryland plants. Please remember that these endemic plants are very rare and often extremely slow growing, so you should always take great care to minimise your impact upon them and their habitat; the endemics are protected by Ordinance and there are fines for damaging them. In fact, unless you have a serious interest in botany, these rare plants are better and certainly more easily seen in the island's gardens such as in the public gardens in Jamestown, the George Benjamin Arboretum and the headquarters of the Agricultural and Natural Resources Department at Scotland.

Conservation

There has long been concern at the disappearance of the native flora, and rare endemics have been propagated and grown in attempts by a few individuals to save them, but it was only in the 1950s, upon the initiative of N R Kerr, St Helena's then Superintendent of Education, that real conservation work began. Beginning in the 1970s and especially the following decade, cooperation between the Agricultural and Forestry Department, the Foreign and Commonwealth Office, the Fauna and Flora Preservation Society, the WWF and the Royal Botanic Gardens, Kew saw attempts to propagate many endemic species. Species have been retrieved from the edge of extinction, in at least one case literally from the very last surviving plant, while others have been down to the last handful; some have been extinct in the wild and only survived as rare specimens in gardens. Certain species have proved exceedingly difficult to propagate or, while possible to raise from seed, have proved intractable in cultivation. Mercifully, others have been very successful and sufficient numbers have been built up to allow planting in public places and in some cases even experimental planting on a larger scale, while local people are encouraged to buy native plants from the Environmental Conservation Section of the Agricultural and Natural Resources Department to plant in their gardens. In March 1996 Diana's Peak was proclaimed St Helena's first national park, covering 64 hectares of tree fern thicket on the three main peaks along the central ridge; one of the principal management tasks is to control and eliminate the alien invaders, buddleja, solanum, flax and whiteweed, *Eupatorium pallidum*.

The island has recovery programmes for 14 species that involve monitoring, propagation, establishment of and maintenance of seed orchards, seed collection and storage, and re-introduction. The millennium was marked with a project to plant a forest of the national tree, the gumwood, on wasteland around Horse Point. To date, around 4,400 trees have been planted by islanders for friends and relatives overseas, as well as by visitors and for others who have bought trees to be planted on their behalf.

Several endemics are desirable ornamental species – 'old father live forever' has been grown in English greenhouses since the 18th century – but as with all plant species under threat it is their unique chemical compounds that are potentially most important to save for future generations. It is these compounds, too, that may in time reveal important properties for humans. Although some species have been 'saved', for the moment at least, all too often it is from the last remaining plant/s and thus from a very narrow genetic base so that the important genetic diversity of the species has in any case been lost.

For details of conservation programmes, see *Appendix 2*, page 158.

Fauna

The first Portuguese who explored the island found an abundance of seabirds, sea-lions, seals and turtles. No other animals were said to have been found. Today, the fauna on the island largely comprises introduced species: cattle, sheep, goats, donkeys, cats, dogs, rabbits, mice, rats and various types of fowl. There are no snakes, but there is one type of frog, which was probably introduced to St Helena along with the mynah birds in 1885 by Miss Phoebe Moss. There are, however, a good variety of endemic invertebrate fauna, including some unusually large examples of their species.

Birds

There is only one bird indigenous to St Helena and that is the wirebird. Other native species of birds died out long ago due to natural predators (rats, cats and humans) and the environmental changes that these brought to the island. All the other birds now to be seen have been introduced to the island from other countries, although they can be just as interesting to observe for the avid birdwatcher.

Wirebird *Aegialitis sanctae-helenae* The wirebird, the national bird of St Helena, is a small, long-legged, grey-brown plover with white underparts and a black mask extending to the sides of the neck. It is the last surviving bird native to St Helena, the only place where it can be found. These birds prefer flat areas of short grassland with patches of bare ground. They eat mainly caterpillars, beetles and snails. They breed throughout the year, but most nesting occurs from October to March, during the dry season. They usually lay two eggs at a time. The success rate of both chicks living to maturity is somewhat low due to predators. The most common of these are cats, rats and dogs, who tend to chase away the adults, then take the eggs or the young chicks. Mynah birds are also known to raid the nests of the wirebird. Other factors which have contributed to the disturbance of the wirebird's habitat are livestock and vehicles, the construction of new buildings and the overgrazing of pasture land.

There is strong evidence that Prosperous Bay Plain was once the nesting ground of the wirebird, and this was probably its original habitat. The plain is now designated as part of the Crown Wastes, so grazing of domestic stock is prohibited. As for human activity, there is some small-scale rock-quarrying, and vehicles have access for fishing, hiking and motor-cross.

The 'Wirebird Project' is a Darwin Initiative-funded project supervised by Dr Neil McCulloch and Dr Ken Norris of the University of Reading. The aims of this project are to:

- estimate the number of wirebirds on the island and see how this compares to the census, which was done in 1989
- determine environmental changes in the wirebird sites since 1989
- determine birth and death rates of the wirebird
- identify the main threats to the wirebird
- train ECS (Environmental Conservation System) staff in the survey-techniques and methods of monitoring the habitat and tagging of the birds
- raise public awareness of the wirebird and its conservation problems

The project was started in November 1998 and was scheduled to run until the year 2001.

Two censuses have already been carried out and have revealed a substantial decline of about 20% in the number of birds.

Yellow canary, *Serinus flaviventris*, comes from southern Africa and is quite common throughout the island. The male is the more attractive of the species, with streaked green upper parts. The breast-belly and band above the eyes are yellow. The female is grey-green streaked, and has a short stubby bill. They are about five inches (13cm) in size. They feed mainly on seeds which they find in gardens and in the undergrowth, but also on fruit and insects.

Madagascar fody *Foundia madagascaniensis* Known on the island as 'cardinals', these small red birds originated in Madagascar. They are easily recognised, especially during the breeding season when the head and breast turn an intense scarlet colour.

Chukar partridge *Alectoris chukar* These birds were probably brought to the island, from the Persian Gulf area, in the late 16th century by the Portuguese. Captain Thomas Cavendish reported a large quantity of these birds during his stop at St Helena in 1588. Today they can be found in the more remote parts of the island, preferring the more arid areas. They are mostly grey all over with a black band from the eyes, down to below the neck. They also have several black bars on the flanks. They have a bright red bill and legs. The females of the species have a smaller knob on the legs and are smaller than the males.

Peaceful dove *Geopelia striata* Known locally as 'turtle doves', these dusty grey birds can be found in drier areas where open woodland and scrub predominate. On St Helena they can often be seen along the wooded roadsides in the centre of the island, and picking up fallen seeds in the public gardens in Jamestown. They are native to Australia and were probably introduced to St Helena during the early 18th century.

Fairy tern *Gygis alba* Considered the most elegant and beautiful of all seabirds, the fairy tern is called locally the 'white bird'. They have delicate, translucent wings and large, jet-black eyes. They are a seabird, but strangely enough, they build no nest. Instead they lay their eggs in trees, the egg usually precariously balanced in the hollow of a branch, or on buildings or cliff faces. Eggs have even been found on the ledges of the windows of St James Church in Jamestown. Not surprisingly, many eggs are lost in high winds. They are extremely inquisitive and think nothing of flying close over the heads of passers-by.

Java sparrow *Padda oryzivora* These attractive bluish-grey birds, with their distinctive black head and tail, white cheek patches, lilac breast and heavy red bill, are relatively common to the island. They were introduced to the island from Indonesia in the early part of the 19th century.

Noddy terns There are two species of noddy found on St Helena. The black noddy, *Anous minutus,* may appear to be black, but on closer inspection is actually a very dark brown, with a white cap and a long fine bill. They build their nests on sheer cliff faces out of guano and seaweed. The brown noddy, *Anous stolidus,* is the larger of the two species. It is almost entirely chocolate-brown in colour and has a greyish-white cap extending from its forehead to its crown. The wings are a darker brown at the tips and edges. They prefer sandy beaches and trees, but on St Helena usually frequent rock crevices or ledges.

Madeiran storm petrel *Oceanodroma castro* This is one of the rarer seabirds to be found on St Helena. It is known to breed on George, Shore and Egg islands, and possibly on Speery Island off the southwest coast of St Helena. This small bird is about eight inches (20cm) long. It is mainly dark brown below, but with a black back and a clear white patch on the rump. The bill is short and black and the tail is slightly forked. It nests in crevices in rock piles and stone walls, or burrows in soft earth. Madeiran storm petrels like to fly close to the tops of the waves. They are rarely seen away from their breeding grounds, but occasionally one has been spotted in James Bay at dusk.

Sooty tern *Sterna fuscata* Also known as 'wideawakes', sooty terns are quite numerous on Ascension Island, but some use Speery Island as their breeding ground. In recent years, the population on St Helena has been declining and no one knows why. These beautiful birds are black on the upper parts, legs and bill. Their underparts and forehead are white. They have long narrow wings and a forked tail. Their face is white with a black stripe running across the eyes to the base of the bill. They are about 28 inches (44cm) in length. They skim the water to obtain their food, primarily fish and squid.

Ring-necked pheasant *Phasianus colchicus* The first mention of these birds was by Captain Thomas Cavendish when he visited the island in 1588. They were probably brought to the island from China by the Portuguese. Despite being actively hunted during the open season, there still remains a healthy population. They prefer the thick cover of the woodland, making it difficult for the casual passer-by to spot them. The male of the species is green, red and copper in colour with a long tail. The female, on the other hand, is a dull greyish-brown.

Red-billed tropicbird *Phaethon aethereus* These are known locally as 'trophy birds'. They are pelagic birds which nest on St Helena and Ascension Island, and are about the size of a large gull. The body and head are white with fine black barring on their back. The outer feathers on the wings are also black. A dark patch around the eye sometimes extends across the nape. They have a dagger-like scarlet bill and spectacular long white tail streamers. They tend to inhabit almost inaccessible places like the cliffs between Breakneck Valley and Jamestown. Their diet consists of small fish and squid.

St Helena waxbill *Estrilda astrild* Locally they are called 'avadavat', and are one of the most common birds on St Helena. These members of the finch family are the smallest of the bird species on the island. They originate in tropical and southern Africa, but no one knows for sure when they were first introduced to the island: most likely some time during the 19th century. The common waxbill has very pronounced dark, cross-barring on its dark-brown upperparts and flanks, a brown rump and a dark-brown tail. It has a beautiful scarlet colour down the centre of the belly, a waxy, coral-red bill and a crimson stripe through the eye. These tiny birds measure about four inches (9.5cm) and are usually seen in large flocks of up to 200 birds. They inhabit open grassland, farmland, cultivated fields, marshes, grassy clearings in forests, and areas near human habitation, especially abandoned farms.

Common mynah bird *Acridotheres tristis* This is probably the most common bird on St Helena. They were introduced to the island in 1829 in order to try to control cattle ticks and other pests. By 1875 they had almost totally disappeared. In 1885, five mynah birds were brought from India by Miss Phoebe Moss, a naturalist, and released near her home at The Briars. Since then, the mynah birds have multiplied out of control to become a pest due to the loud noise that they make and the serious menace they pose to fruit-growers. These birds are about ten inches (25cm) in size. Their bodies are black and brown with white wing patches and the bill is an orange-yellow.

Rock dove *Columba livia* This bird is also known as the 'feral pigeon'. It is found in certain limited areas such as the cliffs of Briars Valley. The rock dove has a dark bluish-grey head, neck and chest, with glossy yellow, green and reddish colouring along its neck and wing feathers. The bill is dark greyish-pink. Two dark bands across the wings are seen in most birds of this species, with one bluish-grey band across the tail.

Earwigs, spiders, insects and other small creatures

Giant earwig *Labidura herculeana* Probably the world's largest earwig, this measures up to 3 inches (8cm) in length. It usually occupied the damp environment of the gumwood forest floor, but has not been seen in over 30 years. Some years ago there was a big expedition launched to search for evidence that there are any of these rare insects remaining. Unfortunately the search was fruitless and none were discovered.

Blushing snail *Succinea sanctae-helenae* These little snails can be found in three different habitats: the cool Peaks, the stream gorges and the arid plains. This particular species, richly pink in colour, is quite common and can be seen crawling along the flax. It is the only remaining species of snail left on the island that is considered to be common; most other species are now extinct.

Spiky yellow woodlouse *Laureola atlantica* This creature, along with related species from places as far apart as South America, Madagascar, Australia and South Africa, is a relic of creatures from millions of years ago. Today they are found only on the endemic plants of Diana's Peak National Park, mainly on High Peak, living on the tree fern, redwood and dogwood.

Golden sail spider *Argyrodes excelsa* This is one of only 45 or 46 endemic spiders on St Helena, none of which are known to be poisonous. It has long fragile legs and hangs upside down on the endemic ferns.

St Helena also has about 77 endemic species of **weevil**. From just a few early ancestors which landed on St Helena millions of years ago, these weevils have evolved into different species with different roles.

It is estimated that 61% of the 256 species of beetle found on the island are endemic to St Helena. The **giant ground beetle**, *Anthina thoracica*, which once occupied the drier scrub land, has not been seen in over 30 years and is thought to have become extinct due to loss of habitat. Another probable victim of extinction is the **St Helena dragonfly**, *Sympetrum dilatatum*.

Marine life

Of the wide variety of marine life to be seen off the shores of St Helena, the following are endemic:

St Helena deepwater scorpionfish *Pontinus nigropunctatus* These fish are found only off the coast of St Helena and the Bonaparte Seamount, about 81 miles (130km) west of St Helena. The species was discovered in about 1868. They can live in both temperate and tropical waters and are carnivorous. Typical characteristics of scorpionfish are their venous spines. They have a bony ridge under their eye which has four spiny points. Many small teeth occupy their jaws. Their bodies are whitish in colour, with numerous dark-brown spots on their back and yellow-brown spots on their underside. The head and fins are reddish. They can reach a size of 14 inches (35cm) in length. Occasionally a fisherman will catch one. The soft white flesh is considered excellent to eat.

The spotted scorpionfish, *Scorpaena plumieri*, is more widely spread, and may also be found off the coast of Ascension Island.

Silver eel *Ariosoma mellissii* This rare eel was discovered in 1870, and is known only on St Helena. To date there have been three instances where one has been caught: once in 1909 and twice in 1930. It has pectoral combined dorsal fins that are continuous around the tail. Its powerful jaws have small teeth at the front and one or two rows of teeth at the back.

Bradt Travel Guides is a partner to the new 'know before you go' campaign, recently launched by the UK Foreign and Commonwealth Office. By combining the up-to-date advice of the FCO with the in-depth knowledge of Bradt authors, you'll ensure that your trip will be as trouble-free as possible.

www.fco.gov.uk/knowbeforeyougo

History

Once an isolated 'piece of rock' located in the middle of nowhere, St Helena slowly gained importance as a supply stop. After the island was settled, numerous important events took place. Much has been written on Napoleon's exile on St Helena, of course, but there are many other events that have shaped St Helena into what she is today.

DISCOVERY AND THE PORTUGUESE

On May 21 1502, the Portuguese admiral João da Nova, who was returning home from the west coast of India after defeating a fleet belonging to the Zamorin, came upon the island. The day of its discovery was the anniversary of St Helena, the mother of Emperor Constantine. In honour of her he called the island Santa Helena and claimed it in the name of the king of Portugal.

Da Nova anchored on the leeward side of the island opposite a deep valley. A timber chapel was built in the valley which later became the site of Jamestown, the capital of the island. It was originally called 'Chapel Valley'. When he set out to explore the island, he discovered seabirds, sea lions, seals and turtles, but no inhabitants were found. The interior of the island was covered by dense forest and the cliffs with gumwood trees. The only landbird he found was supposedly the wirebird, which is still in existence today (see page 11).

The Portuguese soon realised the significance of the location of this island, between the Cape of Good Hope and Cape Verde. It would serve them well as a calling point to replenish the supplies of ships sailing home from the east. The island was also used to offload sick crew members; if they survived, they were taken back on the ships upon their return to the island. They were able to keep the existence of the island a secret for over 80 years.

The English explorer, Captain Thomas Cavendish, landed on St Helena on June 8 1588 while on the last stage of his voyage around the world on his ship *Desire*. He remained here for 12 days, and found that the island had been regularly used by Portuguese sailors on their voyages from the East Indies. He discovered that a church, as well as two houses, had been constructed, and there were three Negro slaves living there. Vegetables and herbs (parsley, sorrel, basil, fennel, anise seed and mustard seed) had been planted, and many trees (fig, lemon, orange, pomegranate, and date) grew there. The island was also home to many pigs and goats which had been left to breed to provide food for the ships' crews which made a stop there.

The island was now no longer the secret of the Portuguese. In 1592, King Philip II of Spain and Portugal warned his fleet not to stop at St Helena on their return from Goa. Through Cavendish's discovery, English captains had learned of the heavily laden Portuguese ships returning from India and were lying in wait at St Helena to attack these ships on their way home.

The Dutch, too, now had an interest in the trade route once dominated by the Portuguese. One Dutch expedition called at St Helena on April 13 1601, on their way back to Europe. The two ships came under fire from a Spanish ship and, after an earnest fight, the Dutch ships retreated and sailed away towards Ascension Island.

Little by little the Portuguese drew back from the island, and they called less and less. They felt that the English and the Dutch had destroyed the peaceful and unspoiled place that the island had once been.

By the beginning of the 17th century, Portugal no longer laid claim to St Helena, and no one power formally occupied the island. On April 15 1633, however, the Dutch proclaimed their possession of St Helena in the name of the United Provinces, although there is no evidence that they settled or occupied the island.

THE EAST INDIA COMPANY AND ST HELENA

The East India Company made the decision formally to take possession of the island after the Commonwealth, under Richard Cromwell, granted a charter to the company. The charter gave them the right to fortify and colonise any of its establishments, and to transport settlers, stores and ammunition. The company saw the potential importance of St Helena as a fortress and supply stop for ships on their way home from India.

In 1659, Captain John Dutton, along with his wife, was ordered to go to St Helena, where the East India Company appointed him governor-in-chief. On May 5, he took possession of the English East India Company's first settlement – the still uninhabited island of St Helena. The building of the fort (now the Castle) was completed, reportedly, within a month. There are three plaques within the walls to confirm that this was in fact the first seat of government on the island. The original name of the building was Castle St John, but it was changed shortly afterwards to James Fort. The little town which sprang up in Chapel Valley was named James Town in honour of the Duke of York, who later became King James II.

Because of the change in the English government in 1660, the charter in the name of Richard, Lord Protector, entitling the East India Company to govern the island, had become of little value. The first royal charter of King Charles II confirmed the company's right to possess, fortify and settle the island of St Helena on behalf of the Crown. The new charter declared that all people born on or inhabiting the island, and their children, would be subjects of England and would enjoy all liberties within any of 'Our Dominions'.

When Captain John Dutton departed during the summer of 1661, many settlers went with him. His position was taken over by his lieutenant, Robert Stringer, who was left with only 30 men to look after and guard the island.

DESPERATE TIMES AND THE DUTCH ATTACK

By 1666 there were only 50 white men and 20 white women left on the island, falling to 48 whites and 18 Negroes four years later. The company did all it could to attract new settlers but had little success: colonists came only in small numbers. At this time there were no landholders among the island's inhabitants. Instructions were sent to Governor Stringer to give those willing to remain on the island a parcel of land, and the island was divided up into 150 parts. Fifteen parts were reserved for the company, a further five reserved for the governor, and then one share was allotted to each planter, his wife and his servant. In return for his freedom and his land, the landholder had to be ready to assist in the maintenance of the fortifications and to act as part of the defending force. He was also required to give a small donation of his produce as rent.

By 1671, there was discontent on the island because of the shortage of food and other necessities. Problems in agreement between the government and the people of the island are nothing new; even in the 17th century, the governor always seemed to take power away from the people, even though there was an elected council on St Helena. The people as well as the governor sent complaints to the council in London. The governor even complained that he couldn't defend his island in the event of general war. In response, the council sent 80 men, 240 rounds of shot and two barrels of gunpowder. At this time, the East India Company, thinking of the spiritual needs of its employees, sent the first of many Church of England chaplains, and a modest little church was erected, to be replaced in 1674 by a slightly larger one. It was probably not called St James' until replaced again by the present church in 1774. Another church was constructed shortly afterwards near the present St Paul's.

On August 21 1672 a mutiny broke out. Three St Helena councillors, with the support of the rest of the council, seized Governor Cony and kept him prisoner until October when they shipped him home and elected the island's clergyman, Chaplain Noakes, as its governor. By this time the East India Company had already sent out his replacement, Governor Anthony Beale, a former ship's carpenter and assistant surveyor of shipping. Governor Beale ordered that the island be fortified and that guns be erected as quickly as possible in readiness for an attack. But the preparations started too late. At the end of November, the Dutch decided to launch an attack on St Helena. A Dutch squadron arrived in December, but it took them a few days and several attempts to secure a landing. Reputedly, on December 31 1672 a party of five hundred Dutch landed at Bennett's Point and, by climbing up the steep Swanley Valley, marched unhindered up to High Peak where they overpowered a small English detachment. The Dutch marched without further opposition to Ladder Hill, above Jamestown. They proceeded to descend on the capital. Here, they were met with strong resistance and repulsed. In the end the Dutch took possession of the fort on Ladder Hill.

On January 1 1673, the Dutch force successfully captured St Helena in an almost bloodless victory. The governor saw the situation as hopeless, so escaped with his people on the *Humphrey & Elizabeth* and set sail for Brazil.

He spiked the guns, leaving the Dutch with very little booty. The Dutch occupation was short lived. Two weeks after the capture of St Helena, Captain Richard Munden sailed from England towards the island. On May 4, a few leagues from the island, he met former Governor Beale who, after arriving in Brazil, had immediately hired a sloop to sail towards St Helena to warn approaching English ships of the Dutch occupation. Munden made plans to retake the island and, on May 15, forced the Dutch to surrender. This was the last, and indeed only, dispute concerning possession of the island. Since then St Helena has been firmly in the hands of the United Kingdom. The second royal charter of Charles II to the East India Company, which was issued on December 16 1673, dealt specifically with St Helena, and sought to correct the mistakes shown by the Dutch capture. It confirmed more clearly the significance of the island as a fortress, and emphasised its importance to the Crown. Captain Richard Keigwin of the ship *Assistance* was appointed the new governor.

Unrest once again broke out in 1674 and there was a mutiny. The governor was seized and taken to the interior of the island where he was kept under guard and wasn't even allowed ink or paper. The mutineers elected Lieutenant Bird to fill the post of governor. Governor Keigwin was charged with intending to desert the island by the first ship which called and also of abusing the soldiers without cause. He was cleared of all charges. Chaos ensued as soldiers threatened Keigwin, but a visiting captain, William Basse, was able to restore order and Keigwin was reinstalled as governor. Not long after, however, Captain Richard Field was named as his successor.

He was replaced by Major John Blackmore in July 1678; due to the threat of war with France the company chose to appoint a military man to the post.

SLAVERY AND FURTHER UNREST

It appears that slavery was instituted on St Helena around the time of the first settlement by the East India Company. In 1679, there were about 80 slaves. Because of fears of a possible uprising, restrictions were put on further importation of slaves, but they were still brought in from time to time.

Discontent among the colonists reached boiling point in 1684, the result of a 'minor incident' involving Deputy-Governor Holden and a soldier, Adam Dennison. Dennison publicly accused the deputy-governor of purposely misconstruing words used in an argument five weeks before. Holden was cleared of the charges, but Dennison was immediately committed to prison to wait until the next ship would leave for England. The planters and some of the soldiers drew up a plot to seize and imprison the deputy-governor. They demanded to have Mr Holden delivered to them and when they were refused, they stormed the fort, but were repelled. Six of the rebels were arrested and sentenced to death by hanging – although two threw themselves at the mercy of the court and were banished to Barbados. After all this, the company implemented a policy of stricter discipline on the island.

As a result of the outbreak of war with France in 1689, ships no longer visited the island, and necessities ran out. The jackets of the soldiers were so worn, they had nothing to cover their backs and no cloth to make new ones. It was almost six years after the war started before a supply ship was allowed to stop at the island.

In 1693, the growing desperation at poverty, caused by isolation, led to a sudden outbreak of mutiny. Sergeant Jackson led a group of 27 soldiers who seized the fort. As a result of this, Governor Johnson was killed, and they took 50 prisoners whom they imprisoned in the dungeon. Five of the prisoners were ordered to go with Sergeant Jackson and his men as hostages. The acting governor, Captain Poirier, was able to bargain with the mutineers and he received seven of his men back in exchange for supplies. The mutineers escaped from the island on the company ship *Francis and Mary*.

It was rumoured in 1694 that the slaves had decided on a conspiracy to kill every white man on the island. Word of this plan got around one Friday night in November and this caused a great panic. By seven o'clock the following morning, every slave had been taken into custody and nothing came of this plot. Eleven of the slaves were convicted in the conspiracy and sentenced to death. In the end only three were put to death and the others were punished severely.

On June 1 1706, the French managed to steal two company ships which lay at anchor in the Roads. The French arrived in two ships which were flying the Dutch colours. This caused so much confusion that they were able to escape with the stolen ships before there was a chance of retaliation from the island.

Following commercial rivalries between the original English East India Company and a New East India Company created in 1698, the companies were merged in 1708 forming the United Company of Merchants of England Trading to the East Indies. St Helena was then transferred from the old to the new, and the United East India Company became Lords Proprietors of the island. They retained possession of the island until 1834, when it was transferred to the Crown.

GOLD FEVER AND PEACEFUL TIMES

Towards the end of 1708, gold and silver were believed to have been discovered by Captain Mashborne, a member of the council, who had been looking for limestone. A short time later another soldier discovered what he believed was gold and copper. On February 22 1709, Governor Roberts issued a declaration encouraging people to find a gold or copper mine, with a reward of £250 for the gold and £150 for the copper mine. Thus started the short-lived 'Breakneck Valley Goldrush'. Unfortunately, the gold turned out to be iron pyrites, but something positive did come out of all this: in Sandy Bay, a good quantity of lime was discovered.

The first St Helena-born governor, John Goodwin, took up office in August 1737. It seems that he was governor in name only, because the real power on the council was held by Duke Crispe, who started out as the governor's steward and eventually worked his way up to a seat in council. He and Goodwin were reportedly involved in some shady business. When Goodwin died, Crispe was officially appointed governor, but his crimes were soon found out and he was declared no longer in the company's service. His successor,

Governor Thomas Lambert, established the first hospital in 1741, on the site of the present hospital at Maldivia.

Charles Hutchinson was appointed governor in 1746 and St Helena enjoyed a prolonged period of tranquility and prosperity. He held the position for 18 years, deciding to retire when he became old and infirm. The peaceful time on the island continued throughout the term of the next governor.

However, the frequent desertion of soldiers from the garrison was a persistent problem, and measures were taken to try to improve conditions and discipline. The company decided that alcohol was probably responsible for the soldiers' behaviour. They decided to forbid the soldiers from visiting the punch houses and instead allowed them to drink only at the military canteens. These new rules and regulations further aggravated the situation and the anger of the soldiers. On December 27 1783, the 'Christmas Mutiny' erupted when the governor would not agree to the demands of the soldiers. Two hundred men armed themselves and marched out of their barracks, having planned to take possession of the post on Ladder Hill, where they would have complete command of the town below. The governor was able to appease them and convince them to lay down their arms. The punch houses were once again open to the soldiers, but alcohol consumption was limited. The soldiers demanded more liquor and this time they took over the Alarm House. Major Bazett, leading a troop of three officers and 70 men, regained control of Alarm House. Ninety-nine men were condemned to death, but in the end lots were drawn and only ten men were executed.

In June of 1787, Mr Robert Brooke was appointed governor. He brought about a lot of change on the island and was able to improve the situation of the garrison. He instituted a system where the bad characters were separated from the rest of the soldiers and given the worst provisions and were deprived of many valued privileges. This brought the desired effect and with time he had the military under complete control. Minor offences were now punished by hard labour and no longer by lashings, bringing improvements in many ways. Through these labour punishments, waste land was converted into a parade ground for the soldiers, gardens were created, and the appearance of the soldiers greatly improved. Men were now eager to become soldiers and serve in the garrison.

Governor Brooke also improved the lives of the slaves. He was aware that although the majority of slave owners treated their slaves decently, there were many who did not. In 1792, he drew up a code of laws for the control and protection of slaves, which limited the authority of the master and extended that of the magistrates. The Court of Directors did not totally agree with the governor's system, but passed a similar set of laws. A master could punish his slave with 12 lashes, but if the owner felt the offence warranted more severe punishment, it would have to be approved by a magistrate and the governor. The importation of slaves was now forbidden.

There were other improvements credited to Governor Brooke. He was responsible for the conducting of water from some springs below Diana's Peak to Deadwood. This proved valuable in many ways, and saved a large stock of

Above A view of Jamestown from the deck of *RMS St Helena* (US)

Left On board *RMS St Helena* (NR)

Below The settlement of Jamestown, nestled in a long valley between two steep-sided cliffs (NR)

Above The endemic wirebird,
Aegialitis sanctae-helenae, also
known as the St Helena plover,
is today endangered. (NR)

Right Diana's Peak with tree ferns,
Dicksonia arborescens, and exotic
fuchsia, *Fuchsia coccinea*,
in abundance (HM)

Below View towards Sandy Bay
and Lot from Sandy Bay Ridge (HM)

the company's cattle during the drought period by turning useless waste ground into good grazing land. The governor also helped arrange a group of St Helena volunteers who were part of a corps which took part in the capture of Cape Town from the Dutch in 1795. After 14 years of service, Brooke retired due to illness and subsequently returned to Ireland.

Colonel Robert Patton was the next man to assume the post of governor. One of his first actions was the establishment of telegraphs to replace signal guns previously used to warn of attack. In 1806, a group of 282 recruits from St Helena joined a British detachment which attempted to capture Buenos Aires. Although the expedition failed, the St Helena Brigade fought bravely and steadily. However, the governor came under heavy criticism for involving St Helena soldiers in this ill-fated mission.

In 1807, measles were brought to the island on board a slave ship which made a stop at St Helena with the home-coming East India fleet. There was no warning of the impending danger until the ship had dropped anchor. Three weeks after the initial contact, the disease broke out in two families. Initially, this did not cause alarm on the island, as the disease was yet unknown to St Helena, but the epidemic soon spread to great numbers. Public and government offices, as well as businesses, were closed. Within two months, 160 people had died and many more were to follow. Until this, the people on the island had believed that their climate was much too healthy for the spread of infectious diseases.

Governor Alexander Beatson had the desire to improve the cultivation of the island, but there was a shortage of labour. In May 1810, the first consignment of Chinese labourers arrived on the island, followed by another consignment in July 1811. They were used as labourers and mechanics. At one time, the Chinese colony of the island numbered up to 650, but was later reduced to 400.

The next threat of discontent on the island was on December 11 1811, when the governor received an anonymous letter threatening a rebellion by the soldiers, because of the new rules implemented by Governor Beatson in regard to the supply of liquor and provisions. The governor took the necessary steps and all the mutineers were captured.

In 1814, a Benevolent Society was founded by Governor Mark Wilks to provide education for the children of the slaves, free blacks and the poorer classes of the community. Also credited to Governor Wilks' term in office was the establishment of a public library in Jamestown.

NAPOLEON

October 15 1815 was the start of the period in St Helena's history with which most people are familiar. This was the day that the *Northumberland* arrived with the island's most famous prisoner. Upon arrival at St Helena, Napoleon scrutinised his 'island prison' with the same spy glasses he used on many battlefields, and is reputed to have said, 'It is not an attractive place; I should have done better to remain in Egypt.' Much has been written about Napoleon and his stay on St Helena. Here I offer a brief description of these six notable years in the island's history.

The year 1815 started a period of prosperity for St Helena. With the arrival of Napoleon Bonaparte and his entourage came many troops to guard him. The population of the island rose from around 6,500 to 8,000, causing a shortage of food and accommodation. To limit the possibility of Napoleon's escape, the government implemented strict measures. Even fishing boats were subject to severe restrictions. Prices of provisions soared and local produce also fetched a high price. Two camps were formed to house the soldiers, one at Deadwood and the other at Francis Plain.

On the day of Napoleon's arrival, there was a crowd of curious people waiting at the wharf to greet him, but all in vain. It was decided that Napoleon should come ashore after sundown on October 16, in order to avoid the unwanted attention of the people. Although it was expected that most people would go home, a troop of soldiers with fixed bayonets was required to force passage for him so he could arrive at his accommodation, the house of Henry Porteous, on Main Street in Jamestown. The house (on the left as you walk up the street, before the Consulate Hotel) was later torn down but is now being reconstructed in similar design. This house was chosen as a temporary residence for Napoleon while preparations at Longwood House, his permanent residence, were being completed. It was estimated the work would take two months.

The Porteous house proved unsuitable accommodation for the entire entourage of 26 people. The French were astounded at the meagreness of the house. They felt that the castle, with its vast rooms, or Plantation House (the governor's residence) would have been more suitable. After a night in the cramped quarters, Napoleon, Sir George Cockburn, and General Bertrand rode about five miles to inspect Longwood House. It is said that Napoleon was disappointed when he first inspected his future residence with its few dark low ceilinged rooms and bare garden. He was assured that it would be transformed into a comfortable residence.

Until this point, Longwood House was used as the summer residence of the lieutenant governor. It was on the return journey to Jamestown, when Napoleon decided he could not spend another night in the house there, that he discovered the beautiful scenery of Briar's Village. He was so enchanted by the estate he saw, that he enquired if it were possible to find accommodation at this location while waiting for the renovations to be completed at Longwood House. The Balcombe family, who owned the house, offered Napoleon the use of their home, but he declined and chose instead to occupy the pavilion, situated on the top of a hill, located about 30 yards (27m) from the house.

Napoleon spent only two months at The Briars. He enjoyed a friendly relationship with the Balcombe family and was especially fond of their 13-year-old daughter, Betsy, who became friends with him. These two months were considered the most enjoyable of his stay on St Helena. At the beginning of December, work had progressed far enough at Longwood House for it to be suitable for Napoleon to live there. With reluctance and sadness, he departed The Briars, to continue his life in exile at Longwood House.

Longwood Old House was originally a cowshed which was later transformed into a five-room house. In preparation for Napoleon's stay, a sixth room was added which was used as a billiard room and ante-chamber. In the bathroom there was originally a large copper tub panelled in oak which was taken to France when Napoleon's body was transported back. It has since been returned to Longwood House. It is said that Napoleon spent long hours in the bath, reading, lunching and chatting, especially in the later years during his illness. The valets would sleep on the sofa in the adjoining room, ready to respond when Napoleon rang the bell.

Although the house was enlarged to accommodate the increased number of people, it was still cramped. Over 20 people at a time were living in this limited space. Napoleon was allowed to walk outside in the gardens and he had freedom of movement. If he went beyond the boundaries of the property, however, he had to be accompanied by a British officer. One may think that this would be a pleasant area in which to have a house, but the weather conditions made it impossible to enjoy at times. In the summer it is subject to fierce sun and in the winter the plateau is swirled in mist, bringing high humidity. In response to Napoleon's constant complaints about the house, plans were made to build an alternative. Longwood New House was brought out from England and assembled opposite the existing building. In spite of this, Napoleon never moved in. The 56-room house was demolished after World War II.

Napoleon's life at Longwood House followed the same day-to-day pattern for the most part. There was always fear that he would try an escape from the island. It was felt necessary that ships be ever present in James Bay, and other ships patrolled the waters around the island, constantly ready in case they were needed. Not only was the sea heavily patrolled, but the island itself was manned with many soldiers. During the day, sentries patrolled outside the boundary walls of Longwood, but in the evening they took up their watch in the gardens, close to the house. Napoleon resented being so closely observed. The ante-room, which also served as the billiard room, was the largest room in the house. In the shutters two peepholes were cut out, and it was believed that Napoleon observed the sentries this way. Every attempt was made to treat Napoleon as a prisoner and to demean him. It was expressly forbidden by Governor Lowe to call him Emperor: he was to be called General Bonaparte. The government censored all correspondence. A curfew of 9.00pm was imposed and no one was allowed to move about the island unless they knew the password. An orderly officer had to report daily that he had seen Napoleon personally. Napoleon had to be accompanied any time he wanted to go for a ride. At first these regulations were implemented rigidly but were later slightly relaxed. However, with the arrival of the new governor, Sir Hudson Lowe, in April 1816, life became more difficult for Napoleon.

From the start of his governorship, Hudson Lowe had a bitter relationship with Napoleon Bonaparte, probably because Governor Lowe strictly enforced the regulations and restrictions. The last time the two men met was on August 17 1816. The following October, the area in which Napoleon was allowed to go out

DAILY LIFE FOR NAPOLEON

Napoleon's life continued to follow the same day-to-day routine. He would get up at dawn and, after his morning routine, would set out for a ride in the cool of the morning. The limited area in which he was permitted to go alone angered him at times, but since he preferred the company of his own people to that of an English officer, he remained within his prescribed boundaries.

Mostly Napoleon lunched alone or in the company of one of his entourage. If weather permitted, he partook of his meal outdoors in the garden. In the afternoon, he dictated his memoirs or other works. Napoleon still thought of himself as the 'Emperor' and etiquette was observed in the evening. At 5.00pm, the officers would assemble in the living room in full dress uniform and the ladies in evening gowns. A game of chess or cards was played until dinner was announced punctually at 8.00pm. It is said that the crystal chandelier which once hung in this room is now in the dining room at the governor's residence, Plantation House. The meal was served in the dining room, by liveried servants and the table was set with gleaming silver and fine porcelain. Every evening the same custom was observed and the cuisine and the wine were always excellent. Coffee was served in the drawing room and then there would be further games of chess or cards, or perhaps some singing or reading. Over the years, the routine became tedious.

unassisted was reduced by a third. He was also forbidden to speak to anyone unless in the presence of an English soldier. Now the sentries posted outside took up their post close to the house at sundown, instead of at 9.00pm as previously.

Little by little Napoleon's entourage grew smaller. Marquis de Las Cases, who thought of himself as Napoleon's closest confidante and to whom Napoleon dictated his memoirs, was arrested on November 25 1816, and was sent from the island in January of 1817. His crime: that he attempted to evade the censorship of all correspondence by the government by dispatching secret letters to London through his former servant. He was caught and immediately removed from Longwood House. Las Cases was the first of Napoleon's entourage to leave St Helena.

The next to leave Longwood was General Gaspar Gourgaud. During the time of the exile, there seemed to be a continual jealousy between Las Cases and Gourgaud for Napoleon's attention. Even after the departure of Las Cases, his jealousy still flared and he seemed to take out his frustrations on everyone. He became quarrelsome and self-absorbed. In February 1818 Napoleon and Gourgaud had a furious exchange in the drawing room. This resulted in the general going to Plantation House to get the governor's authority to leave Longwood House. Only after a letter was written claiming illness as the reason for departure, did Governor Lowe permit him to stay elsewhere on the island until passage could be arranged.

The year 1818 was not a good one for Napoleon. His illness plagued him and he became moody and irritable. Franceschi Cipriani, the major-domo at Longwood House responsible for the smooth running of the household, died after suffering from a four-day illness. Around the middle of that year, four other members of the staff left with their families. On August 2, Napoleon's personal and trusted physician, Barry O'Meara, left the island after a row with the governor. Dr O'Meara had an arrangement for a time with the governor to report on Napoleon and his entourage. Gradually he got tired of the restrictions put upon him by the governor and he stopped his reports. The governor and doctor quarrelled and the governor attempted to have the doctor replaced, but Napoleon refused any other physician. Dr O'Meara resigned before the governor could dismiss him. Napoleon was without medical care for six months and his condition continued to deteriorate. By this time it had been determined that Napoleon was most likely suffering from chronic hepatitis. The governor, afraid that people would feel this ailment had something to do with the unsuitable conditions on St Helena, decided to suppress this information. A naval surgeon brought to the island after Napoleon suffered one of his painful bouts of illness confirmed Dr O'Meara's diagnosis. The doctor was dismissed by court-martial and Napoleon again refused medical care for several months.

During the time of his illness, Napoleon was weak and in bad spirits. He took little exercise and he seldom went out into his garden. It seemed he was losing interest in life. On September 20 of that year, five people arrived to assume the vacant positions in the household: a cook, a major-domo, a doctor and two priests. These newcomers were sent by Napoleon's mother, but they did not live up to the expectations of the exile.

Over the next few months, Napoleon seemed to be regaining his health. In March 1820, he started taking a keen interest in gardening and drew up plans to remodel the garden. When he had first arrived, it was just a small arid garden with a few bent trees. The Chinese gardeners set out to improve it. A lawn was sown and flower beds were added. Orange and lemon trees were planted. A vegetable garden was set in front of the house, but the wind, heat and lack of water ruined it. The work on the gardens was finished in May. There was a square pavilion built from where he could view the sea and follow the progress of ships arriving from South Africa. A small park was built complete with some small ponds where Napoleon walked a lot and ate lunch sometimes under the arbour. In 1990, the gardens were completely renovated to restore them to how they were in 1821.

Unfortunately Napoleon was not to enjoy his improved health for long. His bouts of illness returned with increased frequency. The last excursion that Napoleon made was on October 4 1820, when he, Bertrand and Montholon rode five miles to Mount Pleasant, Sandy Bay, to have breakfast on the lawn with Sir William Doveton, the estate's owner. After this, Napoleon only took short, slow rides in the carriage. In mid-March 1821, Napoleon could no longer leave the house, due to his failing health. The sickbed was then moved into the drawing room. He spent most of his time in bed as his condition rapidly got worse. On May 5 1821, Napoleon died surrounded by members of his entourage. The body lay in state in the drawing room. Governor Lowe and large numbers of prominent officials were received. Hundreds of people filed through the room to mourn or observe Napoleon in death.

Much controversy exists as to the official cause of Napoleon's death. An autopsy was performed shortly after his passing and the official cause was said to be stomach cancer and a perforated stomach ulcer. There has been speculation that Napoleon may have been gradually poisoned by arsenic and this is now generally accepted.

Napoleon was buried in a simple tomb in Sane Valley. On either side of the grave was a willow tree. It is said that Napoleon himself chose this peaceful setting as his last resting place. As he was in life, Napoleon was also guarded heavily after his death. There was a guardhouse stationed close to the tomb and the entire garrison lined the funeral route from Longwood House to Hutt's Gate and to the specially built road to the tomb. Napoleon's remains rested here until 1840, when they were returned to France. The tomb is still there, though it has long been empty.

It was mentioned that Governor Hudson Lowe and Napoleon Bonaparte did not get along well, during the latter's imprisonment on the island. This was not the only important event to happen during Governor Lowe's term of office. In August 1818, following an incident when a slave owner was fined for whipping a young slave girl, Hudson Lowe convened a meeting of the inhabitants, urging the abolition of slavery on the island; as a first measure, all children born of a slave woman from or after Christmas Day 1818 were to be free, but considered as apprentices until the age of 18 for males and 16 for females. Masters were also to enforce the attendance of these freeborn children at church and Sunday schools. Slavery was finally completely abolished in 1832, during the term of Governor Dallas.

After the death of Napoleon, many of the troops were sent away from the island. Governor Lowe was among those who left the island. He and his family sailed on July 25 1821. Although he was a fine soldier, a good linguist, intelligent, hardworking and kind, he was not suited for the job he had been chosen to do, acting as jailer for the French exiles. Before he departed, Sir Hudson Lowe was presented with an address from the island's inhabitants. In it, he was praised for his work to abolish slavery and the gratitude and the affection of the people was conveyed to him.

THE CROWN TAKES OVER

Under the India Act dated August 28 1833, the island was no longer to be ruled by the Honourable East India Company which had governed St Helena for 182 years, for the most part successfully. From April 22 1834, His Majesty's Government took over. Radical changes took place at once. Some say the island never fully recovered from the change in government. The annual subsidy of £90,000, which it had cost the East India Company to maintain the island, was removed. The garrison was disbanded and the new governor was under orders to cut expenses. As a result this left most people on the island in a state of near poverty. There were many cases of hardship when company servants were dismissed from their posts. Whole families and over a hundred young men, finding life so hard and with no prospect of improvement, emigrated to the Cape of Good Hope. With no old-age pensions, friendly societies were founded to provide sickness, death and old-age benefits on St Helena, as in England. The Mechanics and Friendly Benefit Society was instituted this year followed by the St Helena Poor Society in 1847, the Foresters in 1871, and the St Helena Church Provident Society in 1878.

Early in the new regime, in 1833, the whale-fishing industry was introduced to St Helena. Like many industries launched to boost the welfare of a place, it wasn't as successful as was hoped. In 1875 another attempt was made to relaunch whaling, but this venture failed as well, probably because the South Atlantic whale fishery was on the decline during this period.

In 1840 there occurred two events which have historical importance to St Helena. Her Majesty's Government established a Vice-Admiralty Court on the island for the trial of vessels engaged in the slave trade on the west coast of Africa. Large numbers of ships were captured and brought to St Helena during the following ten years. The ships were to be sold or broken up while the human cargoes were fed, clothed and kept at the Liberated African Depot in Rupert's Valley. Most of the slaves who recovered were given passage to the West Indies or British Guiana as labourers; some chose to remain as servants or on various public works.

This work of liberating slaves brought money and employment to the island, but also the scourge of white ants (the termite). These minute creatures were among the timbers on a slave ship from Brazil, which was broken up and stored in Jamestown. Their destructiveness was so great and their appetite for timber, books, furniture and paper so ravenous that a very large sum of money had to be spent over the next several decades to rebuild property in the town. They destroyed the reception hall at the Castle, and a significant portion of books in the public library, among other structural and material damages.

The other important event which occured was the exhumation of Napoleon and the transport of his remains back to France. The French frigate *La Belle Poule* and the corvette *Favorite* arrived at the island on October 8. Among those on the ship were several of the former French exiles who lived at Longwood House with Napoleon. The coffin was placed aboard the French frigate on October 15 with appropriate ceremony. Coincidentally this was the same date that Napoleon arrived at St Helena in 1815 on the *Northumberland*.

On March 7 1847 the first Bishop of Cape Town, Robert Gray, arrived (St Helena had been included in the See of Cape Town when it had been established two years previously). This was the first visit by a bishop and thus the first chance for confirmations on the island – a total of 366 people, about a tenth of the island's population, were confirmed. Bishop Gray made two further visits, in 1852 and 1857.

In 1858, Queen Victoria granted France the right to buy and hold Longwood House and the tomb of Napoleon III of France and his heirs indefinitely. Today, the *tricolore* flies over '*La Domaine française de Ste-Hélène*', and over The Briars, acquired by the French in 1959. A French *conservateur* resides at Longwood.

The Diocese of St Helena was established in 1859 by Queen's Order in Council, and included the islands of Ascension and Tristan da Cunha, and until 1869, the British residents of Rio de Janeiro and other towns on the eastern seaboard of South America, as well as the Falklands. The first bishop, Dr Piers Claughton, was consecrated in Westminster Abbey and arrived in late October that same year, remarking in a letter home that the island was so English in its character that it made him feel at home. In 1861, the island was divided into three parishes; St James', St Paul's and St Matthew's.

Through the years of its history, St Helena has tried many new schemes to boost the economy. This was the case in 1868 when a skilled gardener from the Royal Botanical Gardens at Kew was sent to the island to superintend the planting of cinchona trees for quinine production. A plantation of 10,000 plants sprang up on the side of Diana's Peak. The project promised to bring much profit to the island, but unfortunately the plantation was not properly cared for and it was ultimately abandoned.

In 1873, the second and last St Helena-born governor, Hudson Ralph Janisch, took office. He is most remembered for his *Extracts from the St Helena Records and Chronicles of Cape Commanders*, which was printed and published in Jamestown in 1885. It was said that he was a good governor and wanted only the best for his island homeland. The lack of funds at his disposal prevented him from being able to bring much benefit to the island during his term in office. One thing which stands out about Governor Janisch is the fact that his salary was extremely low compared to other governors. There is speculation that the reason for this is because he was native to the island, but he also had the misfortune to be governing the island during one of its economic depressions. With the opening of the Suez Canal in 1869, ships called less and less at St Helena and as a result the economy suffered with the decrease in income. The island fell into a state of poverty and the situation just worsened. With the decrease in ship traffic, the island once again found itself becoming isolated. Nearly a quarter of the poorest section of the community left the island for the Cape in order to escape the poor economic conditions. Hudson Janisch died in office on March 10 1884.

NEW ZEALAND FLAX AND MORE PRISONERS

An attempt to establish the flax industry was started in 1874 when 100 acres of New Zealand flax were planted by the Colonial and Foreign Fibre Company. The first mill was established in Jamestown, with a seven horsepower steam engine and three stamping machines. The problems of transport from the country into town and the sudden fall in price for the fibre were the reasons for the failure of this first attempt at this industry. Even though it wasn't successful initially, another attempt was made in 1907 and eventually it became the only staple industry of the island and sustained the working population for over 50 years.

The island's next prisoner arrived in 1890. Following the Zulu Wars, Chief Dinizulu, son of Cetawayo, and his family were exiled to the island for seven years. He was very cooperative during his captivity. He did as he was told, never quarrelled, and wandered around the island making friends with all he met. Dinizulu became a convert to Christianity, and was baptised and confirmed by the bishop.

In November of 1899 the first submarine cable was landed by the Eastern Telegraph Company. This connected the island with Cape Town and was the first stage in the link north to Ascension and then to Europe and England.

Once again St Helena became an important place of imprisonment when the first of some 6,000 South African Boer War prisoners arrived in April of 1900. The principal camp was at Deadwood Plain and a second camp was established at Broad Bottom. During the next two years ship after ship arrived bringing new prisoners. A temporary wave of economic improvement came to the island, as the population reached its all-time record of 9,850. The prisoners who died on the island were buried at the Baptist Cemetery at Knollcombes.

After much debate, in 1904 compulsory education was introduced for all children up to the age of 14 years. This applied to all schools whether run by the government, the Benevolent Society or the Hussey Charity. Later the age for compulsory education was raised to 15 years old.

With the re-establishment of the flax industry in 1907, the government had hopes that, at last, they had found a way to build up the economy. Lace making, introduced to the island in 1900, was an industry with a lot of potential. Sadly, at this point no-one took this to be a serious endeavour and it wasn't properly encouraged, at first. In 1907 an effort was made to resurrect the lace-making industry. An expert was sent to the island for six months in order to teach the women several patterns and to try to establish it as a potential profit-making business. This gave some of the neediest women on the island potential to earn money to support their families. Possibly because of the boom in flax growing, the island neglected the lace-making industry and the Government Lace School was closed. As had happened many times before, due to improper supervision, something with so much potential benefit to the islanders' well-being was ignored to the point that the venture failed.

In 1909, another attempt to garner a harvest from the sea was commenced by a private investor. This time the idea was to establish a factory for canning freshly caught fish, particularly mackerel. The canning factory was opened in Jamestown on February 26 that year. To the dismay of everyone involved, the mackerel did not appear as expected. It was always thought there was an abundance of fish in the water surrounding the island. After ten months of waiting and hoping, the factory was shut down. Another endeavour to help St Helena had failed.

In 1911, a potentially tragic event happened, but luckily the circumstances were favourable and a terrible tragedy was avoided. The *SS Papanui*, en route from Britain to Australia with emigrants, arrived in James Bay on fire. The ship burned out and sank, but its 364 passengers and crew were rescued and looked after on the island.

With the outbreak of the Great War in 1914, the defunct St Helena Volunteer Corps was re-established. In 1915, the Imperial Government constructed certain military defences and enlarged the wharf. This gave the island's inhabitants badly needed employment opportunities. As a result of the war the price of the flax fibre soared and the industry flourished. New mills were being constructed and this was a boon to the economic life of St Helena. Because of the very favourable prices being garnered for New Zealand flax, many St Helenians decided they wanted to be a part of this profitable business. They became so fixated on the planting of flax, that they seemed to ignore the planting of other beneficial crops. Instead of growing their own food, they now bought their food at exaggerated prices with the money they earned.

The island of Ascension became a dependency of St Helena in 1922. It was leased out to the Eastern Telegraph Company (later Cable and Wireless). This was probably when the first St Helenians left their island to take up employment on Ascension as servants and labourers.

In 1928 the Motor-Car Ordinance was passed which made it legal to import automobiles to the island. In reaction to this, 60 miles (97km) of road was prepared. The first motor vehicle to run on the island roads was owned by the Honourable H W Solomon OBE.

World War II brought a period of prosperity for the flax industry. Although the war was taking its toll all over the world, St Helena suffered very little hardship. There was a garrison maintained on the island, as well as a local defence force. However, the war did come uncomfortably close to the island when the Royal Fleet Auxiliary ship *HMS Darkdale* was torpedoed off Jamestown by a German submarine, killing 41 people. In another incident, a German Navy vessel, the *Graf Spee* was sighted off Jamestown, but it disappeared again without incident.

Over the next few years the island was enjoying some prosperity as the price of flax increased, reaching its peak in 1951. During that year, the island's exports exceeded its imports. This was the first and only year that this occurred. The island continued to do well through the beginning of the 1950s. During the later years of the decade things started to take a downward turn. A fish cannery, which was opened in 1957, was forced to close due to failure. In 1958, the Union Castle line decided to cut its passenger carrying schedule so that only one in three vessels southbound and two of three vessels northbound, made a call at the island. This decrease in services led to the total withdrawal of the Union Castle line in 1977. To provide access to the island, the first *RMS St Helena* was acquired by the government and run on their behalf by Curnow Shipping until August 2001. Today, it is run by Andrew Weir Shipping (see page 60).

The last exiles to be imprisoned on St Helena arrived there in 1957. Three Bahraini nationalists remained on the island until 1960 when they were released by a writ of habeas corpus.

The reduction in shipping services to the island compounded a dismal economic outlook for St Helena. Then in 1966 the flax industry collapsed, due to government wage rises and loss of contracts with organisations such as the British Post Office. St Helena hemp, which had long been used to tie their mail bags, was replaced by synthetic fibres. The mills had to close and about 250 people lost their jobs.

THE FALKLAND CONFLICT AND BRITISH CITIZENSHIP

Through the 1970s many official visitors came to the island to advise on a variety of topics. Several schemes were started in order to get the economy stabilised, but they were slow to start and many failed. After the closure of the flax mills, there was no significant development realised.

During the Falklands conflict, the first *RMS St Helena* was requisitioned by the Ministry of Defence to help in support of the Falklands, and sailed south with many of the crew volunteering for duty.

A very important event on January 1 1983 had a highly emotional impact on inhabitants of St Helena and those connected with the island. The British Nationality Act of 1981 came into effect, stripping the Saints of their rights of British citizenship, though this had been granted to them by Royal Charter in 1673 by King Charles II. Through this, they lost the right to live and work freely in the United Kingdom, although they were still considered subjects of the UK and her colonies, as 'British Overseas Territories citizens'.

Prince Andrew launched the second *RMS St Helena* on October 31 1989 at Aberdeen. The vessel was specially built for the Cardiff–Cape Town route, and features a mixed cargo/passenger layout. At the same time, a shuttle service between St Helena and Ascension was planned, for the many St Helenians working both there and on the Falklands. The idea was finally abandoned in 1994, although the *RMS St Helena* does make a shuttle voyage to Ascension when it is at St Helena. The island was left with fewer transport links to the rest of the world than it had 200 years ago.

The 1990s saw some attempted changes in the status of St Helena. The Bishop's Commission on Citizenship was established in 1992 by the Anglican bishop of St Helena, Bishop John Ruston, to give support to the island council to restore citizenship rights for the people. Later it was redesignated the Citizenship Commission and the mandate extended to include constitutional development. The commission has 13 members on St Helena including the speaker and two elected members of the island's legislature and two junior representatives from the island's high school, Prince Andrew School. The work of the commission has the support of islanders and formal support of the legislature. It has an active youth group and a branch in the United Kingdom. It is gaining support from a number of UK MPs across the political spectrum and an all-party group has been formed specifically to help the island and the people.

The main activity of the commission centres on bringing about public awareness locally, nationally and internationally about matters concerning citizenship and constitutional development of the territory of St Helena, which includes the dependencies of Ascension and the islands in the Tristan group. The commission is self-supporting and gets its income from fundraising and public subscription. There is widespread support for islanders in their drive to restore full citizenship rights and move towards constitutional development that will ensure a viable economy. The two major activities undertaken by the present commission are to seek legal advice regarding the Royal Charter of 1673, and to communicate with elected Members of Council in holding constituency meetings throughout St Helena to respond to the UK Government White Paper on the Overseas Territories, which was published in March of 1999.

The White Paper was welcomed by the people of St Helena as it set out policies for the future of the territories and its people. It promised that full British citizenship would be offered to those British Overseas Territory citizens who wished to have it. This is now expected to occur some time in 2002.

In March 2000, an unusual occurrence took place. A 16-year-old man from the Central African Republic of Burundi stowed aboard the *RMS St Helena* while she was docked at Cape Town. He was discovered in the afternoon before the ship was to arrive at St Helena. He had a sad tale to tell of the atrocities he and his family had suffered. The passengers on the ship held a collection and then it was decided that this young man should apply for political asylum on St Helena. (This is probably the first time in recorded history that something like this has happened on St Helena.) He was warmly received on the island, and St Helena government officials did everything they could to assist and make him comfortable. After much effort and much interviewing, the youth decided to withdraw his application for asylum. When he first decided to stow away aboard a ship, he saw the word 'London' written on the stern of the ship and thought the ship was headed for the United Kingdom. He was surprised and disappointed when he arrived on St Helena. He didn't understand or speak the language and he became very homesick. He was eventually transported to the UK. Thus ends the story of St Helena's first political refugee.

FAMOUS VISITORS TO ST HELENA

When you ask someone who they associate with St Helena, many people would say Napoleon. What they don't know is that there were quite a few other well-known and important people who paid a visit to the island. Some of these people helped shape the history of the island, others just used the island as a temporary stopping point on their way to another destination.

Dom Fernando Lopez

As far as anyone can determine, Dom Fernando Lopez, a Portuguese officer who was tortured for being the leader of the renegades during fighting at Goa between the Portuguese and the local inhabitants, was the first 'resident' of St Helena. In 1515, he managed to stow away aboard a vessel sailing for Portugal and got off the ship when it stopped at St Helena. He escaped and hid on the island. His companions searched for him unsuccessfully and the ship left without him. Before they departed, they left behind some supplies for him. Here the mutilated man found solace and peace during his self-imposed exile. There was no one to be disgusted by his appearance or to condemn him for his earlier actions. He made his 'home' by scooping out a cave in the side of a soft bank of earth. He lived from herbs which he found in the forest and also from fish when he was lucky enough to catch one. He lived in constant fear of being discovered. Whenever he spotted a ship in the waters off the coast, he would hide. Many of the ships which stopped would leave behind fresh supplies; one even left a rooster which he adopted as a pet.

Lopez continued living on the island in isolation for ten years. Little by little he gained trust and was assured no one would hurt him if he returned to Portugal. After his return to his home country, he made a visit to the Pope in Rome to confess his earlier sins and seek absolution. More and more he longed for his island home and eventually he returned to the peace and solitude of St Helena. Passing ships' crews continued to bring him supplies. He died in 1545 after living on the island almost 30 years.

Edmund Halley

In 1676, the 20-year-old astronomer, who we now know as the discoverer of Halley's Comet, came to St Helena for a year to work. His small stone observatory was on a northeast spur of the central ridges, which is called Halley's Mount today. While on the island he did some important work mapping the stars of the southern hemisphere. He was the first scientist to have visited St Helena. He returned in 1699 as the commander of the expedition ship *HMS Paramour*.

William Dampier

The famous explorer and navigator came to St Helena on June 20 1691 with his ship *Defence*. He stayed five or six days. In his account of the island, he makes some points which are still true today: in order to give the inhabitants a decent standard of living, outside support and money would be needed.

Dampier called again at St Helena early in 1701 in the *Roebuck*, which later sank off Ascension Island.

Dr Nevil Maskelyne

Maskelyne was sent to St Helena in 1761 to observe the transit of Venus passing over the sun which was to take place in June of that year. The observatory was set up on the high ridge behind Alarm House. Unfortunately, shortly before the event was to occur a passing cloud obscured the view. However, it was reportedly seen by several people down in James Valley.

Captain James Cook

Captain Cook arrived at the island in May 1771 on *HMS Endeavour*, bringing the naturalists Sir Joseph Banks and Daniel Solander. On his second visit, on May 16 1775 on the *Resolution*, he was received ceremoniously by the Castle with a 13-gun salute and was greeted by the governor personally. Captain Cook was attracted to the island, like most visitors before and after him, but he observed that so much more could be done with the place. In his journal he wrote:

> Whoever views St Helena in its present state and can but conceive what it must have been originally, will not hastily charge the inhabitants with want of industry. Though, perhaps, they might apply it to more advantage, were more land appropriated to planting, corn, vegetables, roots, etc., instead of being laid out in pasture, which is the present mode.

He remarked that the beef on the island was very good and was the only nourishment worth mentioning. After a stay of six days he left St Helena, stopping at Ascension on his way back home to England.

Captain William Bligh

Captain Bligh arrived at St Helena on December 17 1792 with his ships *Providence* and *Assistant* while on his way to Jamaica. He too had a positive impression of the island. The governor personally received him and he was honoured with a 13-gun salute. He presented the governor with ten breadfruit plants so as to provide St Helena with a lasting supply – although they died later from lack of attention. He also left a quantity of mountain rice seed.

Duke of Wellington

Sir Arthur Wellesley, as he was known in 1805, arrived in the *Trident* on his return voyage to England after his victory at Assaye. Local tradition has it that he slept his first night on shore in the same house that Napoleon Bonaparte, his opponent at the famous Battle of Waterloo, spent his first night. Another local tradition says that he stayed at the house on Main Street which is now a guesthouse known as Wellington House. In fact, he stayed at The Briars.

William Thackeray

This famous English novelist was six years old when he visited St Helena on a voyage from Calcutta to England in 1817. While he and his black servant were walking about the island, the island's famous prisoner, Napoleon Bonaparte, was pointed out to him. The servant told the little boy that Napoleon ate three sheep a day and all the children he could get his hands on. Later Thackeray referred to the incident in the *Roundabout Papers*.

Charles Darwin

The famous English naturalist came to the island on the *HMS Beagle* on July 8 1836. He stayed for six days and made a thorough examination of all he saw. Copies of his work, *A Naturalist's Voyage Round the World* are kept in the Castle. Darwin presented these to the governor to commemorate his visit. He also visited Ascension in 1836 and wrote an account of its geology. He remarked on the Welsh character of the scenery on St Helena. He commented on the poverty of the lower classes and the many emancipated slaves who didn't have work. He noted that the working people could only afford rice and a small bit of salt meat. Darwin liked the islanders who he found to be gentle and pleasant. He found abundant partridges and pheasants but he failed to sight the wirebird, the official bird of St Helena. At the end of his description of the island, he expressed some sorrow for having to leave.

Prince Albert
The second son of Queen Victoria arrived on the *HMS Eurylaus* in September 1860. He came to present new colours to Her Majesty's St Helena Regiment. This was the island's first royal visit.

Princess Elizabeth
The future queen, with her parents King George VI and Queen Elizabeth, arrived aboard the *HMS Vanguard* on April 29 1947, during a royal tour to South Africa.

Duke of Edinburgh
During his round-the-world tour on *HMY Britannia*, the duke made a stop at the island in 1957.

Prince Andrew of England
The second son of Queen Elizabeth II visited St Helena in 1984 to celebrate with the Saints 150 years under the Crown. The approval of funds to build Prince Andrew School was announced during his visit.

WHERE TO FIND OUT MORE ABOUT HISTORY
Those interested in island history would do well to make their way either to the St Helena Government Archives (see page 86) or to the museum in Jamestown (see page 85). See also *Further Information*, page 164.

DISCOVER THE SECRETS OF ST HELENA

Two secrets, actually: A ship and an island

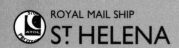

People and Politics

POLITICS

St Helena, Ascension and the Tristan da Cunha group are three UK overseas territories which form a single territorial group under British sovereignty known as St Helena and Her Dependencies. Although both Tristan da Cunha and Ascension have island administrators, the jurisdiction of these islands falls under the governor of St Helena.

Government – past and present
East India Company

When the East India Company administered the island, a governor and a council were appointed by the company's directors in London. Before 1673, a majority of the members of the council were chosen by the settlers. This provision was later revoked and the councillors were appointed by the company. Even after the British government took control of the island, it was still run by a governor and an executive council. Some observers remarked that the British attitude toward the island differed from that of the East India Company. The company ran the island as more of a fortress and important defence point in the South Atlantic, while the UK government's aim was to force the island to self-sufficiency.

The first non-official members of government were brought into the council in 1878 and a separate advisory council was formed in 1939. This new council allowed for a small group of locals to be represented. This group was enlarged in 1956 when unofficial members were introduced into the Executive Council.

Legislative and Executive Council

The General Workers Union was formed in 1958. They helped bring a major constitutional advance in 1963, when the island's first general elections, to form a newly constituted advisory council, took place. In 1966 the Advisory Council was reorganised and formed into the Legislative Council (or LEGCO). In the updated constitution of St Helena in 1988, the governor administers the government assisted by the Executive Council (EXCO) and the Legislative Council (LEGCO).

Today LEGCO and EXCO have a majority of non-official members. The island's executive authority rests with the governor in council, which is composed of ex-officio members as well as elected heads of LEGCO committees. There is no ministerial system on St Helena. The governor has a number of reserved powers with respect to defence, external affairs, internal security, justice, finance and shipping. Her Majesty the Queen has absolute authority over the island. There have never been any moves made to gain independence from the United Kingdom. Actually, St Helena has always tried to bring itself closer to the UK and its inhabitants consider themselves to be loyal subjects of the Crown.

The St Helena Constitutional Order provides for a Legislative Council consisting of the speaker, 12 elected members and three ex-officio members (the chief secretary, the financial secretary, and the attorney general). Elections are held by secret ballot at intervals not exceeding four years. Those aged 18 and over are eligible to vote. At the last general election, in June 2001, about half the seats were contested, representing an increased interest in politics. All contestants are independent; there are no political parties. There are eight electoral districts, four of which are represented by one councillor each. Jamestown, Half Tree Hollow, St Paul's and Longwood each have two councillors. The governor enacts law with the advice and consent of LEGCO and receives advice from an Executive Council of five elected members of LEGCO and the ex-officio members. The Attorney General doesn't vote in EXCO or LEGCO. Policy decisions for each government department are made by committees. The chairpersons from these committees are elected members of LEGCO, nominated by councillors to represent LEGCO at Executive Council.

LAW

St Helena has its own legislation. Although the laws of England as of January 1 1987 are in force on the island, they apply only where they are not inconsistent with any Act of Parliament or Order in Council which extends to St Helena.

The laws and legal system are based on those of England. The court system on St Helena is much like that of the justice system in the United Kingdom. The St Helena Magistrates' Court sits in Jamestown, normally on Thursday, and hears minor cases. There is also a Juvenile Court. Usually three lay magistrates sit in both the Magistrates' Court and the Juvenile Court. The St Helena Supreme Court is for serious cases. A non-resident chief justice visits the island once or twice a year to hold sessions of the Supreme Court. A Court of Appeal, consisting of a president and two justices of appeal, all of whom are non-resident, was held in St Helena for the first time in 1998. There is a resident attorney general who is responsible for legal matters relating to the St Helena Government.

There are no lawyers in private practice on St Helena. In minor cases the defendant is represented by a lay advocate. These lay advocates have been properly trained and instructed on how to do their job. They provide legal advice and assistance to the public in addition to representing people in appropriate cases. For serious cases, a lawyer for the defendant is sent out from the UK.

The St Helena police force currently has 29 officers, whose duties include running HM Prison. The police log appears in the *St Helena Herald* each week.

ECONOMY

St Helena was originally intended as a military base. It was never the intention that the island become self-sufficient. During the 19th century, the economy evolved around supplying provisions for shipping and the local garrison. In 1802 a total of 169 ships called at the island. In 1830, the number had increased to 367 and in 1860 it was 1,040. With the coming of the steamship, the number of ships stopping at St Helena began to decrease. The opening of the Suez Canal cut the number even further. In 1865, 850 ships called at the island, but in 1910 there were only 51. With the decline in shipping traffic came the virtual collapse in the island's economy. The establishment of the flax industry did help boost the economy and it resulted in one profitable year for the island. Since the demise of the flax industry, there has been very little influential industry on St Helena.

Aid

St Helena is heavily dependent on outside aid. Most assistance is received from the UK under four main categories. **Budgetary aid** supports the recurrent budget of the St Helena Government. The **shipping subsidy** covers the loss on the only ship serving St Helena. **Development aid** finances development projects on grant terms. **Technical co-operation** finances expatriate contract officers, consultants and overseas training for Saints. The amount of revenue raised locally by duties and taxes is insufficient to cover the local services provided by the government. This deficit is made up by budgetary aid from the UK.

Employment

Today the economy of the island is depressed. There are many people without jobs, and those who do have jobs may be severely underpaid.

A large proportion of the population, some 70%, is employed either by the St Helena government, or by the parastatal organisations supported by the government. A large number of St Helenians work on a contract basis on Ascension, the Falklands and in the UK. The numbers employed overseas have risen steadily, particularly on the Falklands and in the United Kingdom.

Cost of living

The cost of living is very high for most of the Saints considering the salary that they earn. In 1987/88 an average household spent £73.92 per week as compared with £95.67 in 1993/94. The proportion of income that was spent on food by the average household did not change significantly between 1987 and 1993. In 1997/98, the average pre-tax income was £2,843 per tax payer per year, or £54.67 per week, and the average post-tax income was £2,569, or £49.40 per week.

Recently the cost of fuel has increased, sending the price of petrol up about 50% and the price of diesel about 40% higher. This, in turn, will raise the prices of other goods and services such as taxis, bread, fish and other commodities. In 1999 inflation was measured at about 4%. As so few goods are produced in St Helena, changes in the local retail price index are affected considerably by UK inflation, South African inflation (allowing for changes in the exchange rate between the pound and the rand), and freight rates to St Helena.

The fact that St Helena can only be reached by ship does not help the economy. Only the *RMS St Helena* has a regular service to the the island.

Offshore workers not only provide for their families, but the money which they transfer to St Helena from their place of employment is very important to the economy. It is estimated that £1,500 per year flows back into the St Helena economy for every employed person offshore.

Imports and exports

Throughout recent years the island has been visited by a lot of economists and experts, whose job it is to conduct studies to determine the feasibility of certain projects or to find the 'key' solution to the problem of guiding St Helena to self-sufficiency.

Since St Helena has no airstrip, all goods are carried by ship. Fuel imports are brought in by chartered tanker. All other imports and exports are carried by the *RMS St Helena*, or ships chartered by the St Helena government in the case of emergencies.

St Helena has to import a large percentage of its goods: 60–65% from the UK and 35–40% from South Africa. There are some fruits and vegetables grown on the island today, but this is only a fraction of what is needed. Fresh meat is also available on the island, as cattle, pigs, sheep, goats and poultry are kept.

The island earns income from fishing (skipjack tuna, wahoo, mackerel and grouper), the sale of fishing licences to foreign fleets, the sale of postage stamps, tourism, customs duties and wharfage, and the export of St Helena coffee. All this accounts for more than half of the island's operating costs. The remaining costs are directly met by the UK government. There are also several projects underway which many hope will assist in giving the economy a needed lift. Most of these schemes are supported by the St Helena Development Agency.

St Helena Development Agency

The St Helena Development Agency (SHDA) is the island's first-stop shop for business development. Prominently situated at 2 Main Street, SHDA offers business development advice, information, training and finance for the island's growing private sector. In addition, SHDA is the first port of call for any inward investors who are visiting the island.

SHDA has been in operation since 1995 and has a strong record in delivering financial services for local businesses. In addition, the agency offers a comprehensive range of support services, making it very much part of the local business scene. The agency is heavily involved in the attraction of inward investment and in 1999 was instrumental in bringing Argos to St Helena, the largest single inward investor the island has seen, revolutionising the island's fishing industry.

Whilst SHDA welcomes visitors from outside of St Helena wishing to discuss business ideas informally, it is highly recommended that contact is made prior to arrival on the island, so as to ensure that the maximum benefit can be had from time available on the island. Thus, appointments with government officials or visits to particular points of interest relevant to the potential business venture are best arranged through SHDA in advance of visiting the island.

For more information about SHDA and the services that it offers, visit the agency's website at www.shda.helanta.sh. If you have a business venture that you would like to discuss in confidence, telephone Lyn Thomas, managing director, on 00 290 2920.

Fishing

The sale of fishing licences to Japanese tuna fishing vessels began in June 1988. By the end of 1993, around £2.9 million had been raised from the sale of 414 licences. In 1999, 59 licences were sold, raising a total of £733,781. Revenue collected from the sale of fishing licences by the St Helena Government is estimate at around £700,000 per annum, a contribution that is very important to the island's economy.

Argos Atlantic Cold Stores is a fish-processing plant located in Rupert's Valley. They export various types of fish, including tuna, to the European Union and the Far East. They work closely with the St Helena Fisheries Corporation, from whom they purchase their fish, which is caught by local fishermen. The amount of fish purchased by the St Helena Fisheries Corporation varies each year. In 1989, 585 tonnes were purchased but this fell over the following four years. In 1995, purchases rose again to 530 tonnes and three years later to 561 tonnes, but drastically decreased again in 1999. There has been, however, an increase in the amount exported between 1985 and 1995 and in 1998 a record 367 tonnes of fish was exported at a value of around £246,266.

Agriculture

In 1588, the first English visitors remarked on the valleys which were abundantly planted with trees and herbs. Among the trees which they found were fig, lemon, orange, pomegranate and date. The herbs which were discovered were parsley, sorrel, basil, fennel, anise seed and mustard seed. By this time, there were animals roaming the island, goats and pigs, as well as partridges and pheasant, which were introduced by the Portuguese.

Over the years due to soil erosion, which resulted from flash flooding and some aspects of bad husbandry, a lot of fertile ground was lost. Much land was converted into pasture and grazing area and whatever once grew in the earth was then neglected and destroyed. Another factor contributing to the shortage of locally produced goods is the lack of effort shown in some instances. Not enough effort or care is put into certain areas to ensure success. The prosperous valleys which once flourished with groves of fruit trees, are now dried out and stony, due to neglect of the land. Possibly with education and incentives, these problematic areas can be improved and the consumer, the visitor, as well as the grower, could all reap benefits.

There are now many projects underway and many ideas being implemented to try and gain back some agricultural ground for the island. Although the island does import a large portion of food from overseas, some vegetables and fruits are island-produced. St Helena produces about 95 tonnes of bananas a year for sale to the public. The possibility of developing banana plantations on the island is being looked into. There is a great demand for bananas and the hope is to increase banana production to meet local demand and to supply viable markets on a small scale. There is also an overabundant quantity of mangoes being grown. It is a shame to see mango trees full of ripe fruit, but not enough interest being shown to get the fruit picked and brought to market before it rots.

The Agriculture and Natural Resources Department and the St Helena Development Agency have plans in place to develop the local fruit industry to supply local and offshore markets by means of various methods of presentation: canning, drying, alcoholic beverages and juices. This will increase revenue and encourage cottage industries.

Citrus trees have recently been imported from Spain, shipped via the United Kingdom in order to undergo plant quarantine procedures. The programme will provide rootstock and young citrus trees for the development of orchards for smallholders on the island.

In order to avoid the unnecessary import of disease or pests, St Helena imposes very strict limits on goods brought to the island. There is a ban on fresh food being brought ashore. All animals and most produce has to be quarantined due to infestations of pests. Several programmes have been implemented over the years to eradicate certain pests. The programme that most often comes to mind is the attempt to eradicate the fruit fly by means of pesticides. After many years and many unsuccessful attempts, the aim now is to investigate the feasibility of bio-control agents to control these pests.

Coffee

Coffee growing in the private sector is a programme that has been widely embraced. St Helena coffee is much sought after by connoisseurs for its unique flavour. Because of the rarity of this coffee on the world market, it is quite expensive to buy outside of St Helena. The price of the coffee is about £12/kg on the export market. Between 600 and 900kg are sold annually on St Helena. It is readily available in the shops in Jamestown and it makes a special souvenir for those who want a unique reminder of their visit to the island. It is purchased mainly by tourists and local people who send the coffee to their overseas friends and family. Ironically, now that more coffee is being produced, the demand has begun to decrease.

Airport project

At the time of writing, there is no airport or airstrip on the island. Due to the volcanic nature of the island, the terrain is very hilly and rocky and this, combined with the long distance, has made the construction of an airstrip impossible up to this point. There has been a serious proposal in recent years from SHELCO (St Helena Leisure Corporation) to build an airport and resort area for the island. There are many positive and negative factors to the coming of an airport to the island.

SHELCO proposes to form St Helena Airways which would offer flights to six destinations, including fortnightly flights to Ascension Island and the Falklands, twice-weekly flights to Cape Town, and flights to London three times fortnightly. The scheme calls for restricted numbers of 'high-value, low-volume' tourists and for as much tourist-related internal economic activity as possible, which would lead to the creation of new business opportunities in the local private sector.

SHELCO does not believe that Ascension can be a stopover for any of their flights, as it is currently closed to civilian aircraft. Until now, talks with the American government have failed to reach an agreement on this issue. The proposed site of the airport on St Helena, Prosperous Bay, is on the east of the island, the only part of the island flat enough to support an airstrip. The main problem is that the area is barely adequate for a runway going from north to south, which provides the safest take-off and approach path. It is assessed that, even with substantial rock-blasting and earth-moving, a runway of barely 4,900ft (1,500m) could be created, reduced to about 4,100ft (1,250m) of useable length once the appropriate safety areas had been erected. The northern end of the proposed runway is bordered by a sheer drop to the sea of over 820ft (250m). At the southern end is an unfillable ravine more than 328ft (100m) deep, running from east to west. Another obstacle to the airport is the prevailing southeasterly wind which would affect a north-to-south runway with a permanent crosswind. Many studies have been made and various options have been considered. SHELCO has designed plans to try and overcome some of these obstacles.

Another problem would be trying to find a suitable aircraft, since St Helena requires something capable of flying extremely long distances over the ocean as there is no place to stop and refuel. The aeroplane must also be capable of landing and taking off on a short runway.

The advantages of the project would be to make the island more accessible to tourists. It may also help encourage locals to grow produce for export, hence giving a boost to the economy. People with serious health problems would be able to be flown to a hospital so that proper medical treatment could be given. The building of and running of an airport would provide local people with jobs. It is assumed that during the construction phase of the airport and facilities between 550 and 600 people would need to be employed. During the period of construction the government would benefit from additional taxes, customs and excise benefits, with additional electricity, vehicle hire and miscellaneous revenue which could benefit the economy. When all construction was completed, there would be between 100 and 200 jobs for locals. With the creation of a large number of jobs on St Helena, there would be less requirement for offshore employment.

Looking at the other side of the coin, the airport could also bring some disadvantages. St Helena is a quiet, peaceful place and many fear that the noise from the airport would spoil the tranquillity. Much construction and earth removal would have to be undertaken and it is felt that the delicate balance of nature would be affected by this. St Helena is home to many endemic species and there is a danger that, if their environment were disrupted, it could have a detrimental effect on these species and the island could lose the few plants left of that kind. Many studies have been done and are still being done to measure the environmental impact of an airstrip. There is also the fear that, with more tourists coming to the island, there would be a widespread problem of pollution, be it air pollution from the aeroplanes or simple pollution from people not disposing of their rubbish properly. One of the fears on the mind of the people who truly love St Helena is that, with increased access, the island would lose some of its alluring qualities as a unique destination. Part of the attraction of St Helena is that it isn't easy to get to. When this factor is taken away, will the island lose some of its fascination? If the airport comes to be, the *RMS St Helena* would probably no longer be required and the 80–90 St Helenians employed on the ship could lose their jobs.

In addition to the airstrip and the forming of St Helena Airways, SHELCO also propose building a resort hotel and an 18-hole golf course. An additional facility has also been proposed by SHOOT (St Helena Oasis for Optimal Training), to build a professional football and sports training retreat complex. This would be designed to host training camps for international-class football and sports teams from clubs in Europe, Africa and South America. This is all subject to the approval of the St Helena Government, and as yet no decisions have been made one way or the other.

Shipping

From its earliest days, St Helena has been a refuge for shipping. During the years 1659 to 1834 the East India Company operated St Helena as a restocking base for its East Indiamen, returning from the East. Napoleon's presence on St Helena from 1815 to 1821, resulted in a sharp increase in shipping calls. In addition the liberalisation of the shipping trade meant a dramatic increase in the number of calls, even before the East India Company relinquished St Helena to the Crown in 1834. St Helena was also used as a base for the Navy from which to capture slave ships, and a transit base for the whaling industry in the South Atlantic.

The busiest years for shipping were 1845–62, when over a thousand shipping calls per year were recorded during most years. The opening of the Suez Canal in 1869 and use of steamships meant that fewer ships visited St Helena. In 1977, commercial ships stopped calling at St Helena altogether. The second *RMS St Helena* (built in 1989), a passenger and cargo ship, is now the only regular supply ship. She is financed by the British Government. The ship sails a route from Cardiff/Falmouth to Cape Town via Tenerife, Ascension Island and St Helena, making occasional cargo stops at Vigo in Spain. It also sails once a year from Cape Town to Tristan da Cunha and return.

There was talk for a short time about alternative forms of transportation to the island. Some people recommended that there be a shuttle ship service which only serviced the route Ascension–St Helena–Cape Town–St Helena. Studies were done on this possibility but nothing concrete ever materialised. Even though this would increase the frequency of ships' calls at the island, it was felt the solution wasn't adequate to fill the needs of the island. Another idea which was considered was that of a zeppelin service.

Throughout the island's history, St Helena has been used as a place for passing ships to offload crew members who are ill, and this is still true to this day. In the earlier years there was no hospital, and crew members would stay on the island until they recovered, then sail home with the next ship. Today, patients have the benefit of being treated in the hospital, but then they must either wait for the *RMS St Helena* to make her scheduled stop, or for one of the company's ships on a return route, before they can return home. There have been instances when an ailing crew member has had to spend an extended amount of time on the island, due to the ship being full or being back on her way to England at the time of the person's recovery.

THE PEOPLE AND THEIR WAY OF LIFE
Cultural mix

Every person on St Helena has a story to tell, and each is interesting in his or her own right. St Helenians are tremendously committed to their island, and many work tirelessly for the good of the community in the fields of education, local history, music, arts and craft, as well as in government positions. Others spend considerable time fundraising for local charities. There are thriving youth groups on the island, including organisations affiliated to the Scout and Guide movement. But perhaps just as important is the contribution made by those who are prepared to share their knowledge and love of the island with visitors, drawing them into the island's way of life.

The people of St Helena, or Saints as they call themselves, represent a mixture of many different nationalities and influences. Every period in the island's history has brought new people from different parts of the world. The first settlers were European and with them they had their slaves who came from the Far East. Later, Chinese labourers came to the island, and then Boer War prisoners. St Helenians are a mixture of all these. There is no racial discrimination on the island and no racial distinction. The Saints are proud of both of their identities, as British subjects and as Saints. When asked to describe the Saints, most people's answer would be warm and friendly. They are very helpful and they enjoy getting to know visitors and to become familiar with other parts of the world. Another characteristic of the Saints is that they are very patriotic and loyal to Britain. The queen's birthday is celebrated on the island, and in honour of the Queen Mother's 100th birthday a tea was held for the senior citizens on the island.

The language of the Saints

English is the only official language of St Helena. The dialect spoken on the island still has remnants of older English with some South African influence.

It has a kind of musical lilt to it, not dissimilar to a West Indian dialect. There are certain phrases which are common on the island. You may still hear, for example, 'How is you be?' Sometimes the non-British visitor may have difficulty understanding all that is being said, but you do get used to it after spending some time among the people.

A close-knit community

As a whole, the St Helenians are a close-knit community. The island has an air of small town life. Everyone knows everyone else's business, and word travels fast on the island. The people are reluctant to speak publicly, perhaps because the majority are employed either directly or indirectly by the government. They may be afraid of affecting their employment status if they complain openly. One does feel, however, the effect the dependency on Great Britain has on the people. The UK does have a control on these people's lives to some extent. The government does help support them, but it doesn't give them ample opportunity to try to stand on their own by making a life for themselves. Many conditions in their lives are dictated according to what the money being injected into St Helena is being used for. Many young Saints are aware that there is very little opportunity for them on the island, so they make plans to leave, be it to study, serve in the military, or take up employment offshore.

What is really nice about the people on St Helena is that they help their neighbours. The average person may not have much, but there is never hesitation when someone is in need. A heartfelt example of this was when a young girl who was gravely ill with leukaemia had to be transported to the hospital in Cape Town. At the time both of her parents were working on the Falklands and she was being cared for by her grandmother. The islanders, feeling deep sympathy for the family, pulled together and raised money, through cake sales and other events, in order that her parents and siblings could join her while she was receiving treatment in Cape Town and also to help defer some of the costs. Tragically she passed away soon after she arrived in Cape Town.

The children of St Helena

According to the 1998 St Helena census, the number of children is decreasing and the figures of the middle-aged population have increased. As overseas workers retire, the middle-age bulge will become an old-age bulge. Since the 1980s, the birth rate has fallen considerably. At present there are about 12 births per thousand population. The infant mortality rate has declined over the years from 50 per thousand live births in 1950 to ten per thousand live births in 1999. The death rate on St Helena has remained fairly consistant over the years.

A disturbing part of the society of St Helena is that many children are growing up without the benefit of being able to live with one or both of their parents. The economic situation and the high unemployment rate force people to look for jobs offshore in order to support their families. There are a number of children living in one parent households. Most of the time it is the father who has to seek employment on Ascension, the Falklands or in rare cases, the United Kingdom. There are also families where both parents work offshore in order to earn enough and the children are being brought up by their grandparents. It is estimated that over one hundred children are being cared for by adults who are not their parents. Many people, including the Education Department, feel that this is detrimental to the welfare of the children. Some people feel it is the cause of behavioural problems which have been observed. They feel that this situation gives the children very little hope for a successful future and that they will have to struggle, as have their parents and grandparents, in order to make ends meet.

Education and job opportunities
Schooling
The education system on St Helena is adequate. The schooling on the island largely follows the British system, with local variations as appropriate. Students work towards GSCE and A level examinations. The system of education changed from a two- to a three-tier system in 1988, with the completion of Prince Andrew School, which was funded by a development aid project. There are four first schools, covering the ages between five and eight years old: Half Tree Hollow First School, Jamestown First School, Longwood First School and St Paul First School. There are three middle schools, for children ages 8–12 years: Harford Middle School, Pilling Middle School and St Paul's Middle School. Children aged 12–16 attend Prince Andrew Central School. A pre-school is available for children from the age of three and a half years. Many of the teachers in the schools are Saints, but in recent years, teachers have had to be brought in from outside St Helena, due to local teachers leaving the island for better-paid jobs offshore.

Options after school
St Helena doesn't have much to offer in the way of further education. There is a teacher's college, which many attend. If someone wants to learn a specific job or trade, they usually have to go off the island in order to attend training school. Suitably qualified students are able to take university and college courses in the UK, under a number of scholarship schemes. The British Armed Forces regularly send recruiters to the island looking for interested youths. There are also several schemes which have been planned in order to educate young people to do certain jobs. Students who wish to follow a vocational training are given the possibility of participating in vocational courses in the UK, under the Training and Work Experience Schemes (TWES). Other vocational training is available from experts on the island.

Job opportunities
Most of the jobs available to Saints are for unskilled positions, despite the fact that many of the people who take these jobs are well trained (nurses, teachers, police etc.). Unfortunately, they can't find a well-paid skilled job on the island,

so they are forced to take unskilled work offshore for higher pay. Only 25% of the offshore posts are considered skilled.

The UK government has had to bring in teachers and nurses from Great Britain and South Africa to fill the jobs being left by the Saints. The shocking number is that 80% of teachers have left the profession in the last ten years and 50% of the current teachers have less than five years' experience. This includes the two years of teacher's training, which starts at the age of 18. The loss of experienced teachers has resulted in poor student performance. The quality of health care has also fallen due to the large number of trained nurses leaving the island for higher paid unskilled jobs offshore. There is a real lack of qualified nursing staff.

There is a noticeable difference between the wages of a local and that of an ex-pat worker. A former local teacher who was department head at one of the schools told us that she earned £800 a year before taxes compared with an ex-pat with the same qualifications reportedly earning £5,000, plus travel expenses. These differences in salaries are an important factor for many Saints and sometimes quite a sore subject.

Religion

There are several religious denominations represented on St Helena. The majority of the inhabitants belong to the Anglican Church, being members of the Diocese of St Helena, which includes Ascension Island. The Bishop of St Helena resides on the island. This Diocese is part of the Church of the Province of Southern Africa. Less than 1% of St Helenians belong to no religious group or say they have no religious belief.

The Baptists are the second oldest denomination on the island. They were founded in 1845 when a Scottish evangelist arrived at Jamestown from the Cape. In 1846 the Baptist mission house was purchased, and in 1854 four Baptist churches were opened. Since 1852, a succession of Catholic priests have been sent to St Helena, initially as military chaplains. The history of the Salvation Army starts in about 1884. Many other religious faiths have also established themselves on the island over the years: Seventh-Day Adventists, Jehovah's Witnesses, New Apostolics and Bahaii. Details of most church services are published in the island's weekly newspaper, St Helena Herald.

Cultural and sporting activities
Music

The musical group called The Get-Togethers Orchestra, formed by a St Helenian, plays at functions and takes in the annual Christmas Parade in Jamestown.

In 1996, the St Helena Young Musicians was established. This is a group of young people brought together to encourage them to pursue their interest in music and hopefully to develop their talents so that they can use music to build a life for themselves.

In 1999, the St Helena Ladies' Orchestra was formed. They usually practise once every other week, increasing to once a week if a performance is nearing. The members of the orchestra choose the songs that they wish to play. Two shows are organised a year. At the time of writing this book, the orchestra consists of 16 dedicated members, most of whom are termed as 'middle-aged'. They would welcome any new members wishing to join, especially younger women over the age of 16 years. With such a small group, when a member leaves they find it difficult to replace that person, partly because people may not have their own musical instrument. Through fundraising, the orchestra has been able to buy four of their own instruments so far, and with future performances, they hope to raise enough money to purchase more.

Sport
St Helenians enjoy and participate in various spectator and team sports.

Cricket
There is a cricket league involving about nine teams. Although the turf is not of the quality you would find in South Africa or England, the Saint Helenians adjust well to the demands of the terrain, and it is a much loved sport of the islanders.

Island games
St Helenians became involved in international sport in 1985 when they accepted an invitation to participate in the newly organised Island Games held on the Isle of Man. The Governor's Discretionary Fund as well as voluntary donations and various fundraising activities helped send a team of athletes and a manager to the games. At these games a runner from St Helena won a bronze medal in the 100m race. Two years later another team was funded and sent to the games on Guernsey. St Helena wasn't able to participate in the games again until 1997 for financial reasons. The island of Jersey took it upon itself to help raise money so that a team of six competitors and their manager could travel and take part in the Island Games. The Foreign and Commonwealth Office set aside some money and helped finance St Helena's participation in the Island Games held in Gotland, Sweden in 1999. Fundraising continues for participation in other island games.

Sailing
Another sport which has put St Helena on the world map, to a small extent, is yacht racing. In 1996, the first Governor's Cup Race took place. The race starts in Cape Town and finishes in St Helena. Between 20 and 30 yachts take part in the race, which is held every two years. In the year 2000, the crew of *Beluga* included four young people from the island who trained for two months in preparation for the race. This was only the second time that islanders actually participated in the race. There is a programme set up to train other Saints to take part on the crew of a yacht in future races. This gives these young people exposure to an international sport and gives them pride that they have been chosen to represent their island. The next

Governor's Cup is scheduled to commence on November 30 2002, from Cape Town.

Fishing and other watersports
Not only is fishing a source of income for some islanders, it is also one of the most popular pastimes. Scuba diving is something of an adventure here, with a diverse abundance of marine life. Swimming is popular in the Olympic-sized pool and from some coastal areas.

Skittles
Skittles is popular and there are many teams which participate in the league. Skittles is a form of bowling, using wooden pins and rubber balls. It is actually a lot of fun. Many people take it quite seriously though, as you may see if you decide to participate in a skittles match on the ship.

Football
Football is also played on the island, on Francis Plain. The official football season is August to December, and there are two divisions of teams.

Golf
Golf is very popular on the island and there are various competitions held. The golf course is unique in that it is probably the most remote golf course in the world. Though not long, at just 4,783 yards (4,374m), it can be challenging. Visitors are always welcome, even at weekends.

Rifle shooting
Rifle shooting is also a well-known sport on St Helena; a few young Saints have competed at international level in the Island Games, and have done very well. Full-bore competitions for first-, second- and third-class competitors and small-bore competitions are held each year. In 1999 at the Island Games held in Gotland, Sweden, a young man from St Helena brought home a bronze medal in 300m rifle shooting.

Social events
The Saints are a sociable people; there are many dances and fundraisers held, all well attended. The money raised at these events is used to support projects like Meals on Wheels, renovations on the churches and various other charities. There are also sport days where the school children compete against each other in various disciplines.

Christmas is a festive time on the island. The schools hold an annual Christmas pageant and Jamestown is brightly lit and decorated. It seems everyone gets into the Christmas spirit. There is a parade with musicians and Father Christmas makes a special appearance as well. There is dancing in the street and the community comes together to celebrate the holiday. The day after Christmas there is a sports day held in the centre of Jamestown. Market Street is closed to traffic in the afternoon as various games and competitions are held. It is great fun to watch as well as to participate. The Miss St Helena pageant, sponsored by local businesses and organisations, takes place in May.

Public holidays
New Year's Day (1 January)
Good Friday
Easter Monday
St Helena Day (May 21)
Whit Monday (day after Whitsuntide)
Queen's Birthday (second Saturday in June)
August Bank Holiday (last Monday in August)
Christmas Day (25 December)
Boxing Day (26 December)

Food
Like most communities, the Saints have their own traditional dishes. The most popular is fish cakes, quite often served with a tomato sauce. In addition to this, a very popular dish is pilau, which is a curried rice and meat or fish dish, served piping hot with or without vegetables. Other dishes which are typical of the island are black pudding, coconut fingers, pumpkin pudding and pumpkin fritters. The standard of food in restaurants and hotels is generally good, but not outstanding by international standards.

Social problems
Throughout the history of the island, there have been small incidents of social unrest. In recent times these are on a much smaller scale than during the times of the military garrison on the island. One incident which happened in 1996 still stands out in people's minds today. There was a debate on the government's plan to cut the meagre social services pensions. This enraged a group of St Helenians and they marched their way into the governor's office and demanded improvements. During the incident it is said that someone grabbed the governor by the tie. No-one was hurt in the confrontation, and it was settled within a short period of time, but the media got hold of the story and brought it to the attention of the world. In the end, the changes demanded were made.

One thing that is evident on the island is that some people drink out of boredom or to forget their troubles. A problem which has started to become serious in recent years is under-age drinking, with youths of about 15 or 16 years of age seen in bars and pubs. To alleviate this problem, personal identification cards have been issued, as in most European countries.

Another increasing complaint on St Helena is about noise pollution: the most frequently reported incidents are booming stereos, either from cars or homes. Until recently, the Consulate Hotel held a disco every Saturday night and the music could be heard well all over Jamestown centre. Now, in consideration for their guests, they have ceased having the disco if the ship is in port.

Above The eye-catching Wellington House, now a well-known hotel on
Main Street in Jamestown (NR)

Below left Entrance to the Castle in Jamestown, with the coat of arms of
the East India Company above the archway (NR)

Below right Jacob's Ladder leading up from Jamestown to Ladder Hill Fort (US)

Above Longwood House, Napoleon's home for most of his period of exile (NR)

Right Cannon and other military hardware are to be found all around the island (HM)

Below Napoleon's campaign cot on display at Longwood House museum (NR)

Practical Information

In recent years, St Helena has been trying to find ways to boost its tourist services in order to offer more to the visitor as well as to encourage other people to visit the island. Many improvements have been made and, though there are still many things which could be done, progress is definitely being made and in a beneficial way.

The **St Helena Tourism Association** (Main Street, Jamestown; tel: 2158; fax: 2159; email: StHelena.Tourism@helanta.sh) was set up to involve members of the private sector in the development of tourism on the island. Things that have been done to improve St Helena include the Jamestown Beautification Project, improvements to Sandy Bay Beach, and erecting signs and clearing walking trails. More practical information for excursions to take on St Helena may be found in *Chapter 5*.

WHEN TO GO

The main 'tourist season' on St Helena is from November to March, when it is summer in the southern hemisphere and the days are sunny and hot. Those wishing to visit the island at this time need to make sure that they reserve their ship's passage and accommodation as far in advance as possible as space is limited and fills up quickly. Often you will be put on the waiting list, which is usually long and the chances of getting a passage can become quite slim. Summer is also the time of year when cruise ships make their stop at the island.

During the off-season, it is fairly easy to get space on the ship and a place to stay on St Helena. There are less tourists during this time, but this is also the time of year when the most rainfall occurs and it is noticeably cooler than in the summer months. This doesn't mean one can expect bad weather every day. It simply means that the chances are higher for unfavourable weather. The heaviest rainfall occurs July through September.

PLANNING A VISIT

Everyone has their own reason for going to St Helena, which makes it difficult to suggest the ideal way to see the island. Many people who have visited St Helena will agree that you need at least a week to really experience what the island is about. This gives time to ease yourself into the island lifestyle and to get to know some of the locals. It also allows ample time to plan various excursions to the different points of interest on the island without trying to crowd them all into a short time-span.

SAILING TO ST HELENA
Anchorage
St Helena has only one harbour, The Anchorage in James Bay. There are a limited number of orange mooring buoys available for yachts off West Rocks.

Clearance
St Helena Port Control may be contacted Monday to Friday, 08.30–16.00, on VHF channel 16. Formalities are simple, but should be done in working hours. No overtime is charged, but clearance on weekends is only done by arrangement. All persons must remain on board until cleared by the harbour master, customs and police. Clearance for departure at weekends can be given by customs on the Friday before departure.

Customs
Animals, plants, vegetables and fruit are prohibited without proper import documentation and must not be brought ashore. A declaration of bonded stores is required to be handed to customs on arrival.

Fees
The entry fee for all persons over 12 years is £11. Harbour dues of £17.50 are payable on arrival. Payment can be made in local currency, sterling, Visa or MasterCard.

Coming ashore
Commuting ashore is sometimes a problem due to surge at the landing pier. The local government has introduced a ferry service from 04.00 to 20.00. Arrangements can be made with the ferry operator for transportation to and from the yacht after these times. The regular fee is £1 per person per day.

Supplies
Yachting facilities are scarce. Water can be obtained at the landing steps (bring your own container or hose). Diesel fuel, petrol and bottled gas can be obtained from Solomons Fuel Station, Narra Backs (tel: 2259). Delivery to yachts can be arranged. Visiting boats are not allowed to come alongside the dock so all fuel has to be transported by launch or dinghy.

Repairs
Simple repairs can be carried out on the island. Contact the Harbour Office for information (tel: 2750).

For further information, see www.noonsite.com

There are no package or organised group tours available to St Helena, although a few cruise ships and research vessels make an occasional stop at the island as part of their itinerary. Other than that, a trip to St Helena is an independent undertaking.

For **tourist information** on the island, contact the St Helena Tourist Office, Main Street, Jamestown; tel: 2158, fax: 2159, email: StHelena.Tourism@ helanta.sh.

Getting there and away

Getting to St Helena is almost as adventurous as being on St Helena. One needs plenty of time because there are a limited number of possibilities to reach this isolated destination in the middle of the South Atlantic Ocean.

RMS St Helena

At the moment, the only way to reach St Helena is by sea. The **RMS St Helena**, which is now being run by Andrew Weir Shipping, is only the second ship to bear this name. The present ship was brought into service in 1989 and has 56 officers and crew members. She is 344ft (105m) long and over 63ft (19.2m) wide and has the capacity to hold 128 passengers in 49 cabins. The ship makes the round trip between the UK and St Helena four times a year. The voyage from Great Britain to St Helena takes about two weeks. The ship makes calls at Tenerife (Canary Islands) and Ascension Island before arriving at St Helena. Then it makes its way to Cape Town, South Africa, and stays in the South Atlantic for about six weeks doing the shuttle St Helena–Ascension–St Helena and St Helena–Cape Town–St Helena. Once a year she makes the voyage to the remote island of Tristan da Cunha, departing from and returning to Cape Town.

On arrival at St Helena, the ship is anchored offshore and passengers are brought ashore by tender.

Passengers are required to have full travel insurance for all medical and repatriation liabilities. Cancellation insurance, which can be obtained by UK citizens through Andrew Weir Shipping, is also strongly advised.

Fares on the ship vary according to cabin category and the voyage. To give an idea of costs, one-way fares for a two-berth cabin are as follows:

UK port–St Helena (15 days)	£1,055 (this fare is heavily subsidised)
UK–Ascension (13 days)	£1,670
UK–Cape Town (duration varies on schedule of RMS and time spent on St Helena)	£2,835
Cape Town–Tristan da Cunha–Cape Town (5 days each way)	£960 each way (since this has be purchased as a round-trip the price would be £1,920)
Ascension–St Helena (48 hours)	£440
Ascension–Cape Town (8 days)	£1,250
Cape Town–St Helena (5 days)	£640

A DAY ON THE RMS ST HELENA

The atmosphere on the RMS St Helena is informal. There are plenty of activities to keep everyone happy, but nothing is forced. For quieter passengers, there is nothing more relaxing than sitting on deck and trying to catch sight of a school of dolphins playing with the ship. If you are really lucky you may even see a whale.

There is no better way to start the day than to have your morning tea and the day's copy of the onboard newspaper, Ocean Mail, brought to your cabin around 07.00 by your cabin steward or stewardess. The paper contains a list of the days planned activites, some helpful hints, and the suggested dress code for dinner, according to the captain's 'Officers' Rig of the Day'.

For those who prefer to start their day active, there is almost always a 20-minute workout video being shown in the main lounge at 07.40 which helps to get the circulation going and build up a good appetite for breakfast. The video is suitable for all age groups.

Breakfast can be taken in either the sun lounge, where a continental breakfast is served from 07.30 until 10.00, or in the dining room where a sit-down breakfast is served from 08.00 until 09.15.

There are a number of ways to spend the morning. The main lounge has a small library of books which can be signed out and returned by the end of the voyage. The cupboard nearby contains a number of board games (Scrabble, chess, draughts etc.). For those who like to give their brain a good work-out, there is a daily crossword puzzle which can be obtained from the shelf outside the chief purser's office.

If you feel the need to work off the great breakfast you just enjoyed, there is a small exercise room set up during the day with a rowing machine and exercise bicycle in the quiet lounge at the aft end of A deck, on the port side. After 17.30 this room becomes a quiet room for card playing, letter writing, etc. What about a quick dip in the ship's salt-water pool? It is rather small, but it can be quite refreshing, especially on a hot day. The morning is also a great time for a stroll around the deck and maybe a quick stop on the bridge to talk to the officer on duty and check the ship's current position.

Fares are applicable in either direction of travel. The fare for a round trip is calculated by adding the two legs of the trip together.

Private yacht

A few visitors reach the island by **private yacht** (see box, page 56). Some participate in a yacht race, like the Governor's Cup which starts in Cape Town and finishes at St Helena. The island has also been a stopping point for some round-the-world yacht races, with crews using using their time at the island to do their laundry and replenish their supplies. There are quite a few people who make a stop at St Helena while sailing the world on their private yacht.

Feeling like you need a bit of nourishment but it isn't yet time for lunch? At 10.30 there is beef tea (a beef bouillon) served in the sun lounge.

Before lunch, various knock-out tournaments, such as deck quoits, scrabble, chess, cribbage, eucre and ping pong, take place. At the end of the voyage the winners of the individual tournaments and competions receive their prizes in a special awards ceremony.

Like breakfast, there are two lunchtime options. For those who wish something light, there is a salad bar set up in the sun lounge between 12.00 and 13.15, while in the dining room lunch is served from 12.00 until 13.30.

After lunch you may wish to take a nap or enjoy some peaceful moments with a book on a chair on deck. Every afternoon there is also a video shown in the main lounge, with details listed in the *Ocean Mail*. Sometimes it is a movie, at others it may be a documentary film. At 16.00, tea and sandwiches are available in both lounges. This is usually followed by a programme of classical music from CD or tape in the main lounge. The main lounge is also the location of the very popular team quiz, at 18.15. Over the course of a few evenings, teams of three compete against each other in a general knowledge knockout competition. The winning team from each evening goes on to the final round which determines the 'brains of the *RMS St Helena*'.

You are all ready for dinner, but the chimes have not yet sounded. How do you fill the extra time? What about a walk on deck to watch the sunset? When Mother Nature co-operates, the colours can make a spectacular show. Or you could enjoy a pre-dinner drink at the main lounge bar, which is open from 18.00–23.30. There is a second bar in the sun lounge, open 11.00–13.30 and 18.00–23.30.

Dinner is served in two sittings, at 18.45 and 20.00, which are assigned to passengers before they board the ship. Later, at 21.15, there are organised activities. Sometimes there will be a film shown in the sun lounge. Other evenings there may be games: table quizzes, frog racing, or a tombola.

If you aren't ready to go to bed, head for the sun lounge, where there is either a film or a disco from 22.30. And if you are in the mood for something quieter, what about some star-gazing while strolling along the deck? They say salt air makes one sleep better.

Cruise ship

A few cruise ships make a brief stop at St Helena, including the *QE2*, which anchors here periodically. Ships which make regular stops include the expedition vessels *Professor Molchanov* and the *MV Explorer*. For details, contact one of the following cruise operators:

Cunard Line Mountbatten House, Grosvenor Sq, Southampton S015 2BF, UK; tel (reservations): +44 0800 052 3840; fax: +44 023 8022 5843, web: www.cunard.com
Explorer Shipping Company 1520 Kensington Rd, Oak Brook, Illinois 60521, USA; tel: +1 630 954 2944; fax: +1 630 572 1833; web: www.explorership.com

LONG-HAUL FLIGHTS

There is growing evidence, albeit circumstantial, that long-haul air travel increases the risk of developing deep vein thrombosis. This condition is potentially life threatening, but it should be stressed that the danger to the average traveller is slight. Visitors flying to South Africa en route to St Helena, or direct to Ascension, should be aware of this.

Certain risk factors specific to air travel have been identified. These include immobility, compression of the veins at the back of the knee by the edge of the seat, the decreased air pressure and slightly reduced oxygen in the cabin, and dehydration. Consuming alcohol may exacerbate the situation by increasing fluid loss and encouraging immobility.

In theory everyone is at risk, but those at highest risk are shown below:

- Passengers on journeys of longer than eight hours duration
- People over 40
- People with heart disease
- People with cancer
- People with clotting disorders
- People who have had recent surgery, especially on the legs
- Women who are pregnant, or on the pill or other oestrogen therapy
- People who are very tall (over 6ft/1.8m) or short (under 5ft/1.5m)

A deep vein thrombosis (DVT) is a clot of blood that forms in the leg veins. Symptoms include swelling and pain in the calf or thigh. The skin may feel hot to touch and becomes discoloured (light blue-red). A DVT is not dangerous in itself, but if a clot breaks down then it may travel to the lungs

Hapag Lloyd Cruiseship Management Ballindamm 25, D-20095 Hamburg, Germany; tel: +49 040 3001 4764; fax +49 040 3001 4761; web: www.hlkf.de
Holland America Line 300 Elliott Av W, Seattle, WA 98119, USA; tel +1 206 281 3535; fax: +1 (206) 281 7110; web: www.hollandamerica.com
Oceanwide Expeditions Bellamypark 9, NL-4381 CG Vlissingen, Holland; tel: +31 118 410 410; fax: (+31) 118 410 417; email: expeditions@ocnwide.com
Radisson Seven Seas Cruises 600 Corporate Drive, Suite 410, Fort Lauderdale, Florida 33334, USA; tel (toll free): 800 477 7500 or +1 877 505 5370; web: www.rssc.com
Seabourn Cruise Line Mountbatten House Grosvenor Square Southampton S015 2BF, UK; tel: +44 0800 052 3841; fax: +44 023 8022 5843; web: www.seabourncruiseline.co.uk
Silversea Cruises 77/79 Great Eastern St, London EC2A 3HU, UK; tel +44 (0) 870 333 7030; fax: +44 (0) 870 333 7040; www.silversea.com

Tour operators

There are some tour operators which can make arrangements for people to go to St Helena. As the island is slowly discovered as a tourist destination,

(pulmonary embolus). Symptoms of a pulmonary embolus (PE) include chest pain, shortness of breath and coughing up small amounts of blood.

Symptoms of a DVT rarely occur during the flight, and typically occur within three days of arrival, although symptoms of a DVT or PE have been reported up to two weeks later.

Anyone who suspects that they have these symptoms should see a doctor immediately as anticoagulation (blood thinning) treatment can be given.

Prevention of DVT
General measures to reduce the risk of thrombosis are shown below. This advice also applies to long train or bus journeys.

- Whilst waiting to board the plane, try to walk around rather than sit.
- During the flight drink plenty of water (at least two small glasses every hour).
- Avoid excessive tea, coffee and alcohol.
- Perform leg-stretching exercises, such as pointing the toes up and down.
- Move around the cabin when practicable.

If you fit into the high-risk category (see above) ask your doctor if it is safe to travel. Additional protective measures such as graded compression stockings, aspirin or low molecular weight heparin can be given. No matter how tall you are, where possible request a seat with extra legroom.

perhaps more travel agencies will take an interest in the island. Note that at present there is only very limited accommodation and services available to group tours.

In the UK
Andrew Weir Shipping Ltd Dexter House, 2 Royal Mint Court, London EC3N 4XX; tel: 020 7265 0808; fax: 020 7816 4835; email: chartering@aws.co.uk
Strand Travel Charing Cross Shopping Concourse, Strand, London WC2N 4HZ; tel: 020 7836 6363; fax: 020 7497 0078

In South Africa
St Helena Line Ltd PO Box 484, Cape Town 8000. Offices: Andrew Weir Shipping South Africa, 1 Thibault Square, 3rd floor, Cape Town 8000; tel: +27 (0) 214 251165; fax: +27 (0) 214 217485; email: sthelenaline@mweb.co.za

In the US
Cruise Freighter Travel Association PO Box 580188, Flushing, NY 11358; tel: (800) 872 8584; email: info@travltips.com

HINTS ON PHOTOGRAPHY
Nick Garbutt and John Jones

All sorts of photographic opportunities present themselves on the islands, from simple holiday snaps to that in-depth study of a rare plant. For the best results, give some thought to the following tips.

As a general rule, if it doesn't look good through the viewfinder, it will never look good as a picture. Don't take photographs for the sake of taking them; be patient and wait until the image looks right.

Photographing **people** is never easy and more often than not it requires a fair share of luck. If you want to take a portrait shot of a stranger, it is always best to ask first. Focus on the eyes of your subject since they are the most powerful ingredient of any portrait, and be prepared for the unexpected.

There is no mystique to good **wildlife** photography. The secret is getting into the right place at the right time and then knowing what to do when you are there. Look for striking poses, aspects of behaviour and distinctive features. Try not only to take pictures of the species itself, but also to illustrate it within the context of its environment. Alternatively, focus in close on a characteristic which can be emphasised.

Photographically, the eyes are the most important part of an animal – focus on these, make sure they are sharp and try to ensure they contain a highlight.

Look at the surroundings – there is nothing worse than a distracting twig or highlighted leaf lurking in the background. Getting this right is often the difference between a mediocre and a memorable image.

A powerful flashgun adds the option of punching in extra light to transform an otherwise dreary picture. Artificial light is no substitute for natural light, though, so use it judiciously.

Freighter World Cruises 180 South Lake Av, Suite 335, Pasadena, CA 91101-2655; tel: (800) 531 7774; fax: (626) 449 3106; email: info@freighterworld.com

In Switzerland
SGV Reisezentrum Weggis Seestrasse 7, CH-6353 Weggis/Switzerland; tel: 041 390 11 33; fax: 041 390 14 09; email: info@frachtschiffreisen.ch

RED TAPE
St Helena is a British Dependency, so overseas it is represented by embassies of the United Kingdom. The St Helena Police handle all **immigration** formalities. When the *RMS St Helena* lays anchor, they come aboard and all passengers, regardless of whether they are residents of St Helena, must be processed through immigration. A visitor's pass is issued to the traveller for a period of up to three months. If the intended stay is longer than the length of the pass, then the tourist must go to the police station to obtain an extension for a period of up to one year, provided that certain conditions are met.

Getting close to the subject correspondingly reduces the depth of field. At camera-to-subject distances of less than a metre, apertures between f16 and f32 are necessary to ensure adequate depth of field. This means using flash to provide enough light. If possible, use one or two small flashguns to illuminate the subject from the side.

Landscapes are forever changing, even on a daily basis. Good landscape photography is all about good light and capturing mood. Generally the first and last two hours of daylight are best, or when peculiar climatic conditions add drama or emphasise distinctive features. Never place the horizon in the centre – in your mind's eye divide the frame into thirds and either exaggerate the land or the sky.

Film

If you're using conventional film (as against a digital camera), select the right film for your needs. Film speed (ISO number) indicates the sensitivity of the film to light. The lower the number, the less sensitive the film, but the better quality the final image. For general print film, ISO 100 or 200 fit the bill perfectly. If you are using transparencies for home use or for lectures, then again ISO 100 or 200 film is fine. However, if you want to get your work published, the superior quality of ISO 25 to 100 film is best.

* Try to keep your film cool. Never leave it in direct sunlight.
* Don't allow fast film (ISO 800 and above) to pass through X-ray machines.
* Under weak light conditions use a faster film (ISO 200 or 400).

All visitors over the age of 12 years disembarking at St Helena must pay a **fee of £11**. You must have a valid passport, show proof of adequate funds to sustain you during your stay on the island, proof of confirmed accommodation for the duration of your stay, and an onward ticket to leave St Helena at the end of your stay. You must also have proof of **medical insurance** with you if you intend to stay for longer than 48 hours.

All luggage from the ship is brought to the customs' shed or tent and, once everything is off loaded, travellers can claim their luggage and be processed through customs. No food may be taken on to the island unless accompanied by both an import permit and export inspection certificates from the country of origin. This is a precaution against potential pests and disease unwittingly being brought ashore. Other goods which are prohibited from being taken on the island are firearms and ammunition, unless accompanied by a valid licence; obscene items or pornographic literature, films or videotapes; animals, unless accompanied by a permit issued by the Chief Agricultural and Natural Resources Officer on St Helena.

St Helena is not a duty-free port. Visitors arriving on the island are allowed to bring the following: one litre of spirits or alcohol over 22% volume and two litres of wine or 340 bottles/cans of beer; maximum 250 millilitres of perfume or toilet water; maximum 200 cigarettes; 250 grams or less of other tobacco goods. People under the age of 18 years cannot claim duty-free allowance of alcoholic products and people under the age of 16 years cannot claim duty-free allowance of cigarettes or other tobacco products.

For people arriving at St Helena by yacht, the formalities are similar. They must register with the police in order to get their immigration permit. The departure formalities are the same. See also page 56.

For passengers of cruise ships/exploration vessels who are only on the island for a very limited time, there are usually special arrangements made between the ship and immigration. Each individual ship informs the passengers about how immigration will be handled.

WHAT TO TAKE
Clothing
For normal day wear on the island, casual attire is appropriate. While formal clothing is not necessary, as the island has a relaxed atmosphere, smart dress is advisable for some evenings. Since the climate of St Helena is almost tropical, it is a good idea to pack loose, comfortable clothes. During the summer it can be very hot in Jamestown, but inland it is noticeably cooler, though the humidity is evident in both places. A light rain jacket and an umbrella are always good things to have. A sweatshirt can also be useful in case the winds play up, cooling down the temperature. If you plan on staying in Jamestown and touring the island by taxi, then normal comfortable shoes would be sufficient. For those who wish to explore the island on foot as much as possible, it is recommended that you bring good sturdy hiking shoes. The terrain is hilly and rocky in some places, while in others the hiking paths are just dirt and rocks, and it is important to have adequate support to lessen the possibility of injuries.

Photographic equipment
As can well be imagined, there are lots of excellent photo-taking opportunities on St Helena. The scenery provides plenty of subject matter, as do the people on the island. Most are quite flattered if you take their picture.

There is only one place on the island to develop photographic film. Even though there are places in Jamestown which sell most popular types of film, prices are expensive. Make sure you have enough film and batteries before you get to St Helena.

HEALTH AND SAFETY
Health
No immunisations or malaria prevention are required. There are plenty of mosquitoes on St Helena, but they do not carry malaria or any other infectious disease.

There are no dangerous wild animals on St Helena; the only animals on the island are domestic. There are no snakes and no poisonous insects. There are, however, centipedes and various species of beetle, but they are harmless, even if they aren't pleasant to have around.

The water on the island is deemed safe to drink.

Health care

Health care today is relatively good when you consider the remoteness of the island and the limited facilities they have. There is one general hospital (54 beds) with four doctors and a trained nursing staff. Every so often a specialist from the UK or South Africa will visit the island and hold special clinics for those requiring treatment. There is also a dental clinic and outpatient services. There is no privately owned pharmacy on the island. Visitors requiring any pharmaceutical supplies should contact the hospital (tel: 2500).

The hospital is equipped with an operating theatre and can handle most general medical problems. Unfortunately, if there is an extremely serious medical case involving complicated surgery or treatment, the hospital doesn't have the appropriate facilities. In cases like this, the patient has to be transported to Cape Town, South Africa, in order to receive proper medical treatment. The patient and his/her family must rely on the *RMS St Helena* and her schedule, which may sometimes mean a prolonged wait and can be very distressing for those involved.

British passport holders are eligible to pay local rates for medical and dental services, but non-UK residents pay higher rates.

Visitors with medical problems or requiring specialised care should make sure they bring more than an adequate amount of any medication with them. Although the hospital is well supplied, there may be certain things that are not available.

Safety

All in all, St Helena is a safe island. Only in very rare cases has a violent crime been committed. In these few instances the crime was not a random one, but occurred between parties who had a dispute with each other. Normal and sensible precautions should be taken here as with any other destination. Make sure valuables are in a safe place and then the risk of something being taken will be minimised. It is safe to walk in Jamestown after sundown. There are normally many people about and being the friendly sort, you will probably be stopped several times to have a chat or a quick hello. Unlike many other places, there are no beggars on the island. The people have much pride in who they are and would not consider becoming a nuisance to tourists by begging. Hard drugs are not a problem on St Helena. Occasionally someone will be caught trying to smuggle marijuana on the ship, but in most cases, the person is caught and the drugs confiscated and destroyed. This is one world problem that the island does not yet have to deal with and hopefully in the future, never will. This is one of the great advantages of having only a restricted number of tourists.

The crimes most often committed are petty theft, public drunkenness and traffic violations. In serious cases, the person is arrested and tried before the proper court. If given a custodial sentence this will be served in HM Prison, Jamestown. In extreme cases they will serve their sentences in the UK.

There was a time when HM Prison in Jamestown was empty. In the past few years this hasn't been the case. One of the advantages of being on an isolated island in the middle of the South Atlantic is that, if a prisoner escapes, he has a very high chance of being caught.

MONEY AND BANKING

The official currency of St Helena is the St Helena pound, which has an equal value to the British pound sterling. Travellers who are in possession of British pounds do not need to exchange them for St Helena currency before they arrive, as every business accepts sterling.

When cruise ships arrive with international passengers, a few businesses will occasionally accept US dollars and euros. Not all businesses will do this, though, so it is best to have either British or St Helena currency.

Within the past two years, major credit cards (MasterCard and Visa) have started to be accepted by most shops and businesses as a method of payment on St Helena, so it is a good idea to ask. There are no facilities on the island to withdraw cash from credit cards or bank cards.

There are no commercial banks on the island of St Helena. The only 'bank' that exists is the **Government Savings Bank** at the Castle in Jamestown (tel: 2470), usually open Mon, Tue, Thu, Fri 11.00–15.00; Sat 9.00–12.00. Visitors can change money at the current rate here. Travellers' cheques can be cashed; a commission of 1% is charged. The bank does not offer the full range of banking facilities, but it serves the needs of the islanders, making it possible for them to receive and transfer money from and to their relatives and families offshore. Some foreign currencies can also be exchanged at Solomon and Company in Jamestown.

GETTING AROUND

Depending upon your needs and requirements, there are many options. There is no scheduled bus service on the island. Most St Helenians get around by car.

Hitchhiking

Some people choose to start walking to their destination, and along the way, there is usually a car which stops and the driver will ask if you would like a ride to where you are going. On St Helena, this is perfectly safe. The people on the island have a genuine interest in tourists and they like to be of assistance if they can. It is all part of the islanders' friendly charm. This is an interesting way to get to know the people of St Helena who can offer an insight to the island.

Car hire

If you have a valid driver's licence, then you might consider hiring a car for a few days; this is arguably the best way in which to get a feel for the interior of the island. It is best to arrange the hire car ahead of time, as there are a limited number of cars available for hire on the island. Most of these are privately owned and used, so may not always be available. Cars may be hired either through the shipping line, Andrew Weir Shipping, or through the tourist office in Jamestown. The rates for hire cars are usually £10–20 per day, which includes insurance. You must make sure that you are named the driver on the insurance policy.

All of the cars on the island have been imported from Europe or South Africa; all are used and in various conditions. Most of the vehicles are manual transmission. Take this into consideration when planning your driving tour. You may have to adjust your driving habits to accommodate the condition of the car.

There are about 60 miles (97km) of surfaced road on the island. Bear in mind that St Helena has a lot of steep hills and the roads have been constructed to fit in the terrain, so drive with caution. Most roads on the island are single track. Steep gradients and hairpin bends are common. Island etiquette dictates that the driver coming downhill should make way for traffic coming up. It's important to note that driving on St Helena is on the left, as in the UK and South Africa. Drink-drive laws are strictly enforced. In Jamestown the speed limit is 20mph. Elsewhere on the island, normal speed limits are 30mph, unless otherwise posted. Road signs are shown in miles. Outside of Jamestown, petrol and diesel can be purchased from Solomon's Fuel Stations in Half Tree Hollow and Longwood.

Hiring a taxi

For those who do not wish to drive and choose to have a relaxing tour of the island, hiring a taxi might be a good option. Taxi drivers offer a round-the-island tour which includes all the important sights. The most important places of interest are: The Briars Pavilion, Napoleon's burial site, Longwood House, and Plantation House (residence of the governor). The duration of this tour by taxi is about three hours. When the weather is good, there can be some wonderful views from the interior of St Helena to other scenic places on the island.

The official taxi stand is located in the centre of Jamestown. You can find it by walking to the tourist information office and following the road to the right. The taxis are usually parked in front of the phone booths. When a passenger ship is in James Bay, you can find taxis parked at the harbour. They do not bear a sign which says 'taxi', but official taxis have a special licence plate on the back of the car. They have the normal licence plate number and then there is a space and an extra number afterwards (eg: 432 4). The number after the space signifies how many paying passengers this car is allowed to carry. The taxis aren't equipped with a meter to calculate the cost so fares are negotiable with the driver. Most drivers charge the same amounts.

Cycling

Since the island is very hilly and not all the roads are in great shape, cycling is not really a feasible option. The hills can be quite steep and the twisting and turning narrow roads make cycling hazardous. There are no bikes available for hire.

Guided tours

For the tourists who come to the island on a visiting cruise ship, there are usually organised tours that can be arranged ahead of time on the ship. The *RMS St Helena* also has some island tours which can be booked by passengers. Usually these tours start in Jamestown and are scheduled to accommodate the person's length of time spent on St Helena. Prices for tours vary according to the number of people taking part. The following companies offer tours:

Magma Tours (Proprietor Basil George)

This company offers different tours for groups, but not for individuals. Tours may be booked on board the ship before arrival on St Helena. Participants are advised to have full personal liability insurance. Magma offer a variety of topics of interest, as follows:

The Historical Town Walk A guided tour of Jamestown. It is for a minimum of five people.

The Coastal Boat Tour A guided small boat tour for a group of 10–12 people. It lasts about two hours and is subject to sea conditions being favourable.

The Endemic Botanical Tour An all day tour guided by the island naturalist, George Benjamin. The tours last approximately six hours and participants have to provide their own packed lunch. It is for groups of 10–30 people.

The Island Military Tour An all day guided tour of the military history of the island, lasting approximately six hours. Participants are required to bring their own packed lunch. The group consists of between 10 and 20 people.

Charabanc Tour (Proprietor Colin Corker)

This tour is in an open 18-seat 1929 Chevrolet and, depending on which tour you book, it takes you to different parts of the island. It is highly recommended.

Solomon's Shipping and Travel Agency

This company offers a variety of walking and bus tours accompanied by a local guide, including: a one hour walking tour of Jamestown; a half or full day bus tour of the St Helena sights; and a walking tour of Diana's Peak National Park.

For suggested sightseeing tours by taxi, see pages 87–9.

WHERE TO STAY

One of the conditions of entry to St Helena is that you have confirmed accommodation. During high season, winter in Europe, there is a great demand for accommodation, especially in Jamestown, so it is a good idea to

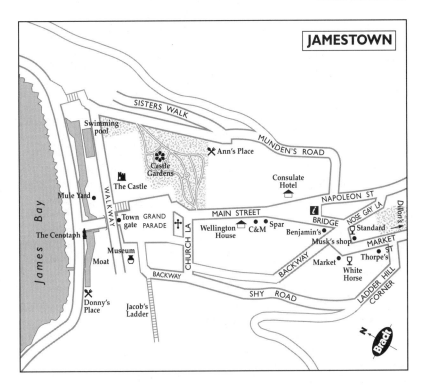

make your reservation well in advance. Because of the limited choices, you should always be flexible with your requirements. Andrew Weir Shipping will automatically make accommodation arrangements through their St Helena agent in one of the island's three hotels, unless specifically requested not to. If you choose to book for yourself, do remember that accommodation has to be booked before setting sail to St Helena.

Hotels

Those who, after a day of sightseeing, appreciate being able to return to a room that has been cleaned, with homemade meals prepared and served on the premises, will probably be happiest staying in a hotel.

Consulate Hotel Main Street, Jamestown; tel: 2962; fax: 2760; email: CON.HOTEL@helanta.sh. Rates per person, per day, single: bed and breakfast £56; half board £67; full board £76; double: bed and breakfast £34; half board £43; full board £49.

Most of the round-trip guests from the *RMS St Helena* are placed by the local shipping agent in this hotel, located in the main street of Jamestown. The largest of the three hotels on the island, all its rooms are twin-bedded, with en-suite bath and shower. Rooms are equipped with wall-to-wall carpeting, a telephone, clock/radio, a fan, and coffee/tea-making facilities. There is a television and video in the main lounge, and a popular bar. There is a sit-down restaurant for hotel guests. The food is good, though simple. The Consulate has an inner courtyard with tables to sit and enjoy a drink. In the basement of the building is an arts and craft centre.

Wellington House Main Street, Jamestown; tel: 2529; fax: 2725 (all double rooms). Full-board rates per person, per day: £62.50 single; £39.50 double. Children aged under two years pay 25%; children aged two and under 12 years pay 50%.

This accommodation is also used by the shipping company. The biggest disadvantage is that none of the rooms have private facilities. The toilets and showers can be found on the second floor. The rooms are on the first floor. The owner of this establishment makes sure the guests are well looked after. The motto of the hotel is 'Your satisfaction – our reward. Just say Wellington House and you are completely at home'. The ambience and the feeling of being at home make the inconvenience of not having private facilities seem not so bad. There is no public bar in Wellington House, so it is quieter than the Consulate Hotel. As a reference, quite often visiting British government officials stay at this establishment when they come to St Helena.

Farm Lodge Hotel Rosemary Plain; tel/fax: 4040 (2 twin-bedded rooms, 2 double rooms, all with en-suite facilities). Fullboard rates per person, per day: £70 single; £55 double.

This newly opened, small hotel is located out in the country, about 20 minutes by car from Jamestown, in a delightful and substantial house, set in its own grounds. There are many places of interest in the interior of the island within easy walking distance. The building was constructed in 1750 as an East India Company planter's house and now elegantly restored to its former glory. Whereas the Consulate Hotel is arguably the 'hotel of the masses', and Wellington House more homely, Farm Lodge is generally more exclusive.

The property is situated at the end of its own road, adding to privacy and peace. The rooms are furnished partially with antiques. In the dining room, silver cutlery is used. The bricks used to build the veranda came from a ship which burned in James Bay many years ago. There are other little classic touches which put this hotel in a class above the others. The owners (a St Helenian and an Englishman) have put a lot of time and effort into renovating this old building, aiming to give guests the most peaceful and memorable holiday possible. If you are looking for something a little bit better and away from Jamestown, then this place comes highly recommended. If you do not have a hire car on arrival, you will be met at Jamestown wharf by car and taken to Farm Lodge. Full English breakfast, as well as mid-morning coffee, are served daily. A light lunch is prepared and packed lunches are available on request for those planning an excursion. Dinner, served at the long dining table with the guests sitting together, is a memorable experience. They use fresh produce from their own garden whenever possible. There is a laundry service. They will also be happy to help arrange walks, tours, car hire etc. There are plans to add a tennis/badminton court, croquet lawn, a swimming pool and two additional rooms.

Bed and breakfast

Those wanting the convenience and services of a hotel, but wishing to have contact with the islanders, may consider staying at a bed and breakfast. There are at present only three properties offering this service, none of them in Jamestown itself, but it seems to be gaining in popularity. A room and

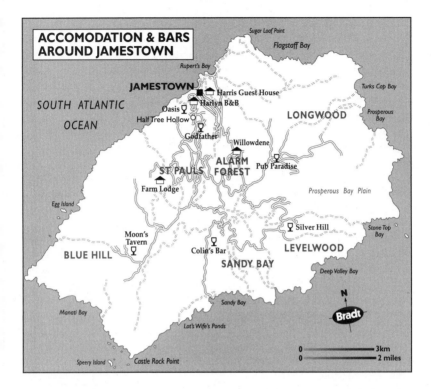

ACCOMODATION & BARS AROUND JAMESTOWN

sometimes a sitting area are provided, as well as breakfast. In most cases, other meals can be obtained by arrangement. It is a good way to get a taste of island life, but with the freedom to come and go, and eat as you choose. Accommodation is best arranged with the tourist office in Jamestown.

Harlyn Bed and Breakfast Half Tree Hollow; tel/fax: 3727 (Arnold Flagg). Daily rates £20 single/ £35 double.
The newly built 'cabin bedroom' is for two people, either bunk bed or twin-bedded, with en-suite bathroom with shower. Private lounge with tea-making facilities, television and video and patio at the rear of the house. Breakfast includes eggs, homemade bread and fruit.
Harris' Guest House Main Street, Jamestown; tel/fax: 2729 (Donald Harris). Daily rates: bed and breakfast: £20 single/ £30 double. Full board: £30 single/ £50 double.
Located in the heart of Jamestown, this guest house is conveniently close to the swimming pool, the library, the shops and the seafront. Guests may use the downstairs lounge, lobby and garden. Accommodation consists of a double room and two family rooms, with shared bathroom. A car is available for hire at a rate of £10 per day.
Willowdene Bed and Breakfast Gordon's Post, Alarm Forest; tel/fax: 4307 (Pat Musk). Daily rates: bed and breakfast £10 single/£18 double; full board £20 single/£38 double.
This home is situated in the country with a spectacular view down to Jamestown and Rupert's Valley. There are three single bedrooms available with shared bathroom.

Self-catering accommodation

For those who don't mind making their own bed or meals, there are a number of flats and bungalows in and outside of Jamestown to choose from. This type of accommodation is more affordable than staying at a hotel with full board. At most properties there is a reduction for longer stays. It is always best to enquire ahead of time for special rates. In some cases the rates for longer lets are negotiable with the property's owner.

The list of self-catering accommodation changes constantly, and prices vary. If you plan on an extended stay on St Helena, it is best to get in contact with the tourist office in Jamestown for a current list (see page 87).

Self-catering establishments are for the most part simple flats, most with washing machines and electrical appliances and sufficient kitchen equipment (pans, cutlery, plates etc). They are furnished adequately but not luxuriously. Most have radios, and some have televisions.

Visitors staying in self-catering accommodation will need to order bread one day ahead from Benjamin's Shop or Musk's Shop in Jamestown. Fresh vegetables may be bought from the St Helena Growers, Thorpe's Shop or Spar Supermarket. For restaurants, see page 72.

Lower Jamestown (the centre)

Self-catering here is recommended for those who prefer to live in a busy little town (Jamestown has 850 inhabitants), having shops close by, and who have nothing against the normal daytime noises of the town. In the evening, you can sometimes hear laughter and music from the pubs, but it is normally under control. Not having to depend on taxis or a car in order to go shopping can be an important factor when deciding on the best place to stay.

Here you will find accommodation for one to four people. Prices range from £15–30 per day to £180–240 per month.

Upper Jamestown (outside the centre)

This area is for those who prefer a somewhat quieter location but is still close to the centre of Jamestown, the heart of St Helena. The properties are located 10–15 minutes' walking distance (going gently uphill) from Jamestown centre. Some of the properties have a veranda or a garden sitting area. There is a small shop in the area, but the majority of the shops are located in the town centre (Lower Jamestown).

Accommodation in this area is also for one to four people. The prices range from £12–30 per day to £180–240 per month.

Half Tree Hollow

Half Tree Hollow is a settlement located about 650ft (200m) above Jamestown, at the top of Jacob's Ladder. In recent years the population has grown quite rapidly. There are a couple of shops in the area, where provisions can be bought. A strong argument for considering staying at Half Tree Hollow is the magnificent view of the ocean and arriving ships. Jamestown is approximately a ten-minute, downhill drive away, on a narrow, single-laned road with two-way traffic. Taxi (moderate prices) or rented car (varying quality) are recommended.

Here you will find accommodation for up to four people. Prices range from £12–25 per day to £200–600 per month.

The interior of the island

Those who would like to live away from it all in the country, particularly nature lovers and hikers, would probably be content in this area. Depending upon the location of the accommodation, it can rain substantially more or be foggier than in Jamestown or Half Tree Hollow. The temperatures are, however, more moderate when the sun shines. Jamestown, with its shops, restaurants and tourist information, is normally no more than 20 minutes away by car. The qualities of individual residential properties can vary from place to place. Some are truly off the beaten track. It all depends on the personal requirements of the tenant and their preferences. It is best to hire a car if staying away from Jamestown.

There are three main areas inland on the island where accommodation can be found: St Paul's, Longwood and Alarm Forest. Larger accommodation can be found in this part of the island. The rates vary from £8–35 per day to £150–300 per month.

WHERE TO EAT AND DRINK

In Jamestown, there are a few restaurants from which to choose. For lunch, there is the choice between cafeteria-style food or a sit-down menu. No reservations are required in the restaurants for lunch; dinners have to be reserved ahead of time. Usually you can tell the owner what you would like, or she may give you a choice of what she has in her kitchen. A meal in a restaurant costs between £5 and £10 per person, exclusive of drinks. Alcoholic drinks are imported from South Africa. Castle beer is available in cans. A bottle of ordinary red or white wine costs about £6 (there is little choice). Spirits are relatively expensive.

Wellington House serves home-cooked, individual meals, as does Farm Lodge. The **Consulate Hotel** food is good. As it is a bigger hotel than the other two, it lacks the really personal and homely touch of the Wellington and Farm Lodge.

Pubs on the island are open Mon–Sat 11.00–14.00, 17.00–23.00. Some pubs are also open on Sunday from noon until 14.00.

If you wish to take an excursion into the countryside, it's a good idea to take a packed lunch with you as there are no restaurants in the interior of the island. The following places will prepare a packed lunch for you: Wellington House, Ann's Place, the Consulate Hotel and Harris's Guest House. Orders should be placed the day before the lunches are required.

In Jamestown
Restaurants

Although several venues serve lunch, only two are open in the evenings for dinners, apart from the hotels: Donny's Place and Ann's Place.

Wellington House Main Street, Jamestown; tel: 2529; fax: 2725. Home-cooked, individually prepared dishes and friendly service are on offer in this family-style restaurant. Morning and afternoon tea or coffee is served from 10.00 onwards.
Donny's Place The Sea Front, Jamestown. Serves hot snacks, soft drinks and alcoholic beverages. Meals are available on request. It is open all day Monday, and Thursday through to Sunday. Highly recommended for those who want to relax and have a beautiful view of the seafront. There may be a disco or 'cinema' in the evenings.
Dillon's Snack Bar The Mule Yard, Jamestown; tel: 2290. Serves hot and cold snacks, drinks and ice-cream. They are open every day.
Ann's Place Castle Gardens, Jamestown; tel: 2797; fax: 2841. A cosy place where the owner runs the kitchen herself, seving home-cooked hot meals and snacks as well as soft drinks and alcoholic beverages. The place is cosy, and its location in the castle gardens means that it has an outside area available for eating. For dinner you need to make a reservation in advance; wherever possible, dishes are cooked to request. Open every day.
C & M's Main Street, Jamestown; tel: 2730; fax: 2340. Serves hot snacks and meals, sandwiches, soft drinks, ice-cream, tea and coffee.
Spar Takeaways Main Street, Jamestown. Serves hot snacks.

Pubs

There are two pubs in Jamestown: the Standard (tel: 2309) and the White Horse (tel: 2843). The visitor should be aware that alcoholic beverages may not be consumed on the streets of Jamestown.

Outside Jamestown

Pubs outside the capital are as follows:

Colin's Bar Sandy Bay; no telephone
Moon's Tavern Blue Hill; tel: 4093
Oasis Bar Half Tree Hollow; tel: 3607
Pub Paradise Longwood; tel: 4083
Silver Hill Bar Levelwood; no telephone

NIGHTLIFE

It is best to check the weekly *St Helena Herald* or at the tourist information office for the nightlife activities planned for the weekend. Some of the venues which have regular programming are:

Colin's Bar Has a DJ on Saturday nights.
Godfather's Rock Club Half Tree Hollow; tel: 3059. Has many planned activities: eucre, country and western night, bingo, skittles, and dances.
Pub Paradise On Saturday nights there is a DJ who plays dance music, and sometimes there are live bands.
Silver Hill Bar Has a disco on weekend evenings.

SHOPPING

The shops in Jamestown sell the normal range of souvenirs, such as T-shirts, coffee mugs, Napoleon memorabilia, stickers, postcards etc. Some special things can be bought which are exclusively St Helenian, like the St Helena coffee and the much-loved St Helena honey. As mentioned before, the post office in St Helena sells stamps and first-day covers. For those who are interested, Eva Benjamin's shop sells old first-day covers.

Shops are usually open Mon, Tue, Thu, Fri 09.00–13.00, 14.00–17.00; Wed 09.00–13.00; Sat 09.00–13.00, 18.30–20.30. A few shops operate longer hours on Saturday.

Fresh vegetables can be bought from the St Helena Growers, Thorpe's Shop, or Spar Supermarket.

MEDIA AND COMMUNICATIONS

St Helena has one official newspaper, one radio station and no local television station. Don't expect to find international newspapers or magazines on sale; they are not imported as they would be long out of date before they arrived.

Print media

The St Helena News Media Board came into operation on October 15 1998. The board was established to remove the media, which includes Radio St Helena, from government control and thus create an independent media. On June 1 2001, the island's newspaper, the *St Helena News*, was renamed the *St Helena Herald* and the paper took on a new look. The paper is published every Friday, price 20p.

To launch the new look, a limited edition of the first *Herald* was produced in partial colour with photographs of the island. Like its predecessor, the *St Helena Herald* contains mostly local articles of general news but also some human interest stories as well. There is a good editorial column, as well as a section with letters to the editor entitled 'Write On'. Those within the government service are not entirely free to use the press and are bound by Public Service Orders. For this reason, many Saints are hesitant to come forward and express their views. Having said that, people are challenging the government and addressing other issues in the 'Write On' page, which on average has five to ten letters each week.

The board would like to implement other improvements and modernisations to the *St Helena Herald*, such as printing in colour, but at the present time finances are not available to support this. The *Herald,* which prints 1,500 copies a week, and usually consists of about 16 pages, is still collated and folded by hand.

On October 1 2000, the newspaper made its debut on the worldwide web (www.news.co.sh), so more people who are interested in the island now have access to the current goings-on. The site has been quite successful, logging about 800 hits a week.

Radio

Radio St Helena, opened on Christmas Day 1967, is the only station on the island. It is officially registered in London as the 'St Helena Government Broadcasting Station', but has always been known as Radio St Helena on the island. When it first opened, the station operated at a frequency of 1511 kHz,

200 metres on the medium wave band. On November 1 1978 it was changed to the present frequency of 1548 kHz, 194 metres.

The radio station was established under the control of the education department, as part of a ten-year plan for education. Prior to the official opening, a number of programmes for schools and adults were broadcast as test transmissions for a period of about six months. In July 1969 overall administration of the station became the responsibility of the Information Services. Its aim today is to inform, educate and entertain through a wide range of programmes, although financial constraints limit how far this can go.

When the radio station first started in 1967, its equipment was already old, and by 1977 it could no longer cope. Increased funding since then has led to an improvement in equipment and thus of radio programmes. The original equipment was later brought to the museum in Jamestown.

In the early 1990s, a radio bus was acquired, allowing the broadcast of location transmissions, such as Legislative Council meetings. Over the years, the station has built up an extensive record library and now has some 23,000 records, almost 4,000 single discs and over 350 compact discs.

Since June 1 2001, in a popular extension to its service, Radio St Helena has broadcast 24 hours a day, seven days a week, The station opens at 07.00 and broadcasts throughout the day, with a variety of programmes, including locally produced ones, interspersed with 'canned' material and BBC World Service News. From 23.00 onwards the BBC World Service is broadcast in digital quality until the following morning. During these hours the station is unmanned. Reception is excellent and comes to the island via a satellite dish provided by the BBC. The extended service came into operation on the same day that the island's new newspaper published its first issue. The weekly programming schedule for Radio St Helena is published in the *Herald*.

Television

Television service came to St Helena in 1995, brought to the island via satellite. There are three channels available to viewers, offering a selection of programmes from BBC World, M-net, Discovery Channel, KTV and a sports channel, which brings major sporting events. Plans are in hand to extend the service, but there is no local programming, and no plans for this in the near future.

Before the age of internet communications, St Helenians used shortwave radio to communicate to other parts of the world. For many it is a hobby and gives them access to information about other countries and people.

Postal service

All mail must go by ship, the only physical link with the outside world. Reliance on this mail service for communication has recently lessened with the introduction of fax and email services through the Cable and Wireless satellite link. As well as the postal service, the post office is a major source of government revenue through its philatelic sales overseas. The main post office is on Main Street in Jamestown. All districts on the island have a sub-post office operating in a general store or grocery shop. Postage stamps can be bought at the main post office, as well as at the sub-post offices and at the souvenir shop in Jamestown. The post office sells island maps, and the Philatelic Bureau is located there. The bureau sells stamps from St Helena, Ascension Island and Tristan da Cunha, as well as first-day covers. The post office in Jamestown will gladly receive mail for tourists providing it is addressed Post Restante. After the mail arrives on the ship, there is always an announcement on the radio when it is ready to be collected from the main post office.

Post office and Philatelic Bureau Main Street, Jamestown; tel: 2629, fax: 2242; email: PM.PO@helanta.sh. Open Mon, Tue, Thu, Fri 08.30–15.00; Sat 08.30–12.00.

Telephone

In 1899, the Eastern Telegraph Company (later Cable and Wireless) laid the first telegraph cable in Rupert's Bay. Today, Cable and Wireless employs almost 40 people on the island. In December 1989, St Helena acquired international direct dialling plus fax and data transmission worldwide. Before this date, international calls had to be booked days ahead. Calls made on Christmas Day had to be arranged three months in advance and limited to 15 minutes per call in order to ensure that as many people as possible could have use of the service!

Local phone cards can be obtained from Cable and Wireless, the post office, Ann's Place, the Standard, and the Consulate Hotel. Telephone booths are located in Jamestown, and in various places in the country. The use of AT&T phonecards is possible for calls to the USA, Canada and the United Kingdom. Eurocard, MasterCard and Visa are accepted for payment of telephone calls and other services from Cable and Wireless. Cell phones do not work on the island at present.

Emergency telephone numbers

Police/fire/ambulance 999
Hospital/dentist 2500

Internet

Internet service was brought to the island in 1998 through Ascension Island. The costs for this service were very high and not many private citizens could afford it. In September 1999, St Helena received its own server, which decreased the service fees. Although many people feel the costs are still a bit high, this hasn't stopped them from acquiring an internet connection.

There are no internet cafés as such on the island, but members of the public can go to **Cable and Wireless** (Napoleon Street, Jamestown; tel: 2900; fax: 2094) to send or receive emails. There are two computers available for use. The disadvantage is that you only have access to the internet during business hours – Mon–Fri 9.00–15.30; Sat 9.00–11.30 – but that is the price you pay for being so far away from the rest of the world.

OTHER PRACTICALITIES
Churches
Details of most church services are published in the island's weekly newspaper, the *St Helena Herald*.

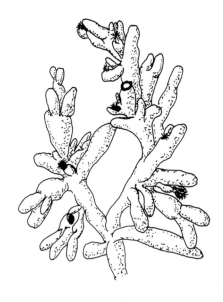

Visiting St Helena

From the sea, the island looks bleak and forbidding, with little sign of habitation. Inland, however, it has something of the rolling hills of Devon, while Jamestown could almost have been plucked from a 19th-century Jane Austen novel.

ST HELENA FROM THE SHIP

Since the discovery of the island in 1502, James Bay has been the place for almost all ships that have stopped at the island. You can see many of St Helena's attractions while still on the ship, especially with a pair of binoculars. Depending on the exact position of the ship while it is at anchor, you may even be able to get a view into Bank's Valley or Rupert's Valley.

When standing on the ship, looking towards the island, here is what you see: to the far left (to the northeast), you can see the prominent 700ft (213m) **Sugar Loaf.** It is a part of the ridge of a volcano which was extinguished 11 million years ago. The British used Sugar Loaf as a signalling station until 1877. The sailing ships could only reach James Bay by rounding Sugar Loaf Point because of the prevalent southeast trade winds.

If you bring your gaze down from the top of Sugar Loaf towards the ocean, you can see the military fortification **Middle Point** which is located about 160ft (49m) above sea level. A little further over to the right is **Half Moon Battery**. They were both erected by the British at the beginning of the 18th century. The oldest defences were already standing by 1678 at the lower right along the bay, named **Banks' Platform** in honour of the commanding officer. The original fortifications were continually battered by the heavy breakers which eventually destroyed them. During Napoleon's stay on the island and the accompanying military build-up, these fortifications were rebuilt. Looking towards the left side of the valley, you see a fortification wall with an outlet of water. There are a variety of other ruins which are scattered about this valley.

The next bay looking in the direction of Jamestown is **Rupert's Bay**, most likely named in honour of Prince Rupert, the famous cavalry leader in the English Civil War. Rupert's Valley is the industrial centre of St Helena. There is a fish-processing plant, the power station, and the white fuel-storage tanks which dominate this valley.

The old fortress wall on the left side of the valley is the remainder of the British defence installations which were built and improved during the 18th century. The 9,000 slaves who were freed by Her Majesty's Navy between 1840 and 1847, were also accommodated in Rupert's Valley. The **chimney** between the two white fuel tanks is a part of the desalinisation plant, which was built at the beginning of the 20th century, in order to provide potable water for the Boer War prisoners who were being held in the interior of the island. Other than for trial purposes, the plant was never put into operation.

The hill between Rupert's Valley and Jamestown is **Munden's Hill**. This hill was named after Sir Richard Munden, under whose command the British won back St Helena from the Dutch. Immediately after taking back St Helena, the first fortresses were built along the rock's ledges. The buildings which can be seen from the ship, are defence installations which were used during World War II. The **dilapidated houses** located above, are also a part of these defence installations. From 1957 to 1961, three princes from Bahrain, the last people to be exiled to this island, lived in these houses. In the middle of Munden's Hill, looking close to sea level, you can make out **old cannons** on the rocks. To the right of the dilapidated houses, there is a sign, that states, east of this point is where the **first telegraph cable** between England and Cape Town came on shore in 1899.

Well visible are the connecting roads and paths from Jamestown to Bank's Battery and up the ridge to the fortification of Upper Munden. In previous centuries, these were well-developed roads. Today they are partially disintegrating. With good hiking shoes, you can still manage these roads and paths with little problem. The patches of green along the ridge of Munden's Hill are prickly pear cacti, a widespread species of cactus found around the island.

Several yards from the ledge at Munden's Point lies the wreck of the Dutch ship *Witte Leeuw*, which sank in 1613 after combat with a Portuguese ship. The ship was carrying cargo of porcelain, diamonds and spices which went down with it.

Jamestown and Jacob's Ladder, which leads up to Ladder Hill, are described in detail in the following section. Between Munden's Hill and Ladder Hill, you can see a small portion of the hilly interior of the island. About halfway up this section you see a group of houses. This area is called **The Briars**. The summer pavilion where Napoleon spent his happiest time on St Helena is located in this area, behind the houses which are visible.

Ladder Hill is crowned with a flagpole which belongs to an earlier signal station on the cliff. To the left of Jacob's Ladder you can see, quite clearly, the old road leading up to the Hill. Directly underneath the flagpole you see two white triangles. Today these are used to help the ships find their anchor position in James Bay. The old layers of lava, which have been cooled down for about ten million years, are visible. The prominent house with the white stone steps, located to the left of the top of Jacob's Ladder is the **Cliff Top House**. It was built in the late 19th century, probably as the military officers' mess. Now it is used as housing for British government employees.

Following the ridge along to the left, you see the ruins of the **old observatory**. The large building with the red roof, which dominates the top of the ridge, is the **New Apostolic Church**. On the hill behind this ridge, you see a part of the **High Knoll Fort**. This relatively new fortress, was completed in 1894 and is in fair shape. Visitors to High Knoll are rewarded with a spectacular view from the top. On a clear day, there is a beautiful 360° view of St Helena which can be enjoyed.

Now we direct our attention back to the flagpole. To the right are the remains of the walls of **Ladder Hill Fort**. To the right of the houses there are two guns which were used during World War II. Further on, the island continually follows the same pattern: a barren hill followed by a lush valley and then another barren hill.

WHAT TO SEE
A walking tour of Jamestown

The steps leading from the water up to the wharf have been the official entrance to Jamestown for centuries. Sailors in the 1700s came on shore in more or less the same way as passengers from *RMS St Helena*, or any other passenger ship or boat. From this point, there is a good view of **Jacob's Ladder** with its 699 steps.

About 50 yards (45m) from the wharf steps, you will come upon a two-storey pink house, built in the late 18th century. It is the closest dwelling house to the ocean on St Helena, and was last inhabited by a fisherman. Today it is used by **St Helena Yacht Club**.

A little further on is the blue-painted **HM Customs House**. It is estimated that this building was constructed as early as the middle of the 18th century. The slightly raised building with the arched roof, behind it, was built in the early 19th century and was once used as a mortuary.

After leaving the harbour area, continue walking along the road and after about 50 yards (45m), on the left-hand side, there is a view of the bastion of the outer town wall of Jamestown. The old cannons are still there. This **defence installation** was built as early as the 17th century. The old **moat**, next to the bastion, is visible along the entire valley.

Walking further along the oceanfront, you come upon the **cenotaph**, a memorial to the men of St Helena who fought and died in the two world wars. Glance to the right over James Bay, where you can just make out a piece of steel jutting out of the water. This is a part of the rudder of the ship *Papanui* which sank in James Bay in 1911. Coal, which was loaded in Las Palmas, caught fire during the journey to Cape Town and the fire just kept getting worse. Three hours after arriving at St Helena, the *Papanui* was fully engulfed in flames. The entire valley glowed in the light of the flames.

Now direct your attention towards the **town gate** and the town's inner wall. The walls are made from basalt stone, which is plentiful, due to the volcanic nature of the island. Until 1935, the town moat was crossed using a drawbridge.

Looking up just before you walk through the town gates, you can see the coat of arms of the last governor of the East India Company, Charles Dallas, who held the office from 1828 until 1836. On the other side of the gates is a

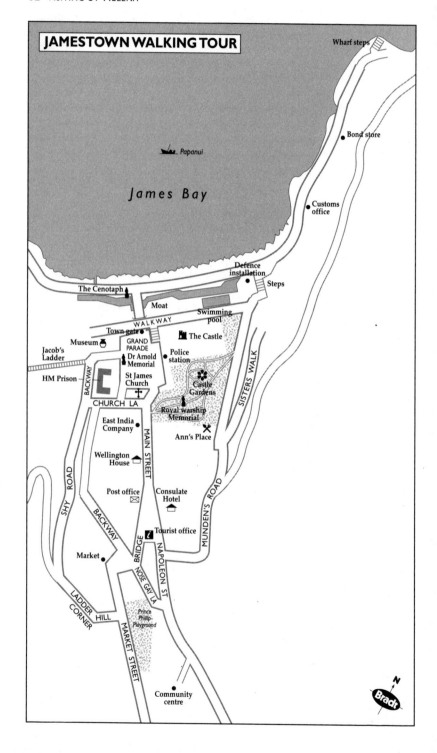

JAMESTOWN WALKING TOUR

picture of the rare wirebird. This is the official bird of the island, as well as its mascot. On both sides of the wirebird, two arum lilies are shown. This is the official flower of St Helena.

The large area you encounter after passing through the town gates is called the **Grand Parade**. This was used in earlier years as the drill ground for the British garrison. The description of this area that follows is in a clockwise direction:

Starting from the left, we see the entrance to the government offices building, the **Castle**. This is the third building which has been erected on this spot. The first was built in 1659 and it was replaced with a new building in 1708. In the 1860s the second building was so badly damaged by termites, that it was necessary to erect the present building in 1867. There are two memorial stone tablets built into the wall to the left of the entrance, which commemorate the buildings which stood in this place, previous to the present one. Other than housing the government offices, the Castle was also once used as the winter residence of the governor. Today there are several government offices housed in the Castle. Above the gates to the entrance, we again see the coat of arms of the last governor of the East India Company.

To the right of the entrance gates, between the two hibiscus, is a **post stone**. Before the island was settled, ships would often leave letters and messages for other ships behind basalt rocks, like this one. Immediately next to this is the entrance to the **former barracks**. The letters 'VR' above the arch is the abbreviation for Victoria Regina, and were probably in honour of the golden or diamond anniversary of Queen Victoria's reign on the British throne, in 1887 or 1897.

The building complex we see to the left was built at the beginning of the 19th century and contains the **police headquarters**, the **court building** and the **public library**. If you look on past the library, you can see branches of the flamboyant tree sticking out of the fence that encloses the castle gardens. This tree is considered one of the most beautiful flowering trees in the tropics because of its bright red flowers. Now look across the street to the memorial which stands in front of the parking area. This **pillar** was erected in honour of Dr Arnold, a colonial surgeon and twice governor of St Helena.

The church here is **St James' Church**, completed in 1774. It is located in the area where the Portuguese erected the first chapel on the island in the 16th century. The small wooden door behind the rows of pews inside the church came from this Portuguese chapel. It gave the valley its name, Chapel Valley, which is still in use today. The clock in the church steeple was brought to the island in 1787. It was first at the court building until 1843, then it was moved to the church. The gravestones in front of the church were brought from another cemetery in Jamestown when the old graveyard was built upon. The steeple was removed in recent years as it was in a dangerous condition.

Behind the church we get a glimpse of **HM Prison**. It was built in the first half of the 19th century. It holds a maximum of 20 inmates. It is never full, but there is often at least one inmate serving time.

If you walk a bit towards the seafront again, you will find yourself between an ecru-coloured warehouse (formerly Lawler's Hotel) and the Public Work's Department (PWD) store. Rising in front of you is **Jacob's Ladder**, completed in 1829, with its 699 steps leading up to Ladder Hill at an incline of 39–44°. The height difference is around 602ft (183m). To the side of the steps there were once tramways, operated by simple machinery worked by a capstan bar and ropes by mules at the top. It was used to transport manure from the stables in Jamestown, and by the military installations to transport ammunition and supplies.

Those who have the time and the stamina to conquer Jacob's Ladder will be rewarded with a fantastic view and ample picture taking opportunities from the top. From Ladder Hill we can look down on Jamestown and out over James Bay. On either side of the ladder an inclined plane was built which consisted of tramways used to transport supplies.

Leaving the Grand Parade and walking towards the centre of town, we find ourselves on Main Street. On the left we pass the **Castle Gardens**, originally the garden of the East India Company. The dominant trees with the grey-green bark and the two-inch-long oval leaves are banyans. Some of these trees supposedly were already here when Napoleon arrived on the island. The gardens are filled with different types of plants and flowers and well worth a look around. At the very end of the Castle Gardens there is a restaurant, **Ann's Place**, which is a favourite meeting place of the people who visit this island with their yacht. The **memorial** in the middle of the Castle Gardens is to the memory of the Royal Warship *Waterwitch* and her Royal Navy crew, who helped fight the slave trade in the middle of the 19th century. The anchor which we see on the grass was found in the bay during construction work.

The building next to the Castle Gardens, **New Porteous House**, was built to replace the one where Napoleon and his entourage spent their first night on the island. The actual house where they stayed burned down in 1865 and the remainder was torn down in 1937. The houses which border this building were all constructed in the first half of the 18th century.

Across the street from the Castle Gardens are three similar-looking houses. They were built in the 18th century, serving both as the dwellings of government employees and also as the **headquarters of the East India Company**.

Staying on the same side of the street, we now come upon a blue building with the name **Wellington House**, also from the 18th century. It is rumoured that the Duke of Wellington stayed in this house in 1805 during a stopover on his way home from India. Today it is a hotel, which offers afternoon tea and coffee.

After passing the next few buildings we reach the **post office**, built in the Victorian-style with its verandas. The building was used as the officers' mess for the British garrison until 1907. After the troops left the island, the post office was set up here.

The cream-coloured buildings with the blue balustrades, on the other side of the street, were for the most part built in the second half of the 19th century. Only the **Consulate Hotel** dates from the middle of the 18th century. The hotel was once the residence of the American vice-consul during the whaling period in the 1850s. The iron railway girders, which support the veranda, were installed after termite attacks destroyed the wooden posts.

The long building which is situated across the end of Main Street, houses the **tourist information office**. The two large trees in front are peepul trees, which are sacred in India. In earlier years, these trees were planted the whole length of Main Street. Before the abolition of slavery in 1832, the slave market was held at this spot.

Walking to the right of the tourist information building (mind the cars!) and stopping at the end of the street, we come upon another square, called the **Bridge**. The cast-iron and wrought-iron building, which dominates the right side of the street, is called the **Market** and serves as the market hall. It was prefabricated in England in 1865 and the individual pieces were shipped to Saint Helena, where it was assembled. This type of construction was chosen because of the termite invasion. In the 1860s termites had done significant damage to many buildings on the island. The clock tower in front was constructed in 1930.

The museum

The St Helena Heritage Society, founded in 1980, maintains a small museum on Main Street in Jamestown, although it is about to relocate to a new home at the foot of Jacob's Ladder. With a lot of work and fundraising, the Friends of St Helena and the Heritage Society are converting the Old Power House into a more modern and suitable museum for the island. The opening of the new museum is set to coincide with the quincentenary celebrations in May 2002.

The museum tries to preserve the island's history and present it to the island's visitors. It holds a number of interesting artefacts from St Helena's past including old coins, Ming porcelain, photographs, items made by the Boer War prisoners, items recovered from the sunken *Witte Leeuw*, old rifles and pistols, musical and scientific instruments, bottles, old radios and jars. It is hoped that the opening of the larger museum will attract many new exhibits and instil greater enthusiasm for the preservation of items of local history.

Open Mon, Wed, Sat 10.00–12.30. When the RMS St Helena is in port the museum is also open on Friday from 10.00–12.30.

The library

The public library (Grand Parade, Jamestown; tel: 2580), supposedly the oldest in the southern hemisphere, is located in Jamestown. It holds an extensive collection of books on St Helena and her dependencies. It also has a wide variety of books on offer for lending.

When you think of what a library might look like on a small isolated island in the middle of the ocean, you picture a small damp room with just a few old copies of books. It is a nice surprise when you enter the library in Jamestown to see a large room with well-organised rows of books. There is a section towards the back with a table where you can sit and read if you wish. At the front of the room there is a section of children's books. Most people are surprised how well the library is stocked and the friendliness of the library staff adds to the enjoyment of the visit.

For the visitor who is staying on the island for more than just a few days, it is possible to take out books. Simply fill out a form and for a refundable deposit of £10, you are free to check out books. Many of the books come from South Africa and England. The library is also happy to accept books from travellers who don't wish to take them back home with them. These donations help extend the library's collection and make it possible for future visitors to have access to a wider variety of reading material.

Open Mon, Tue, Thu, Fri, Sat 10.00–14.00, 16.00–19.00; Tue and Sat evenings open until 20.00

St Helena Government Archives

The government archives, established in 1962, is situated at the castle in Jamestown (tel: 2470), among the government's main administrative offices. The office is open Mon–Fri 08.30–12.30, 13.00–16.00.

The archives consist mainly of records of both the East India Company and the Crown Administration. The East India Company's records date from 1673 to 1876 and include books of letters to and from England, as well as judicial, military, maritime and other administrative records. There are several registers of wills (dated 1682–1839) as well as leases and deeds (dated 1682–1849). The records of the island's Crown Administration date back to 1836 and consist of council records and correspondence between the governor and the Secretary of State for the Colonies; the island's Blue Books; and other miscellaneous administrative records.

The archives also holds copies of many of the island's newspapers and publications. The first newspaper, originally published in 1806, was a monthly gazette. The oldest paper which the archives hold is the *St Helena Advocate*, published in 1851. There were also a number of satirical magazines published. A notable newspaper is the longest-running *St Helena Guardian* (published 1861–1923). Other publications held at the Archives include the *St Helena (Diocesan) Magazine* (1901–15) and the St Helena *Wirebird* (1955–66). A great source of information are the *St Helena Calendar* and *Directory Almanacs*, published from about 1829 until 1842. Its successor was the *St Helena Almanac and Annual Register*, published between 1842 and 1843, with a further issue published in 1913.

The island's Anglican parish registers, which date back to 1680, are a goldmine for family researchers. They are held on loan by the Government Archives, and have been extensively indexed in recent years. The island's Baptist registers are also available.

Another helpful tool for genealogists is the database of existing gravestone inscriptions of St Helena. In the 1980s, children of the Secondary Selective School went around and transcribed as many tombstone inscriptions as they could find. Most likely they were able to get the majority of readable inscriptions down on paper. Other people have added to this project in later years. During a longer stay on St Helena a few years ago, I reorganised and 'cleaned up' all the various inscriptions and placed it in a computer database, of which the archives was given a copy. There are still many records which

Above Speery Island, with kayaker Neil Rusch in the foreground
– the first person to circumnavigate the islands of St Helena,
in 1998, and Tristan da Cunha, in 2001 (NR)

Below Children from St Helena enjoy swimming in the pool
overlooking the sea (HM)

Above Yellow-billed albatross nesting on the steep slopes of
Tristan da Cunha (NR)

Right Albatross chick (NR)

Below left Green sea turtle hatchling emerging from its egg
on Ascension (HM)

Below right Rockhopper penguin on Tristan da Cunha's rocky coast (NR)

would benefit from being indexed and placed in a database, but unfortunately St Helena lacks the personnel or the equipment to do the work.

The current archivist, Mrs Maureen Stevens, is very knowledgeable and helpful to anyone who requires her assistance; many people have benefited from her help.

Other information
Tourist office Main Street, Jamestown; tel: 2158, fax: 2159, email: StHelena.Tourism@helanta.sh. Open Mon–Fri 08.30–16.00.

SIGHTSEEING TOURS AROUND THE ISLAND
Those who travel to St Helena via cruise ship have a short time span in which to experience the island. With careful planning, it is possible to pack a lot of sightseeing into just a few hours and make the most of a short stay. Below are some suggested itineraries for those who want to make the most of their St Helena experience in the least amount of time. Here are some suggestions for excursions by taxi of different durations, depending on how much time you have to tour the island.

One-hour tour
Tour 1 Take the taxi to Ladder Hill Fort. Walk down **Jacob's Ladder** a few steps to get a wonderful place to take photographs of the ship and James Bay. Now, take the taxi to The Briars where you have the chance to view the **pavilion** where Napoleon spent his happiest days on St Helena. On your way back to Jamestown, if the weather co-operates and there is enough water, you have the opportunity to see the **Heart-shape Waterfall** on the left as you drive by. Driving on, you again reach Main Street in Jamestown. If there is time you can quickly take a few pictures before you must return to the ship.

Two-hour tours
Tour 2 Same as tour one, plus a tour of The Briars **Pavilion**.

Tour 3 Taxi ride from Jamestown to **Plantation House**, the governor's residence, built in 1792. On the large lawn in front of the house you will find several giant tortoises. Among them is **Jonathan**, the oldest inhabitant of St Helena. His age is estimated from 150 to 200 years old. He was probably brought to the island from Mauritius when he was fully grown. Some people believe he was already living on the island when Napoleon arrived. Visitors can freely walk on the grass to greet and pet the tortoises, but please do not feed them.

Five minutes walk brings you to **St Paul's Cathedral**, built in 1851. Like the market in Jamestown, it was built mostly from prefabricated materials sent from England and sent to St Helena in individual parts, and then assembled on the island.

The return trip is via Gordon's Post and Side Path. On the way to Jamestown, you may see the **Heart-shape Waterfall** on the left side as you drive by. If you are interested, ask the taxi driver to point it out to you.

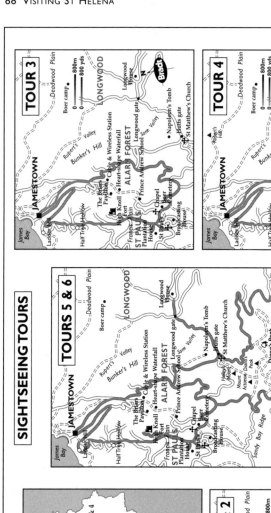

SIGHTSEEING TOURS

TOUR 3

TOUR 4

TOURS 5 & 6

TOURS I & 2

Tours 1, 2, 3 & 4

Tours 5 & 6

Tour 4 Take the taxi to the top of Ladder Hill, as in Tour 1, for a great view of James Bay. Now we drive further to **High Knoll Fort**. High Knoll is one of the best preserved forts on St Helena and offers a spectacular 360° view of the island. There is no better place to view the entire island.

Because of the poor condition of the road, there is about five to ten minutes walking involved from the taxi to the fort. Before you return to Jamestown, if time allows, you could make a stop at **Plantation House** and possibly **St Paul's Cathedral**.

Tour 5 How about a visit to **Napoleon's** original **burial site** in Sane Valley? It is about a ten-minute taxi ride and then about 15 minutes by foot down a wooded path. If the weather is nice, then it would be well worth a visit to see **Longwood House**, where Napoleon spent the majority of his exile. The drive back to Jamestown could be via Levelwood–Green Hill which would give you a chance to see the southeast part of the island.

Three-hour tour
Tour 6 As in Tour 3, plus a visit to the **Boer War Prisoners' Cemetery** and the **Knollcombes Cemetery**. Both of these are located close to Plantation House. Knollcombes is where the last St Helena governor born on the island, Hudson Ralph Janisch, is buried.

If it is fine weather, it is worth a trip to Sandy Bay Ridge–Levelwood to enjoy the view from the southeast of the island. Afterwards, you could visit Napoleon's former residence, **Longwood House**. From here you take the taxi directly back to Jamestown, about a 20-minute ride.

BEYOND JAMESTOWN
With its varying and rugged terrain, St Helena is an experienced walker's paradise. There are a great many places on the island which are not accessible by car and the only way to explore them is on foot. The interior of St Helena holds many secrets to the beauty and fascination of the island. It gives you a chance to experience the diversity of the landscape, to view scenes from nature not found anywhere else in the world, and to get a sense of the part the island played in the world's history.

In this section, I have divided the island into five areas and highlighted the places which are of special interest or have special significance.

Northeast
Banks' Battery
This area consists of a group of fortifications. It was fortified around 1678 and over the next one and a half centuries the fortifications were continually improved. The original fort was named Banks' Platform, after the officer who oversaw its construction. Eventually this was washed away and, during the residency of Napoleon, it was rebuilt. The new fortress was guarded by cannons, which can still be found lying about on the ground and on the platform. There was a tunnel built under the wall to carry storm water. The main battery was built later and is well preserved.

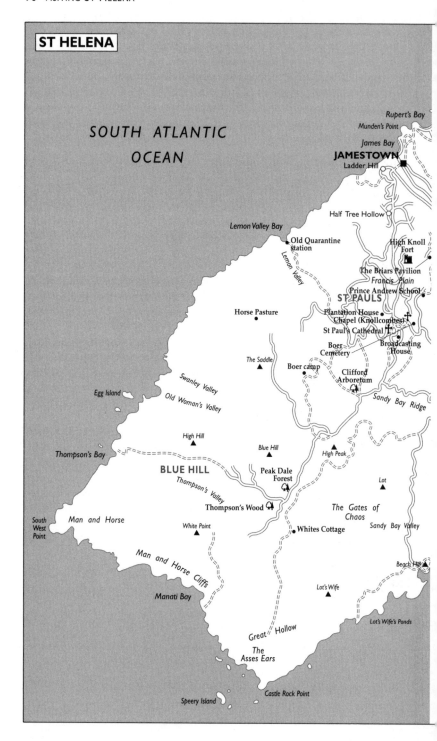

ST HELENA

SOUTH ATLANTIC
OCEAN

Rupert's Bay

Munden's Point

James Bay

JAMESTOWN

Ladder Hill

Half Tree Hollow

Lemon Valley Bay

Old Quarantine
station

High Knoll
Fort

Lemon Valley

The Briars Pavilion

Francis Plain

Prince Andrew School

ST PAULS

Horse Pasture

Plantation House
Chapel (Knollcombes)

St Paul's Cathedral

Boer
Cemetery

Broadcasting
House

The Saddle

Boer camp

Clifford
Arboretum

Swanley Valley

Sandy Bay Ridge

Egg Island

Old Woman's Valley

High Hill

Blue Hill

High Peak

Thompson's Bay

Lot

BLUE HILL

Peak Dale
Forest

Thompson's Valley

The Gates of
Chaos

South
West
Point

Man and Horse

Thompson's Wood

White Point

Whites Cottage

Sandy Bay Valley

Man and Horse Cliffs

Beach Hill

Manati Bay

Lot's Wife

Lot's Wife's Ponds

Great Hollow

The
Asses Ears

Speery Island

Castle Rock Point

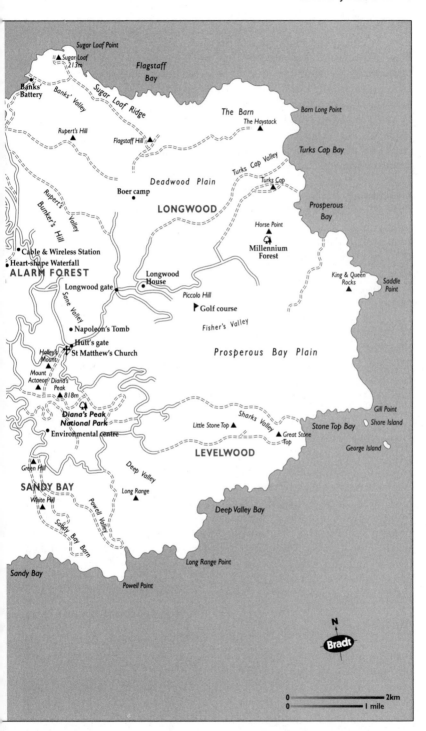

The Barn

Here is one of the more recognised landmarks on St Helena. Along with Flagstaff, it is the first piece of land one sees appearing over the horizon approaching the island from Ascension. This area is believed to consist of the oldest rocks on the island, some formed before St Helena emerged from the sea. The lava from the volcanic eruption which bore St Helena, formed what is called the Barn. During his stay, it was reputed that the sight of the Barn depressed Napoleon. This was also one of the last areas where the wild goats could be found, before they were finally eradicated. For those who are fortunate enough to make it up there, the reward is spectacular views

Deadwood

The plains here were once very populous with gumwoods. Due to the influence of man and wild goats, the original vegetation was virtually destroyed. Today the wirebird inhabits this area, as it is a suitable habitat for this rare species. They prefer the dry grasslands and the semi-desert areas for their habitat. From 1900 until 1902, Deadwood was the site of the main Boer War prisoners' camp. In 1901 it became necessary to build a second camp at Broad Bottom because of conflict between two groups of prisoners, the Freestaters and the Transvaalers.

Flagstaff

This was originally the site of a signalling station, but was not successful because it is frequently shrouded in the mist that covers this area at certain times of the year. During Napoleon Bonaparte's captivity it was briefly used again.

Longwood

Longwood (tel: 4409; fax: 4996) is well-known as the place where Napoleon Bonaparte (see pages 25–8) spent the majority of his captivity on St Helena. Located on an exposed plateau, it can be a depressing place in poor weather. Since 1858, the government of France has maintained the property and the French Vice-Consul Michel Martineau resides here, too, in a section of the property not accessible to the public. A visit to Longwood Old House is very much worth the effort. Most organised tours of the island include this in their itinerary and it gives the visitor a slight idea of what life was like for St Helena's most famous prisoner.

Open Mon–Fri 08.00–12.30, 14.00–16.00; Sat 08.00–11.30. Admission free.

Munden's Point

Munden's Battery was named after Sir Richard Munden, who helped the British regain possession of the island from the Dutch in May 1674. This area was sporadically built up until World War II. From 1957 until 1961, one of the abandoned buildings which formed part of this fortification, was used to house St Helena's last political prisoners – three Bahraini princes. From Upper Munden's, there are good views across James Valley and across to Jacob's

Ladder. Munden's Battery is also a good vantage point to view some seasonal bird visitors. From September to March, the island is visited by skuas, large, dark-brown, gull-like birds which migrate from their breeding grounds in the Arctic to avoid the northern winter.

Piccolo Hill

This is where the island's only golf course is located. At the far side of the golf course is a single gumwood tree. Piccolo Hill was built during the 1960s to house the staff of the Diplomatic Wireless Service. With the aid of an aerial complex on Prosperous Bay Plain, the Diplomatic Wire Service was able to monitor most West African radio communications. This station was made obsolete when satellites and more powerful transmitters were put into operation.

Rupert's Bay

No-one is absolutely positive why this area was so named. There is an entry in the records of St Helena which states that Prince Rupert, the famous cavalry leader in the English Civil War, anchored in this bay during his return voyage from India, in order to refresh his ships company. This story cannot be verified, but it makes for an interesting explanation of the name. Rupert's Valley is considered the industrial centre of the island, as this is the site of ARGOS (the fish processing plant), the bulk fuel farm, and the chimney (which is all that remains of the desalinisation plant which was never put into operation).

Sugar Loaf

It is not easy to reach the top of Sugar Loaf, as the path has eroded, so you almost have to climb up the last bit. Once at the summit, you are rewarded with an extraordinary view. Today you can visit the ruins of the telegraph station that was built atop Sugar Loaf. At one time this was a very important signalling station. Many large ships used this as their navigational guide, as the only way to approach Jamestown was round Sugar Loaf Point. The old flagstaff was considered an important landmark for almost 200 years, until it was taken down and burned in 1877. Sugar Loaf, like the Barn, was part of the original volcano that was centred around the north eastern portion of the island. The last activity is said to have occurred around 11 million years ago, but the areas of the lava flows are still visible, especially between Bank's and Rupert's.

Southeast
Prosperous Bay

As mentioned previously, this is the proposed site of the airport/airstrip which SHELCO is hoping to construct. You can actually see the stakes which have been set to mark the area where the north-south runway is planned. Besides the airstrip, Prosperous Bay is a place of interest for other reasons. A little-known fact is that the gypsum found on Prosperous Bay

Plain was most probably used to make Napoleon Bonaparte's death mask. This area is a good place to catch a glimpse of the white fairy terns. They tend to fly quite close over the heads of people and this provides an excellent opportunity for photographs. Despite the fact that Prosperous Bay was the site where the English landed in 1673, it was considered unnecessary to fortify it, but years later small batteries were constructed and the ruins of these can be seen today.

This is a particularly desolate part of the island, with some cacti and sisal plants but an otherwise rough and cratered appearance. The name is derived from a ship that landed at the bay, and is not a reference to the fertility of the area.

Northwest
The Briars

The Briars was where Napoleon spent his happiest time on St Helena in the pavilion of the Balcombe property. There is now a small museum at this site containing memorabilia from Napoleon's two month stay here. (Open Tue–Thu 08.30–12.30; Sat 08.30–11.30. Admission free.)

In the early 1820s an interesting experiment was carried out here. A Chinese labourer who claimed to understand the breeding and care of silkworms was sent to China to procure some. Upon his return a silkworm farm was started at The Briars. Much to the disappointment of the governor, this project ended in failure.

Francis Plain

Francis Plain was named after Henry Francis who owned this land in 1692. During Napoleon's captivity it was used as one of the main camping grounds. One of the claims to fame of Francis Plain is that it was home to the Zulu chief Dinizulu and his family for seven years. Francis Plain is also used quite frequently for outdoor sporting events, like cricket, football, netball, rounders and other athletic events. The biggest event held here was the annual school sports day which used to take place on January 1. Unfortunately it was abandoned in 1998, thus ending a 50-year-long tradition. At this stage they cannot say where or when future sports days will take place, although there are hopes that some organisation will decide to use the New Year's Day holiday and this venue for fundraising events.

Half Tree Hollow

This is basically a suburb of Jamestown. It is located behind Ladder Hill above Jacob's Ladder. From here there are spectacular views to the ocean. It is an interesting place to be to watch the ship arriving back at the island or to follow the individual private yachts making a stop at St Helena on their long ocean journeys.

High Knoll Fort

The original fort probably stood on this site around 1790. This fort was used not only to help defend the island, but as a makeshift prison in 1811 for a group of mutineers who decided to rebel in protest over the abolition of alcohol for the garrison. The present fort was built somewhere between 1874 and 1894. During the internment of the Boer War prisoners on St Helena, some of the more dangerous people were incarcerated here. Later it was used as a quarantine centre for animals which had arrived at the island, until 1998 when the present facility came into service.

The fort has fallen into serious disrepair. Although repairs have been made to the large section of the wall that collapsed some time ago, unfortunately other sections of the fort's walls have also now collapsed. The authorities would like to repair more of the fort but funding will be a problem. All fortifications belong to the Crown properties for which the St Helena Government is responsible. When you walk along the top of High Knoll, you have a 360° unobstructed view of the island, making it one of the best places from which to view other parts of St Helena.

Knollcombes

For the family historian, this is one of the more interesting places to visit. The Baptist cemetery is here, as well as the Boer War prisoners' cemetery. The neatly organised lines of prisoners' graves make for an impressive sight, even from the road. St Helena's second and last island-born governor, Hudson Ralph Janisch, is also buried here. This is one of the best places to explore if you plan to use a car, as it is accessible by well-maintained roads.

Ladder Hill

Ladder Hill can be reached in two ways, both originating in Jamestown. For those who like a challenge, Jacob's Ladder and its 699 steps will certainly give you one. The alternative route is to take the road up. This is a bit longer, but the climb is more gradual. The roads are narrow, so you must always be aware of oncoming cars. No matter which way you choose, everyone is of the same opinion: the climb is worth the exertion. From the top of the ladder, one can enjoy a beautiful view of the ocean and the harbour and have a very good vantage point over the centre of Jamestown.

Lemon Valley

It is not proven, but this valley was probably so named because of the abundance of lemons found here by early visitors to the island. It was said to contain the greatest population of trees on all of St Helena. Lemon Valley Bay is distinct in that it has the island's only real beach. Quite often a group of people will charter a boat to transport them between Jamestown and Lemon Valley. It is possible to walk down to Lemon Valley from Sarah's Valley and then arrange for the boat to pick the group up later in the day for the return trip to Jamestown.

Plantation House

Plantation House is the residency of the governor of St Helena. The house itself has a certain dignity to it. The main attraction, however, is the giant tortoises which roam the lawn in front of the house. The most famous of these is

Jonathan. No-one knows for sure how old he really is (some estimate him to be between 150 and 200 years old), or how long he has been on the island. Everyone agrees, though, that he is the island's oldest and longest resident. You can tell him apart from the other tortoises because there is a white marking on the front of his shell. All the tortoises are quite friendly and do not seem to mind tourists snapping pictures of them, but please do not feed them. They are well looked after and it is important they are kept on their normal diet to stay healthy.

St Paul's Cathedral
The original church was built in the early 17th century. In 1851, the present church was built, mostly from prefabricated materials shipped from England. The walls, however, are constructed of local stone. It is a simple building which, in 1859, became the cathedral church of the diocese of St Helena. For those interested in old and interesting gravestones, this is the place to come. Unfortunately, care has not been taken of these grave markers and many have been allowed to break; sadly, on some, the writing is no longer legible.

Southwest
Lot's Wife's Ponds
It takes a little manoeuvering to get to this spot, but people who have been here highly recommend it. It is accessible by foot starting just above Sandy Bay Beach. The walk is about 1½ miles (2½ km). The path ends at the top of a low cliff just above the ponds. It takes a bit of negotiating to get down there and a rope can be quite helpful. The ponds are located behind a naturally formed wall of rock and the crashing waves supply the ponds with fresh water. Many people swim in the ponds and it is considered to be safe.

Sandy Bay
Sandy Bay Beach isn't really a beach in the typical sense. It is actually made up of rocks and black sand which were once part of the surrounding cliffs, or carried in by the water. It's an interesting area to explore as there are lots of ruins which allude to St Helena's history. At Sandy Bay Lines, you can see what remains of the old lime kiln. In the early 1700s a great quantity of limestone was discovered here. At the time, it was a great find, because the mortar which had been used in many of the fortifications and building was of such poor quality that the structures had started to crumble. The lime kilns were built so the limestone could be fired and converted to lime to mix with the mortar in order to improve the quality of the buildings. The battery is still standing but much of the wall which once connected the fortifications at Sandy Bay has eroded due to weather, time, and poor construction.

Centre of the island
The Peaks
This particular area contains three peaks: Cuckhold, Diana and Actaeon. The top of Diana's Peak is treeless, whereas both Cuckhold's Point and Mount Actaeon are marked by an old Norfolk Island pine. This is where the only

national park on the island is found. It contains many of the endemic species of St Helena. The last remaining wild specimen of the St Helena olive was discovered on Mount Actaeon in August 1977. This area is also a good place to see the evidence of the failed flax industry. New Zealand flax grew wild over this area for many years, killing many native plants. A lot of work has gone into trying to reintroduce the endemics in this area and control the flax so that native flora have their habitat back.

There are three paths which can be followed, all three starting at Cabbage Tree Road which is the entrance to the national park:

The shortest of the three walks is the **Snail Circuit** which takes about two hours. This path takes you along the trail of the endemic blushing snail, *Succinea sanctae-helenae*. The blushing snail is abundant and can be easily spotted on the cabbage trees. From the top of Diana's Peak, you can enjoy impressive views of St Helena. From the ridge there are cabbage trees, dogwoods and whitewoods to be seen in the thicket below. The highest mailbox in the South Atlantic is located atop Diana's Peak, where there is a rubber stamp which can be used to celebrate reaching the top of St Helena.

The **Weevil Walk** is about three hours in duration and circles the central ridge on the Longwood side and goes through the lush thicket on the Sandy Bay side. Walkers along this path will pass by dogwoods, cabbage trees and an enormous thicket of buddleia.

The **Spider Sprint** is a four-hour circuit walk and will take you to parts of the Peaks that most people don't get to. The walk traverses Diana's Peak, the highest point on St Helena, and Mount Actaeon. Cabbage trees and dogwood still grow in the isolated thicket near High Ridge. This path also leads the walker through Purgatory, where, if you look carefully, you may spot dwarf jellicos on the cliffs.

One thing has to be said about visiting the Peaks: it is best to wait for good weather. Visibility is limited to only a few yards/metres when the mists roll in and this could prove to be dangerous especially for those unfamiliar with the territory.

Halley's Mount

As mentioned previously in the *History* chapter, Halley's Mount was where Edmund Halley set up his observatory in 1677 to catalogue the southern stars and observe the transit of Mercury. The observatory was built on a northeastern spur of the central ridges. Unfortunately this spot is frequently covered in clouds, but despite these Halley was able to carry out a good amount of work. From here, you can enjoy a splendid view of the southeast of St Helena.

Sane Valley

Sane Valley is the original burial place of Napoleon. The guard shack is still standing in its original spot: even after Napoleon's death, the British kept a close watch over the former emperor. This spot is quite well hidden and you must go down a track that was originally cut for the funeral cortege. The tomb was surrounded by willows at the time of Napoleon's internment, but they were allowed to decay. Now the willows have been replaced by Norfolk Island pines. It is said that Napoleon himself chose this spot as his final resting place. There was never any inscription on the tomb; the governor at the time, Hudson Lowe, would only allow the name 'Napoleon Bonaparte' to appear. The body was removed from the tomb in 1840 and taken back to France. His remains are now at Les Invalides in Paris.

Open Mon–Fri 08.00–12.30, 14.00–16.00; Sat 08.00–11.30. Admission free.

ACTIVITIES
Walking/hiking
The most popular sport to be undertaken on St Helena is walking. For those who are spending more than a few days on the island, there are a lot of interesting walks which can be done. It is a good idea to check at the St Helena tourist office to see if there are any organised walks planned for the time you are on the island. These walks are usually accompanied by a knowledgeable guide and are highly recommended. You get a very personal view of the island that you may miss if you go independently.

This is not to say that you cannot get a good experience from a walk taken independently of a group. The option of taking an individual walk or hike has its advantages. You can take things at your own pace and you can set up your own itinerary according to what you would most like to see. There is an excellent book giving suggestions and descriptions of several walking routes called *Exploring St Helena: A Walkers' Guide*. This was written by Ian Mathieson and Laurence Carter and can be ordered from Miles Apart (for contact details, see page 165).

St Helena has steep valleys and beautiful scenery. The walking terrain has varying degrees of difficulty, from gentle strolls along country roads to more adventurous walks along the coast or ridges to view the spectacular scenery and the beautiful flora. For the more experienced hiker, there is ample opportunity to discover more isolated parts of the island, such as Lot's Wife's Ponds, Prosperous Bay Plain or the Barn. Appropriate hiking boots are recommended for these walks. See also page 97.

Golf
There is one nine-hole golf course on St Helena, usually played twice to give 18 holes. Located close to Napoleon's former residence, at Longwood, it is reputed to be one of the remotest and most challenging golf courses in the world. The magnificent scenic surroundings are occasionally 'enhanced' by a roaming donkey in the field nearby. The course is open to the public as well. The fee for playing at the golf course at Longwood is £5 for 18 holes.

Swimming
There is an Olympic-sized swimming pool in Jamestown which is open daily. There is also a small children's pool off to the back of the area. Admission fees for the swimming pool are as follows: children 0–4 years: no charge; children

ages 5–15 years: £0.20; people 16 years of age and over: £0.40. In addition swimming is possible from the wharf and a few other coastal areas.

Scuba diving

The St Helena Diving Club offers the opportunity to enjoy scuba diving and snorkelling; the club can be contacted through the tourist office in Jamestown. A membership fee is required and, with the appropriate certification and equipment, it is possible to scuba dive in James Bay. The water temperature in this area averages around 73°F (23°C). There is diverse marine life and also the remnants of some wrecks which adds interest to this unique diving location. There is much marine fauna to be seen around the island, including butterflyfish, parrotfish, damselfish, trumpetfish, scorpionfish, jacks, puffers and morays. The manta ray is a frequent sight in the summer and sometimes you can be lucky enough to see a whale shark. It is also possible that you might see a hawksbill turtle.

There are no decompression facilities on St Helena, so it is particularly important to follow sensible diving practice. Prices for diving are as follows: shore-based dive £7.50; boat dive £10; air-fill £2; equipment hire: tank £3, wet-suit £4, fins £2, mask £2, weight belt £2.

Fishing

For the avid sports fisherman, there are opportunities to enjoy your hobby. By prior arrangement, you can join one of the local fishermen for a day. The most popular fish being caught in these waters are tuna, marlin and barracuda, but there are also smaller species of fish to be found. Information regarding hiring of boats may be obtained via the Fisheries complex in Ruperts (tel: +290 2430), or ask at the tourist office.

Tennis

At the moment the only tennis court is at Prince Andrew School. Charges are £0.50 per hour but courts are available only after 16.00 and during school holidays. However, another tennis court in Jamestown is shortly to open, although details of fees were not available at the time of publication.

Part Two

Ascension

ASCENSION ISLAND AT A GLANCE

Location South Atlantic Ocean, 700 miles (1,120 km) northwest of St Helena; about halfway between Brazil and Angola

Size 34 square miles (88km²)

Highest point 2,817ft (861m)

Status Dependency of St Helena

Capital Georgetown

Currency St Helena pound or pound sterling. The US dollar is in common use too.

Population 1,008 (2001)

Language English

Religion Predominantly Christian

Time GMT

Electricity 240V, 50Hz. The standard electrical socket is the 13-amp flat pin used in the UK.

International dialling code +247

Background Information 6

For many years Ascension Island was inaccessible to tourists because of the military installations which have their home here. Previously only military personnel, government employees and people employed by companies on the island, were permitted on Ascension. In recent years this has gradually changed and the administration now encourages visitors.

Today the island is used mainly for communications purposes. The American military operates a surveillance station for the US Air Force, a satellite surveillance station, as well as the airport. Cable and Wireless operates an earth station for the European Ariane rockets and a satellite communications centre. The BBC World Service have their Atlantic Relay Station on the Island.

The St Helena Government seconds staff to Ascension to run the administrator's office, the post office, the savings bank and the police detachment. As the Ascension Island Government increasingly takes more responsibility for its own affairs, it has started employing its own staff.

Various private companies keep the rest of the estimated 1,000 inhabitants employed. The majority of the people on Ascension are from the neighbouring island of St Helena. There are about 200 British citizens and about 70 American nationals who make up the rest of the population. They live on the island for anything from a few months to a few years, depending on the individual work contract.

Georgetown is the administrative capital of Ascension. Most of the island's inhabitants live within the four settlements outside of Georgetown. Two Boats village, about three miles (5km) inland and situated at 600ft (190m), is a residential area. Traveller's Hill is where the RAF contractors live. The US base area is located at Cat Hill. On Green Mountain are the Residency, some cottages and the now disused farm.

There is an Anglican church, St Mary's, a small Roman Catholic church, the Grotto (the name is taken from a local fumarole), and the remains of a mosque, which served Muslims from West Africa in the early days of occupation.

GEOGRAPHY AND CLIMATE

Ascension is a rocky peak of purely volcanic origin with its base just west of the mid-Atlantic ridge. It is located 703 miles (1,100km) northwest of St Helena. Geologically Ascension is very young and the possibility of volcanic activity can never be completely ruled out. There are 44 dormant craters on the island. Much of the island is covered by basalt lava flows and cinder cones, giving the impression of a moonscape. The last major volcanic eruption took place around 600 years ago. The highest point on the island is Green Mountain at 2,817 feet (861m), covered with lush vegetation which increasingly spreads throughout the island during the rainy season. The small farm near the peak once produced vegetables, but has unfortunately fallen into disrepair.

The climate on Ascension is sub-tropical, but it is much drier than one would expect. Temperatures at sea-level are between 66–88° F (20–30° C) and are about 10–15°F (4–5°C) cooler on Green Mountain, which receives the greatest amount of rain. Temperatures are kept moderate by the persistent southeast trade winds. The heavy rainfall period is from January to April with showers occurring throughout the year.

NATURAL HISTORY AND CONSERVATION

Before the 19th century, Ascension Island had no mammals and few plants. It was, however, home to one of the largest seabird colonies in the tropical Atlantic, with up to 20 million boobies, terns and frigatebirds nesting there.

Flora

There are 25 species of indigenous vascular plants, of which ten are endemic to the island. Three of these plants have not been seen since 1889, and the Rubiaceous shrub, *Oldelandia adscensionis*, is presumed extinct. Of the seven remaining species, four are listed as rare and three are endangered. There are only about a dozen indigenous and six endemic species of flowering plants. There are also five types of endemic ferns. Since 1815 there have been many introductions of alien species to the island. These were originally brought in an attempt to modify the climate and provide food. It is these introductions that have been mainly responsible for the decline in endemic flora. There are also fears that further extinctions will occur. The vast majority of Ascension's flora has been introduced in the last 150 years or so.

The following is a selection of some endemic plant life which is still surviving at this time:

Euphorbia origanoides is one of the world's rarest plants and endemic to Ascension but the population is declining. This low-growing plant has prostrate vermilion stems with a thick milky juice, small alternate oval, slightly toothed leaves and greenish-red flowers similar to the English spurge. The milky juice is poisonous and can cause blindness if allowed contact with the eyes. Small colonies grow near Letterbox, between Sisters and Cross Hill, near Collyer Point, Comfortless Flats, on the seaward slopes of Devil's Cauldron and near Cotar Hill and South Gannet Hill.

Sporobolus caespitosus is an endangered endemic grass. The last time this species was spotted, there were approximately 70 tufts remaining high on Green Mountain. Since then, no further sightings have been made, and it is quite possibly extinct.

Dryopteris adscensionis is an endemic which can be found in moist ravines. As far as anyone knows, there is only one single plant remaining.

Pteris adscensionis is a rare endemic. There are two populations of ten plants on Green Mountain and in Cricket Valley.

Marattia purpurascens is an endangered endemic fern. In 1976 there were several hundred on the top of Green Mountain.

One of the biggest ecological dangers to Ascension is that of the Mexican thornbush which seems to grow anywhere, is impenetrable, has nasty thorns and is spreading throughout the island at a very rapid rate. A type of beetle which feeds only on the seeds of these bushes was introduced to the island about two years ago but as yet there has been little evidence that this has helped.

Birds

The only known landbirds before the 19th century were the small night heron and the Ascension flightless rail. Both are now extinct. The tiny flightless Ascension Island rail, *Atlantisia elpenor*, was closely related to the Inaccessible flightless rail. The only evidence of the presence of this extinct bird is from a traveller's description of 1656, and skeletons found within the last century.

At the present time, only four non-seabirds exist, all of them introduced. The waxbill, *Estrilda astrild*, and the common mynah, *Acridotheres tristis*, are usually seen in Georgetown. Canaries *(Serinus flaviventris)* were introduced in the 1860s. Red-necked francolin, *Francolinus afer*, also occur. The occasional vagrant birds will also find their way here, for example cattle egrets, *Bubulcus ibis*.

The introduction of feral cats in 1815 has cleared the majority of the birds. Another main reason for the drastic decline in seabirds on Ascension was the arrival of men who harvested birds and their eggs and mined some of the guano. In the 1920s the guano deposits were worked by an English company and some of the remains of the venture still exist. Contributing to this problem were goats and rats. There is little doubt that the continued presence of feral cats on the main island prevents seabirds from recolonising the coastal plain. Most seabird populations are therefore limited by the availability of suitable nesting sites on Boatswain Bird Island.

This effectively limits the proportion of adult birds that can breed, and therefore the total productivity of the populations. The competition for breeding sites is quite intense. Conflicts between rival birds often result in the contents of the nest being destroyed or adults being injured. As a result of this, seabird breeding success on Ascension appears to be lower than comparable seabird colonies elsewhere. The populations of the 11 species of seabirds that are still present have fallen to about 400,000, most of which nest on Boatswain Bird Island, which is cat-free; there are also significant numbers of sooty terns to the southwest of the airfield. Birds do occasionally attempt to nest on the main island, often right across from Boatswain Bird Island, near the path down to the Letterbox Point.

Feral cats are not the only animal which has negatively influenced the population of seabirds, as man has also made his contribution. A Japanese long-line fishery for big-eye tuna *(Thunnus obsesus)* and swordfish *(Xiphias gladius)* has been operating within 200 nautical miles of Ascension since 1988 and this could have severe implications for the frigatebird and booby populations. These species are known to scavenge bait from behind local sport-fishing boats and some occasionally get caught on the hooks. It is also likely that these species are flying out to the commercial fishing vessels as well, in an attempt to take the bait from the hundreds of long lines which are set, and as a result they become ensnared and drown. In addition to long-line fishing, yellowfin tuna *(Thunnus albacares)* are also caught around Ascension using purse-seine nets. Over-fishing of these surface-feeding tuna could have indirect effects on Ascension's seabird populations. All the seabirds on Ascension are surface-feeders and the small fish upon which they prey are usually too deep for capture. Tuna have similar prey to the seabirds and herd shoals of small fish to the surface where they become available to seabirds. Reductions in the tuna populations around Ascension could therefore result in a reduction in food availability for all seabirds on Ascension.

Boatswain Bird Island is a sight worth seeing. The rock lies just off the east coast of Ascension and is a flat topped sheer rock some 400 yards long and 300ft high. Landing is not permitted. It can also be viewed when the *RMS St Helena* passes by on its way to or from Ascension. When the ship blows its whistle, you get a fair idea of just how many birds make their home here, as the skies are filled with their graceful forms. However, this is to be discouraged as it leaves eggs and chicks open to predators and exposes them to the heat of the sun.

Ascension Island frigatebird *Fregata aquila* Boatswain's Bird Island now supports the entire world population of the Ascension Island frigatebird, the smallest frigatebird in the world. It has a hooked beak and forked tail. The males have a prominent red pouch at the throat, which is inflated during courtship rituals. They breed only on Boatswain Bird Island, laying one egg at a time and seem to survive by pirating other birds' food, especially the boobies. They will also take baby turtles and sooty tern chicks.

Masked booby/brown booby *Sula dactylatra* The masked booby and the brown booby are attractive birds and belong to the gannet family. Masked boobies, also known as white boobies, are the farthest ranging of their genus found around the world. They are the largest of the species, with a wingspan of about 5ft. They are brilliantly white in colour with deep-black wing markings and a distinct bluish face mask. Their nests are often located near cliffs or steep slopes. Since these are the heaviest and most awkward of boobies, they need the aid of gravity to take off into full flight. Brown boobies are the most common of the species. They are brown on the top with white underparts. Boobies have a fairly regular breeding cycle. The young are usually born in pairs, with the larger chick frequently killing the smaller within a few months of birth. As they grow larger while still retaining their downy coat, juvenile masked boobies often seem much larger than their parents. Research has shown that only around 40% of the adult population of masked boobies is able to breed each season on Ascension due to a lack of breeding space. Boobies will avoid breeding in years when food supply is poor and those that do have very poor success.

Sooty tern *Sterna fuscata* The breeding season for the sooty tern, or 'wideawake' as it is known locally, varies on a cycle of just under ten months. It is a graceful bird with a forked tail and pointed wings, generally white below and black above with a white patch on the forehead. Their main food is fish and squid. They are widely distributed around the world in tropical latitudes. They breed on the coastal flats. Large numbers of this bird settle on the southwest coast, called the Wideawake Fairs, to hatch their eggs. They are also found in very small numbers on Boatswain Bird Island. The colony, currently about 200,000 pairs, is much reduced from the million plus pairs recorded in the 1950s. This reduction has been caused by cats preying on breeding adults and chicks. It is estimated that approximately 1% of the total population is killed each breeding season.

Fairy terns *Gygis alba* A few fairy terns, also known as white terns, can be found nesting on the cliffs. This bird was probably given the name fairy tern because of its effortless flight and its pure white plumage. Its large dark eyes appear to be surrounded by shades.

Red-billed boatswain/yellow-billed boatswain Ascension is famous for the red-billed boatswain *(Phaethon aethereus)* and the yellow-billed boatswain *(Phaethon lepturus),* also known as tropicbirds. They have magnificent tail feathers, which are over half the length of their body. They are found on Boatswain Bird Island and at Pillar Bay.

Madeiran petrel/black noddy A few Madeiran petrel *(Oceanodroma castro)* nest on Boatswain Bird Island as well as the black noddy *(Anous minutus)* which is very similar to a tern. It is black with a white cap and is more common on St Helena.

The breeding population sizes of these species, with the exception of sooty tern, are poorly documented due to difficulties in accessing many of the colonies.

Feral cats
Domestic cats were brought to the island in 1815 to get rid of the black rats which had survived shipwrecks. The cats, however, preferred the birds, whose populations were drastically reduced to almost nil by the middle of the 19th century. The cats quickly became wild and multiplied rapidly. The cats are the main reason why almost the only place to find full time ground-nesting birds on Ascension Island is on the tiny Boatswain Bird Island.

GREEN SEA TURTLE
Tricia Hayne

The green sea turtle, *Chelonia mydas*, is named after the greenish colour of its fat. Those that nest on the beaches of Ascension spend most of their lives in the sea off the coast of Brazil, returning hundreds of miles to their place of birth to lay their eggs. Turtles are cold-blooded animals, requiring warm water to survive. In fact, water temperature affects the sex of the hatchlings – at 82°F (28°C), a balance between male and female is to be expected; cooler than that and males will dominate; hotter and there will be a predominance of females.

In the wild, the green sea turtle lays between 300 and 540 eggs per season, nesting every three or four years. In their first year, the hatchlings grow up to 6lb (2.7kg), and by the time they are three or four they can be expected to weigh up to 52lb (24kg).

Turtles do not nest until they are at least 25 years old, when they lay their eggs deep in the sand. The eggs take around 60 days to hatch, at which time the hatchlings make their way towards the sea, attracted by the play of moonlight on the waves, and set off for distant climes.

Other wildlife

Also making their home on the island are rabbits of which there are plenty, especially around the RAF base at Travellers Hill. The additional animal inhabitants include sheep, feral donkeys, land crabs, an estimated four species of endemic spider, two species of lizard and assorted rodents. All wildlife except feral cats, rabbits, rats and mice are protected by law.

There is a colony of **land crabs** that lives on the island. In April 1977 they were virtually overrunning the island, invading houses, and in some cases being found in beds. Although they are probably the earliest colonisers of Ascension, relatively little is known about them, their history on Ascension or their breeding habits. On Ascension these crabs breed infrequently. When they feel the time is right, at dusk they will creep out of their hiding places in rocky crevices or holes in the sand. Cautiously they make their way down to the water's edge, their egg pouches bulging with tiny brown eggs. Before the eggs can be laid, the pouch must be thoroughly soaked with sea water. In the past, there have been reports of up to 300 crabs being seen in the surf. After the eggs are laid in the sand or soft ash, the crabs return to their holes. The process is repeated the following evening. Great care should be taken not to disturb them during their time of breeding.

Marine life
Green sea turtles

One of the most renowned attractions of Ascension are the green sea turtles (*Chelonia mydas*). Many tourists flock to the beach after dark during egg-laying season, January to May, to observe the turtles laying their eggs on the beach and then returning to the ocean. It is quite a sight to see according to those who have witnessed it.

Before the arrival of man, the beaches served as the main breeding ground for the Atlantic population of green turtles, most likely due to the fact that there was a minimal number of predators. As long as anyone can remember, these creatures have migrated to the island annually from their feeding grounds along the South American coast. Today, the turtles are not so fortunate as they were in earlier days. The hatchlings face increased danger from feral cats and nest sites are becoming overgrown with Mexican thorn. They are however completely protected and it is an offence to disturb them in any way.

Fish and other marine creatures

In the waters around the island there are bottlenose dolphins, barracuda, sailfish, wahoo, bonita, tuna, marlin and other game fish. Endemic fish which can be found in the waters off Ascension are: combtooth blennies (*Scartella nuchifilis*), resplendent angelfish (*Centropyge resplendens*), and porgies (*Diplodus sargus ascensionis*). The only other endemic animal species found here are two species of inland salt water shrimp, *Typhlatya rogersi* and *Procaris ascensionis*, which can be found in rock pools near Shelly Beach.

Conservation

The RSPB appointed a conservation officer in October 2001 and the Ascension Island Government appointed theirs in November. There is a thriving Ascension Island Society for the Prevention of Cruelty to Animals (AISPCA).

There are two environmental projects underway. In March 2001 it was announced in the House of Lords that the UK government, along with the Royal Society for the Protection of Birds (RPSB), are to help fund a project to clear the island of as many of its feral cats and black rats as possible in an effort to protect Ascension Island's seabird and turtle population. Many of the cats breed in caves high in the volcanic mountains and are proving difficult to find. The eradication of the rats will follow after.

WIND ENERGY

In September 1997, four 225kw wind machines went into energy production to provide energy for the US Base on Ascension Island. The four windmills are located south of Dark Crater. The electrical energy produced is injected into the station's high voltage electrical distribution system and supplements the electrical power produced by the fuel oil engine generators at the power plant.

The average wind speed on Ascension Island of 16–17mph results in an output of 350–400kw, providing an annual electrical production of 3–3.5 million KWHs. The wind farm saves 290,000 gallons of fuel oil every year, which considerably lowers the output of the greenhouse gases, carbon dioxide and nitrous oxides, into the atmosphere.

The Mexican thornbush, accidentally introduced in the 1960s, which gives cover and provides food for the rats, will also be removed. It also denies nesting sites to the birds.

It is estimated that, once these pests are removed or brought under control, the breeding bird populations will move to the island, thus bringing an increase in the numbers of all the bird species that nest here. It is hoped, too, that Ascension might then attract more eco-tourists.

In addition, the Green Turtle Project looks after the welfare of the turtles.

HISTORY
Discovery and a quiet start
Ascension was discovered in 1501 by the Portuguese seafarer João da Nova, who named it Conception. Not until two years later, on Ascension Day 1503, was the island officially claimed and named by Alphonse d'Albuquerque.

During the 17th century, ships started to call at the island to supply themselves with turtle meat and eggs to supplement their shipboard diet. In return they would leave goats behind for ships which called at the island after them. This practice continued into the 19th century. This seemed to be one of the main reasons for ships stopping here, but also there were occasions where a wrongdoer would be marooned on the island as punishment for his crimes.

Also in the 17th century ships passing Ascension would call at the island and leave letters for other ships going in the right direction to deliver. This most likely occurred at a place on the island which is now called Letterbox, but no trace remains today of where these letters could have been deposited.

Captain William Dampier made a visit to the island on February 22 1701 when he arrived in the *Roebuck* on his way from Australia to England. When he arrived, his ship was leaking very badly and unsuccessful attempts were made to repair it. She sunk in her moorings and in April 2001 Australian marine archaeologists led by Dr Mike McCarthy discovered the wreck off Long Beach, Clarence Bay. While exploring the island, Dampier and his men discovered a spring. There is much discrepancy as to the location of the spring. There is a place called Dampier's Spring or Dampier's Drip, but it is more than likely that the actual location was in Breakneck Valley.

First settlers and the military
The fact that it was dry and barren was most likely the reason that Ascension remained uninhabited until Napoleon was sent to St Helena in exile in 1815. During the former Emperor's captivity on St Helena, a small British naval garrison was stationed on Ascension to deter the French. This first settlement was established on the northwest coast of the island and called Garrison. Today it is known as Georgetown, the island's capital.

In later years a village was built at the foot of Green Mountain and named Two Boats. The original site was a stopping place for sailors going for water to Green Mountain. Twenty-foot longboats were set on their ends in the earth with seats across to provide shade and a resting place for those passing by, hence the name Two Boats. By Napoleon Bonaparte's death in 1821, the island had become a supply station and sanatorium for ships involved in the suppression of the slave trade around the West African Coast.

In 1823 the island passed to the Royal Marines and became a base for naval operations until 1922, under the supervision of the British Board of Admiralty. That same year it was made a dependency of St Helena.

Telegraph cable and NASA

The first telegraph cable was landed in 1899, and with this Ascension became an important telecommunications station. From 1922 until 1964, the Eastern Telegraph Company (since 1934 under the name *Cable and Wireless*) 'governed' the island, with the senior manager handling the day-to-day operations of the island.

In 1942, the United States Government, by arrangement with His Majesty's Government, came to the island to build an airstrip, Wideawake Airfield. From 1943 until 1945 over 25,000 US planes made a stopover in Ascension on their way to North Africa, the Middle East and Europe, transporting troops and moving planes to serve in World War II. The US wartime base, holding as many as 4,000 servicemen at one time, was centred on Command Hill overlooking the airfield. American troops left in 1947 and the airstrip fell into disuse.

In 1956 an agreement was signed between Great Britain and the United States permitting the use of Ascension as a long-range testing ground for military missiles. In 1957, US Air Force presence was re-established and the airstrip facilities were enlarged. It is now an ICBM (intercontinental ballistic missile) and space missile tracking station. During the Falklands Conflict, Wideawake Airfield once again proved to be an invaluable asset as a staging post between Great Britain and the Falkland Islands. The British forces and the US personnel on the island co-operated closely with the RAF.

In 1967 a NASA tracking station was built but has since been shut down. Since 1964 an administrator from the British Government has carried out the executive duties of government. In 1982, Ascension became the stopover point for RAF Tristar flights between the United Kingdom and the Falkland Islands in order to provide British Forces support during the Falklands Island conflict. Since 1985 these flights have also been utilised by St Helenians to get to and from their jobs on the Falkland Islands and also by a limited number of passengers from the *RMS St Helena* who travel with the ship between Ascension and St Helena.

Ascension has proved its usefulness as a communications island, military and civilian, many times, especially during the Falklands Conflict. It has been an invaluable source of employment for St Helenians. Yet still, after all these years, nobody 'lives' there. Presently, the only freehold belongs to the Church; no-one can retire there and no-one can buy property. This status of 'a working island' has suited everyone well enough for the past few decades. Slowly, however, things are changing on Ascension and in 2002 it should be possible for people to live permanently on the island and own property there.

GOVERNMENT AND LAW

Executive authority of the island is held by the governor of St Helena. The resident island administrator is responsible for the day-to-day running of the island. A statutory body called Ascension Island Works & Services Agency looks after public services.

Ascension has a limited range of its own legislation. It is based on English law with a mixture of Ascension and St Helena Ordinances, adapted to conform with local circumstances. The administrator is the chief magistrate of the court and four Justices of the Peace have been appointed.

The small court house is attached to the police office, and on the rare occasion when it is necessary to conduct a hearing, it is quickly filled by the participants. The inspector takes on the role of public prosecutor, and the defendant is frequently represented by a lay advocate, someone who has had no formal education in law. Cases are usually heard by two Justices of the Peace. In the event of appeals, or there is a more serious case, it is heard by the chief justice who will stop off during his occasional journeys to St Helena. Needless to say there are many occasions when he passes through without a case to hear.

Government services

In 1984, Ascension Island Services was established to provide and operate the island's common services (school, medical, public works, environmental health, port etc). On April 1 2001 Ascension Island transferred to a new system of organisation. The object of this move was to create a self-sufficient community which would indicate a tendency towards establishing permanent residency. The new structure has been broken down into three organisations.

In addition to its present responsibilities, the Ascension Island Government took over responsibility for Public Health and Environment Services, Education Services, and Fire and Rescue.

Ascension Island Works and Services Agency (AIWSA), which is owned by the Ascension Island Government, was made responsible for public works and the managing of the cargo and passenger facilities at the harbour. The agency is governed by a Board of Management appointed by the governor with a general manager as Chief Executive Officer (whose appointment is also made by the governor), who is responsible for the day-to-day management of the company.

The Ascension Island Commercial Services (AICS), jointly owned by BBC World Service, Cable & Wireless and Ascension Island Government, will be responsible for the running of the guesthouse and the island shop. In addition to this, they will attempt to privatise all businesses by March 2002 and encourage the people of the island to get into the entrepreneurial spirit.

Military

The United States Air Force operates the Ascension Auxiliary Airfield (Wideawake), leased from the British Government in 1956, and the southernmost tracking station of the US Government Eastern Test Range. The USAF contractor, Computer Sciences Raytheon (CSR) manages and operates all the USAF facilities on the island.

Aircraft can land at Wideawake Airfield only with the prior permission of the US Military. Negotiations are underway to allow civilian flights. It is hoped that this will encourage the tourist industry to improve access to St Helena.

The Royal Air Force maintains the air link between the United Kingdom and the Falkland Islands via Ascension. The RAF has subcontracted some operations to various other companies. Turner Ltd of Glasgow maintains the RAF facilities. SERCO Ltd manages the airport. Eurest Defence Services Ltd provides catering and domestic facilities. The Maersk Co (UK) provides a permanently moored 70,000 tonne tanker offshore as the bulk fuel facility.

Police

Ascension Island is reputed to be one of the friendliest police beats in the world. The police force on the island consists of six police officers, four constables, a sergeant and an inspector who are from St Helena. The police officers are initially trained on St Helena. More specialised training is carried out in the UK. The officers are usually sent to the island for a two-year tour of duty, and their families are allowed to accompany them. Many prefer to be posted to Ascension as the salary is higher, though the basic wage is low in comparison to the United Kingdom.

The day-to-day running of the police force is handled by the sergeant. The inspector has overall command of the detachment. He reports to the chief of police on St Helena who in turn reports to the governor of St Helena. A strong emphasis is put on a close relationship with the community by implementing foot patrols and visits to various establishments. Although both the British and American armed forces have their own security forces, the police on Ascension have island-wide jurisdiction.

The police execute various tasks which are not normally associated with police work, such as immigration, vehicle registration and issuing the numerous types of licences (vehicles, driving, firearms, dogs and cats). Other duties include manning Her Majesty's Prison as prison wardens. Fortunately this job is rarely required. The prison cells, which have in the past been used for longer-term offenders, are used today mainly as an overnight police lock-up. The prison has had only ten inmates in the past two years.

A very strong emphasis is placed on maintaining good relations between the police and the people and this has probably been a major contributing factor in maintaining a crime-free environment. The majority of offences reported are traffic offences, mostly failure to renew licences, drinking and driving, or lack of due care and attention. There has been the very occasional case of theft, or of common assault, but fortunately these are very few and far between. The community takes a very dim view of any offence committed, which has resulted in a law-abiding population with a high regard for the local police force. One can really feel safe and secure on the island. There is no need to remember to lock doors, and people feel they can trust each other. Parents need not worry about the safety of their children, as no one on the island will do them any harm. Many young people will visit the island's police station for a friendly chat. The police are also very active in their support of the island's youth groups, such as the Scouts.

COMMUNICATIONS

Besides housing military bases, Ascension is mainly a communications centre. Until recently Ascension Island was a main relay point of the coaxial submarine cable system laid between the United Kingdom, Portugal and South Africa, with links to South America and West Africa. This cable system no longer operates. Cable and Wireless operates an international satellite telecommunications service, an internal telephone service and operates the Ariane Earth Station. In 1967 the BBC opened its Atlantic Relay Station to improve coverage of shortwave broadcasts to Africa and South America. In 1997 the BBC appointed Merlin Communications International to operate its Ascension facilities, including the island's power and fresh water plants. Ascension is also used by the Composite Signals Organisation (CSO), who have been here since 1966. These companies, together with the RAF, finance all non-military activities on the island. Ascension receives no financial aid from the United Kingdom.

In addition to the *RMS St Helena,* the British Ministry of Defence chartered merchant navy vessels run a monthly shipping service from the UK. An American supply ship calls about six times a year. The island also receives the occasional passenger cruise ship and fishing vessels.

Post office and mail

In 1863, the Union Castle Steamship Company began calling at Ascension to deliver and collect mail. There is no national postal service within Ascension Island. Houses have numbers, but few of the roads have names! All postal addresses on Ascension are those of the employing organisations. Representatives from the various organisations collect the mail from the post office, but internal deliveries between organisations are to separate boxes, one for each organisation. These are located outside the administrator's office. As most people within the small communities know each other, personal mail within the island is quite rare.

Airmail is received and dispatched twice a week via the RAF Tristar aircraft that flies between the UK and the Falkland Islands. Surface Mail and parcels arrive every month from the UK on the Ministry of Defence chartered shipping service, also en route to the Falklands. Surface mail to and from Cape Town and St Helena, and surface mail to the UK travels on the *RMS St Helena* as it makes its voyage between the United Kingdom, Ascension, St Helena and Cape Town.

Banking

For many years there was little requirement for a bank on Ascension Island. The numbers of people working there were small and staff withdrew any money needed from their employer. So the various companies and organisations took over the function of a bank.

PHILATELY ON ASCENSION

The first supply of stamps were sent to the island in March of 1867 by the UK Postmaster General. In 1922, in celebration of Ascension becoming a dependency of St Helena, sets of St Helena stamps over printed with Ascension were produced. This was the start of worldwide interest in Ascension philately. Due to the strong interest shown, the island's post office was inundated with requests for these stamps. In August of 1924, the first sets of Ascension definitive stamps were produced, which increased demand. In those days the post office was normally staffed by one or two wives of the workers of the Eastern Telegraph Company, so it must have been quite a task to meet the demand of the public at that time. Since 1966 the post office has been run by a staff of three (the postmistress, a postal clerk and a philatelic clerk) sent from St Helena who usually work on the island in two-year tours.

Stamp designs are agreed upon by the Philatelic Committee, which consists of members of the public, and is chaired by the administrator. The aim of the committee is to issue five sets of stamps per year, although special and commemorative issues may be added if the occasion warrants it. A 'definitive' set is released every five years, and remains on sale until it is replaced, whereas the special and commemorative issues are withdrawn from sale 15 months after their release date. Stamps from St Helena in mint condition can also be purchased, but first-day covers are fully serviced (ie: with stamp and postmarked). The post office operates within the strict regulations of the International Postal Union; for example all first-day covers are actually cancelled in the Ascension post office, situated in the heart of Georgetown. Ascension has up to 400 standing order customers receiving the new issues and new customers are always welcome.

With the expansion of Ascension Island in 1966, the need to make new arrangements became obvious. The Ascension Savings Bank (ASB) was set up as a branch of the St Helena Government Savings Bank. As there is no commercial bank on the island, the Ascension Savings Bank provides the only place on Ascension where the community can safely deposit money. Today many workers have their salaries paid direct to the bank.

The system is not yet completely modernised. Up until quite recently, the bank was still using a manual system; a computer system has now been implemented. Customers could only withdraw their money in cash, as none of the accounts have cheque withdrawal facilities. Deposits can also only be made in cash and there are no credit card processing facilities. Now the modernisation has started services should start to improve in the near future. Although cheques cannot be cashed at the bank, they can, however, be cashed with the government cashier.

EDUCATION

There are about 100 St Helenian children of school age, whose parents are employed on the island. These children attend Two Boats School. The curriculum largely follows that of the UK.

THE FUTURE

For some time there have been negotiations going on between the United States and Great Britain in order to allow civilian charter flights to land at Wideawake Airfield. Commercial aircraft have not been authorised to operate from Ascension, except in emergency, since the 1956 agreement between the governments of Great Britain and the United States. At the time of writing, the talks are still continuing. All signs are that things are still looking positive and that the island will be open to civilian air traffic sometime in the near future, though no definite target date has been discussed.

In the July 12 2001 issue of the weekly newspaper, *The Islander*, the Ascension Island Administrator, Mr Geoffrey Fairhurst, gave his view on how things will develop on the island in the future. As mentioned above, the Ascension Island Services was broken up into three parts as of March 31 2001. The newly formed government body plans to fund itself with the introduction of income tax, customs duties, and possibly some form of property tax. At this time no definite decisions have been made. Whatever is decided, they intend to have it in place by April 2002. It is hoped that eventually a commercial full service bank could be drawn to Ascension. In order to accomplish this they would like to introduce private enterprise to Ascension.

The various components of the old Ascension Island Services (the guesthouse, petrol station, laundry, shop and so on) will be sold off. Recently the savings bank was modernised with a computer system and the post office now accepts Visa and MasterCard. It is hoped that other businesses on the island will take up the opportunity presented by credit cards.

At present, any fishing revenue from licence fees in the waters around Ascension goes to the St Helena government, although this may change.

To improve the economy of the island, a fish trans-shipment business is under discussion, but as the island presently has no fisheries protection vessel, it is questionable whether a fishing company interested in doing business on Ascension would offer the patrol vessel as part of the deal.

For a long time there have been ongoing discussions about the buying of land and the right of abode on Ascension, this will also include the buying of businesses. The administrator hopes to get plans firmly in place by the end of 2001. They are going to start on a land development plan to decide where housing plots might be and where commercial and industrial property could be placed. At the present time, there is a housing shortage on Ascension. They need some inward investment to get these badly needed houses built for the workers, as well as for the visitors.

If the transition from a military controlled to a commercially driven island were successful, and Ascension Island were to become prosperous, this could only be an asset to the people of St Helena.

Visiting Ascension

Ascension Island is a 'working island' although it is now starting to open up and attract visitors who wish to enjoy its rich environment and history. The tourist infrastructure is still rather modest. Thus the visitor has to be prepared to make many of his arrangements himself.

GETTING THERE
By air

Ascension Island's airport is actually a US military base. The RAF flights start from RAF Brize Norton, about 20 miles west of Oxford, in southern England. After a short stopover on Ascension, the plane continues its journey to the Falkland Islands. Normally a RAF Tristar passenger plane is used for this service. Usually only 20 seats per flight are allocated to civilians, therefore advance bookings are recommended.

Flights leave Brize Norton at 23.00, arriving on Ascension at 07.30. Return flights operate from Ascension departing at 22.50, arriving at Brize Norton at 08.15 the following day. There are two flights a week in each direction, with days varying according to the time of year.

An APEX one-way fare (purchased at least 28 days in advance) costs £415. Standard economy fare is £661 one way, plus a £20 booking fee per person. Return fares are charged at double the single fare. There is an entry permit fee of £11, payable at the police station on Ascension. The shuttle service from the airport to Georgetown costs £10.

The above are military flights, which are not normally offered by travel agencies. Flight bookings for tourists are handled by:

Andrew Weir Shipping Ltd Dexter House, 2 Royal Mint Court, London EC3N 4XX; tel: +44 020 7265 0808; fax: +44 020 7816 4835

Getting to and from Brize Norton

A bus goes from Heathrow Airport every half-hour to Reading. From Reading, a train service operates to Swindon, taking about one and a half hours. A coach picks up passengers from Swindon railway station at 20.15 on the day of departure to Ascension, and will take them back to Swindon station on the morning that the flight arrives back at the airport. Usually there is also a coach from Brize Norton directly to London Heathrow Airport to coincide with the arrival of the RAF flights.

Baggage allowance

Ascension Island and St Helena residents/immigrants are allowed 54kg per person (27kg for children which must be requested). All other passengers are permitted 27kg per person (20kg for children). There is one piece of cabin baggage, not exceeding 18 x 12 x 9 inches and 4kg, allowed per passenger.

By sea

The Royal Mail Ship *St Helena* has regular service to the island. You can embark either in Cardiff (Wales); Tenerife (Canary Islands) or Cape Town

SAILING TO ASCENSION

Anchorage

Yachts should anchor in the area north of the Pierhead, in a position which does not obstruct ships arriving, departing or unloading cargo. Yachts must not tie up to any buoy or mooring in Clarence Bay. Landing is permitted only at Pierhead steps. Yachts may normally stay for up to three days. The crew may go ashore between 0700 and 2300, but may only stay ashore if booked into the Georgetown Guest House.

Clearance

No advance notice is required of arrival, but at the earliest opportunity the captain must report to the police, who also act as immigration officials, with the yacht's details, crew list and passports. This must be done within normal working hours; if a yacht arrives outside of these hours, the crew must wait on board.

Clearance for departure may not be done in advance, so visiting yachts must leave on a normal working day.

Fees

All those landing must pay an entry permit fee of £7.50 per person. Light dues are payable at £1.50 per 100 tons (up to 500 tons), minimum charge £10. Medical insurance, sufficient to cover medical evacuation by air, is compulsory and is available on the island at £4 per day. Existing policies are acceptable.

Repairs

Only minor repairs can be effected. In the case of any serious repairs needed, contact the Ascension Island Works & Services Agency in Georgetown (tel: 6346) for advice.

Supplies

Water may not be freely available. Fresh produce and other provisions are sometimes in short supply and may not be available for yachts even if on sale to the islanders. There is no cooking gas on the island.

Above Comfortless Cove on Ascension, a scenic spot for swimming (NR)

Left Ascension Island's hi-tech lunar landscape is somewhat unexpected to the visitor (NR)

Below The view from Green Mountain with Two Boat barracks on the plain and Georgetown in the distance (NR)

Above The rather forbidding sight of Tristan da Cunha, with its distinctive conical shape (NR)

Right Cargo, including fresh fruit, is shipped ashore from the *RMS St Helena* (US)

Below right Tristan's welcoming signpost, erected only when a ship is at anchor in the bay (NR)

Below left Tristan longboats securely staked against the high winds that are familiar to the island (NR)

WELCOME TO THE

TRISTAN DA CUNHA
SOUTH ATLANTIC

REMOTEST ISLAND

IMPORTANT INFORMATION FOR THOSE TRAVELLING TO ASCENSION BY SEA

Please take into consideration while planning your trip that embarkation on the RMS St Helena is only possible for those people who have no difficulty getting into a small motor boat, even with sea-swells. Depending upon ocean swells, people who have trouble climbing stairs or need assistance to walk may not be able to disembark from or be brought aboard the ship.

(South Africa). The journey takes about 13 days from Britain, eight days from Tenerife and about ten days from Cape Town (including a brief stay on St Helena). The standard price for this journey, one way, based on a double cabin with upper and lower berths is £1,670 from Cardiff and £1,250 from Cape Town. For other fares, see page 57. Only passengers who regard themselves to be steady on their feet, should consider going ashore on Ascension Island. The procedure to reach the quayside can be a bit difficult and it is strongly advised that passengers wear sensible shoes to go ashore.

RED TAPE
Immigration requirements
Besides a valid passport, the traveller must also have a valid health insurance policy, which covers transport by plane for medical treatment, if necessary. All visitors must also have written permission from the island's administrator in order to visit the island; this can be organised by Andrew Weir Shipping.

Fees per person for passengers going ashore at Ascension Island are made up as follows: entry permit fee: £11 (free for children under 12); launch fee: £5.50; tour fee: £5. Ascension insurance surcharge for passengers under 65 years: £4; for passengers 65 years and over: £6.

Passengers who already have worldwide travel insurance covering them for amounts of £100,000 or more are advised that they are not required to pay the insurance surcharge.

There is no fee for children aged 11 or under. The entry permit fee is payable on arrival on the ship or at the Airhead, or at the police station as soon as possible after arrival. At this time, evidence of adequate medical coverage must also be produced.

GETTING AROUND
Guided tours
An organised tour of the island is run by the chief purser on the RMS St Helena, during her stopover. The tour is made available since the RMS St Helena has its own minibus on Ascension. It takes roughly three hours, but this all depends on the time available. The route around the island includes Comfortless Cove, Two Boats Village, Green Mountain and the Farm, to the RAF Base at Traveller's Hill, then up to Command Hill from where there is a

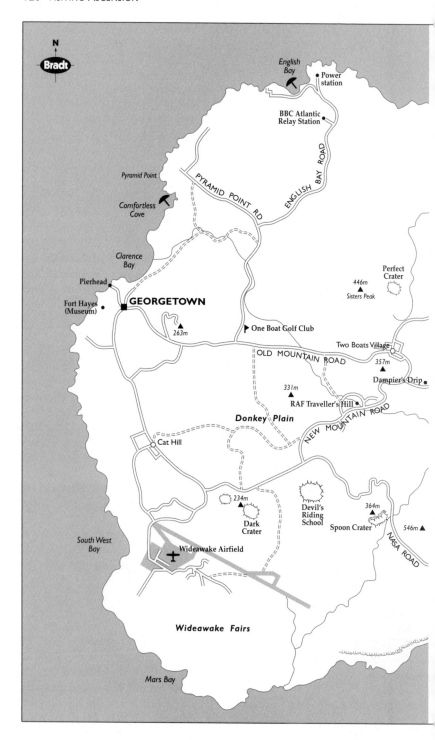

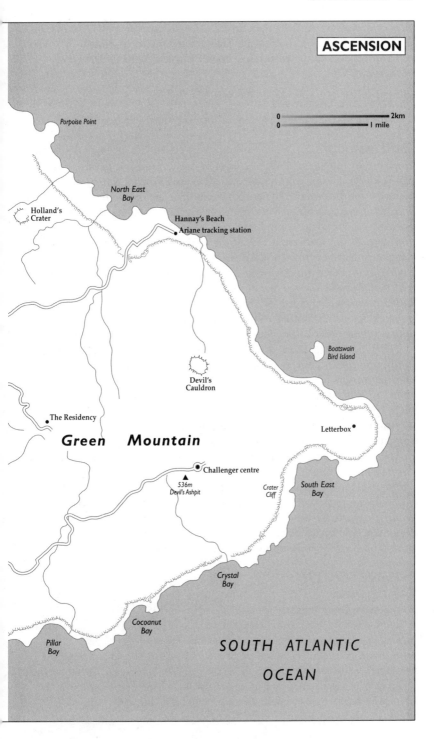

view of Wideawake Airfield, then finally to see the cannons at the foot of Cross Hill. If time permits, a short stop at Georgetown may be included.

Those staying on the island may book a bus tour with Cedric Henry (tel: 6244; fax: 6287).

Taxis/public transport
There is no public transport system or taxis on Ascension.

Car hire
For those wishing to explore Ascension by car, it is possible to hire a car for a day or longer if required. The **Ascension Island Tourist Office** can arrange a hire car for the cost of £20 per day, but as there are only a few hire cars you should reserve your car well in advance of your arrival on the island. You must possess a valid driving licence for your country. Once you arrive on Ascension you need to go to the police station and there they will issue you with a temporary driving permit for the duration of your car rental. The advantage to having a car is that you can explore the island more quickly than you can on foot. But please be warned that not all the roads are regularly travelled and you may find yourself stranded for a long period of time if your car should happen to break down. Always make sure you have enough petrol and the car is in good working order before you attempt to drive off the beaten track.

There are some basic driving rules which should be followed. The maximum speed limit is 40mph. In certain areas this is reduced to to 20–30mph. On hills where there isn't enough room for two cars to pass, vehicles going down must always give way to vehicles going up. It is tradition on St Helena, as well as on Ascension, to wave at cars travelling in the opposite direction while driving. Due to the surfacing on some roads, extreme caution should be exercised in wet weather as they become very slippery.

There are no traffic lights, roundabouts, motorways or traffic jams on Ascension, but driving here poses its own unique challenges. The island's sheep and donkeys have an annoying tendency to wander across the road without warning, especially at dusk or when the roads are wet. Many of the roads are narrow, winding and steep, especially the road up to Green Mountain. Mountain bikes have become quite popular in recent years, so drivers need always to be on the look-out for cyclists.

WHERE TO STAY
Guesthouses
Georgetown Guesthouse Georgetown; tel: 6246; fax: 6356; email: accommodation@atlantis.co.ac. Located in the heart of the island's tiny capital. this is an ideal base for your stay on the island, close to the nine-hole golf course and all Georgetown amenities. The rooms are all en suite, comfortable and well furnished. Single and double apartments are available and cost £40–70 per night. Each room has a television, telephone, fridge and tea-making facility and there are several small self-catering kitchens for use by guests. Meals are available in the nearby Galley.
Hayes House Georgetown; tel: 6246; fax: 6356; email:

accommodation@atlantis.co.ac. This is a comfortable but more basic place to stay than the Georgetown Guesthouse. There are both en-suite and non en-suite rooms. There is a TV lounge and patio area with a small self-catering kitchen. Rates £25–35 per night

Bungalows

Georgetown/Two Boat Village; tel: 6246; fax: 6356; email: accommodation@atlantis.co.ac. There are up to six clean and comfortable self-catering hire bungalows available located at both Georgetown and Two Boats village. These bungalows tend to be booked for longer-stay visitors and get reserved well in advance. Rates are £25 per night minimum one week stay; £300 a month (excludes water and electricity).

All the above prices are without meals. Meals can be eaten at the Galley (a self-service) restaurant, at one of the clubs on the island, or prepared yourself in the kitchen of your accommodation.

Accommodation may only be booked through **Ascension Island Commercial Services** Georgetown, Ascension Island ASCN 1ZZ; tel: 6246; fax: 6356; email: accommodation@atlantis.co.ac. A booking fee of £25 is charged.

Insurance can be bought from Ascension Island Works & Services Agency in Georgetown.

WHERE TO EAT AND DRINK, AND NIGHTLIFE

The clubs provide most of the entertainment on Ascension Island. Purchases can be made by non-members using cash in all the island clubs.

Two Boats Club Two Boat Village; tel: 4621 (office); 4439 (club). Located in Two Boats village, a 15-minute drive from Georgetown. There is a billiard/snooker/pool room, darts, gaming machines and a skittles alley. Live music and a disco are regular events as are the famous Mountain Grill dinners. Lunches are available most days and evening meals can be arranged by prior booking for small and large groups. Open Mon–Sun: 12.00–14.30, 19.30–24.00 (closed lunchtime Thursday)

Saints Club Georgetown; tel: 6344. Located in Georgetown. The lively Saints Club has a charming interior displaying photos of St Helena and historical Ascension Island. There are various gaming machines, darts, pool and snooker tables. Entertainment is available most weeks. Open Mon–Wed: 19.30–23.30; Thu: 12.00–15.00, 19.30–23.30; Fri: 12.00–15.00, 19.30–24.00; Sat: 12.00–15.00, 22.00–01.00; Sun:12.00–18.00.

Volcano Club American Base. It has the style and ambience of a 'real' American bar. There is entertainment every week (discos, country dancing, karaoke, etc). The bar also has several pool tables and gaming machines. Adjoining the bar is the highly popular Snack Bar, which sells a wide variety of American-style food (T-bone steak, burgers, pizzas etc). They accept US dollars, St Helena pounds and British pounds, but change is always given in US currency. Between the snack bar and bar is a gift shop selling T-shirts, postcards and Ascension Island souvenirs. Adjacent to the bar is a 'package store' where various American beers, wines and spirits may be purchased. Opening times are displayed outside the store. Opening times bar: Mon–Fri:16.30–23.00; Sat:

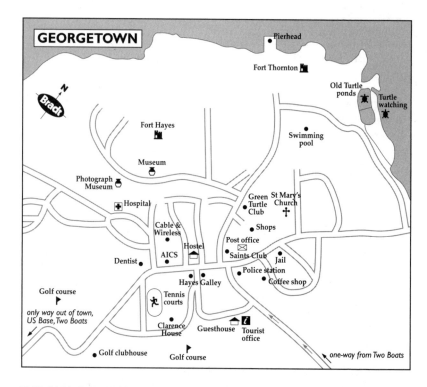

12.00–24.00; Sun: 12.00–23.00. Opening times snack bar: Mon–Fri:16.30–22.00; Sat, Sun:12.00–22.00. Opening times gift shop: Mon, Wed, Fri: 19.00–22.00.

Georgetown Coffee Shop Situated next to the administrator's office in Georgetown, the coffee shop is open most mornings and/or afternoons. You can relax under a shaded patio, and enjoy a variety of cakes and savouries as well as hot and cold drinks and observe the slow pace of Ascension Island. Open Mon, Fri, Sat: 09.00–13.00.

Reflections Bistro During the day, this establishment is known as the Georgetown Coffee Shop (see above for details). It is open once a week, on Wednesday evenings, for dinner. The meals are excellent and usually follow a theme (ie: Indian, Chinese, Italian and even James Bond 007 nights). Meals should be booked well in advance as they are very popular.

Airhead Café Airport. Open Mon–Fri: 08.00–13.00. Also evening of incoming/outgoing flights 22.00–22.30.

Green Turtle Tel: 6778. Located in the former Exiles building, close to the shops, the Green Turtle is open for lunch at weekends, and as a club every evening.

SHOPPING

The **Ascension Island Commercial Services Shop** is in the heart of Georgetown (Ascension Island ASCN 1ZZ; tel: 6246; fax: 6356; email: accommodation@atlantis.co.ac). It is the only shop that sells food groceries. One can usually find most of the basic groceries needed. But as this is a small island there can sometimes be shortages of certain items, especially fresh produce, which is flown in.

The shop also sells non-food items such as toys, gifts, electrical goods, cards, stationary etc. There is a substantial video library, as well. Also available are slightly out of date UK magazines and newspapers which have been brought from England on the RAF Tristar flights. Opening times of main office: Mon–Thu: 08.30–17.00; Fri: 08.30–16.30. Opening times of cash office: Mon–Thu: 09.00–12.30; Fri: 09.00–12.30, 13.30–16.00. At RAF Traveller's Hill there is a smaller **Ascension Island Commercial Services Shop**. Open Mon–Sat: 09.00–13.30, 18.30–22.00; Sun: 12.00–14.00.

The **Turtle Nest Gift Shop** is located on the lower floor of the former Exiles building in Georgetown. They sell cards, gifts, jewellery and other novelty items. Open Wed, Fri: 16.30–18.00; Sat: 10.00–13.00.

The **Rock Shop** is situated behind the Ascension Island Commercial Services Shop in Georgetown. They carry men's, women's and children's clothes of various styles. Open Wed, Fri: 17.00–18.00; Sat: 10.30–11.30.

The **Sue Ryder Boutique** is a charity shop on the lower floor of the former Exiles building in Georgetown. They sell very good used clothing. Open Fri: 17.00–18.00; Sat: 10.30–11.30.

The **RAF Welfare Shop** is situated close to the entrance of RAF Traveller's Hill. They sell sports equipment, video cassettes, postcards, clothing, souvenirs and operate a video rental library. They rent videos at very reasonable prices.

June's Gift Shop is located in Two Boats Village, close to Two Boats Club. They stock a variety of gifts, cards, wrappings etc. as well as a large selection of adults' and children's clothing. Opening times are displayed outside. Open Tue, Thu: 17.00–18.30; Sat: 10.00–12.30.

Volcano Club Gift Shop is found between the Volcano Club bar and the snack bar on the American base.They offer a wide variety of gifts and a wide selection of T-shirts. Open Mon, Wed, Fri: 19.00 – 22.00.

Other practicalities

Georgetown post office Georgetown, Ascension Island ASCN 1ZZ; tel: 6260; fax: 6152; email: PostOffice@atlantis.co.uk. Open Mon–Fri: 08.30–12.30, 13.30–15.30; Sat: 08.30–12.00 (airmail closing times: Wed: 15.30; Sat: 10.00)

Police office Georgetown; tel: 6412 (emergency number: 6666). Open Mon–Fri: 08.30–13.00, 14.00–15.30; Sat: 08.30–12.30.

Savings Bank Georgetown; tel: (+247) 6326. Open Mon, Wed, Thu, Fri: 08.30–12.00, 12.30–15.30.

One Boat Petrol Station One Boat. Open Mon, Wed, Fri: 08.00–12.00; Tue–Thu 16.30–18.30; Sat: 10.00–14.00.

PLACES OF INTEREST

In addition to Georgetown, 44 volcanic craters, the volcanic caves, lava tunnels, old forts, cannons and cemeteries invite the guest to explore the history and the landscape of Ascension Island.

Georgetown

The capital of Ascension is Georgetown. It is more a small village, with the ambience of 1950s England. There is a supermarket, which is normally fairly empty, and some gift shops. There is a guesthouse and some bungalows. The biggest problem in Georgetown is that there is no real restaurant; there is only the Galley. Otherwise you need to buy food and prepare it at your accommodation. The possibilities are severely limited.

In Georgetown there is a small **museum** which is actually very good considering its small size and well-worth the visit. The only church in Georgetown is St Mary's, an Anglican church within the Diocese of St Helena and the Province of South Africa. It serves the whole island community and welcomes people of all denominations. It is open 24 hours a day for private prayer. The door is only closed to prevent sheep or donkeys from entering.

The **turtle ponds**, which were built in 1829, are located on the site of the island's first harbour before the Pierhead was built. They were used for holding live turtles which were later shipped on board to provide fresh meat for the sailors (and turtle soup for the Lord Mayor of London and the Lords of the Admiralty).

Fort Hayes was built around 1860 on the site of an earlier battery. It is now part of the Museum (open Sat: 11.00–13.00). The new building opposite, opened in 1994, houses the Gallery and the *Islander* newspaper. The Gallery is open every Saturday 11.00–13.00, or by appointment. It is manned by a knowledgeable team of volunteers who will be happy to show you around.

Outside Georgetown
Challenger Centre
Many of the island's letterbox walks start from this point. From here, you have magnificent views of the coastline and the mountain. The NASA site was at one time located here. When NASA left the island in the early 1990s, the Scouts took over the building and converted it into an outdoor pursuits centre in 1993.

Comfortless Cove
This small cove is one of the few places on the island where it is usually safe to swim. At the weekends there are many families that come here. The original name was Sydney, which was later changed to Comfort Cove. Beginning around 1830 this inlet was used for landing crew-members from the ships working off the west coast of Africa, who had contracted yellow fever. These sailors were quarantined in this area and the garrison supplied provisions for the ill. Many suffered and died from this disease. During this period the bay was renamed Comfortless Cove, as an indication of the misery that was experienced here. The victims who didn't survive the yellow fever epidemic are buried in the small cemetery, known as Bonetta Cemetery after the crew of *HMS Bonetta*, many of whom died at this lonely spot. Nearby is Trident Cemetery and the *HMS Archer* memorial. Take special notice of the way many of the graves are marked. Instead of a stone, often a plank or piece of driftwood was used.

Dampier's Drip
As mentioned before, this is where William Dampier and his crew discovered a much needed spring of water. According to island mythology, they

PAINTED LIZARDS

On the road between Georgetown and Two Boats is a pile of rocks with the shape of a lizard on top. Tradition has it that people leaving Ascension, never to return, should secretly paint the lizard before they leave. There are many stories that circulate about the rock, one of which is that anyone who painted the lizard then returned to the island would die.

In the early days you actually painted the lizard. Nowadays, though, most people just pour a can of paint over it. The resultant effect is something between a rather gaudy snowman and an ornamental candle.

The lizard rock is on the left of the road between Georgetown and Two Boats, between the junction at Cross Hill that leads to the US Main Base and the junction leading to English Bay.

supposedly buried a treasure there, though it is yet to be found. In the 1820s about 50 men, women and children lived in the caves around the drip, collecting water in casks for transport to Georgetown by donkey.

English Bay
English Bay was the site of the unsuccessful guano-collecting undertaking. Remains of the workings can still be seen here. Today it houses the BBC South Atlantic Relay Station, and the power station and plant which supplies much of the island with electricity and water. It also happens to be the island's only easily accessible beach of any size. Take care when swimming; it can be dangerous.

Green Mountain
This is the area of Ascension that gets the most rain. The peak is topped with bananas and bamboo. There is also an abundance of tropical plants. It is possible to go into a volcanic lava tunnel or a volcanic cave. Some of the most interesting walks, with the best views, can be experienced here. Vehicles are only permitted as far as the Red Lion, the main farm building.

Hannay's Beach
Hannay's Beach is notable for a large and powerful blowhole along with many smaller ones. From its far end one has a view towards Boatswain Bird Island. The building above the beach is the Ariane tracking station belonging to the European Space Agency.

Two Boats
As mentioned earlier, this village takes its name from the longboats that were upended and made into a shady place to rest for those collecting water from Green Mountain. The first boats were erected in 1826 and have been replaced a number of times since then. This is also where the island's only school is located.

ACTIVITIES

Due to its volcanic origins, Ascension Island has many attractions to offer the visitor. The atmosphere on the island is easy going and there is plenty of sunshine. It is located closer to the Equator than St Helena, so the temperatures are usually higher. Most people feel that they can easily fill a week on the island enjoying its wildlife and walks, but for the less active a few days will suffice.

Hiking

There are a lot of different hiking areas on Ascension and a good companion to have along while hiking is the book *Ascension Island Walks*, published by the Ascension Island Heritage Society. This book lists all the walks included in the 'Letterbox Tour'. The idea of letterboxes is not a new one. In the 17th century, outward bound ships would leave messages on the island for the next ship to take home. These letterboxes are set up with the same concept. In 1913, the first letterbox, a green tin box, was placed at Letterbox, at the easternmost point of the island. Notes were left by visitors at this spot and the next person to come along would bring the letter to the General Post. The modern set of boxes was set up in 1979. There is now a handstamp set up next to each letterbox as proof of where the visitor was. These walks cover a good portion of the island and take in 18 letterboxes at various locations.

There are also 12 mountain paths which make a good excursion for those wanting to experience the natural side of Ascension. For those not used to difficult hikes, it is recommended that you walk on the roads as much as possible as some of the paths could be dangerous.

Turtle watching

From January until May, you can observe the green turtles on the beach near Georgetown. It is imperative that the nesting turtles are disturbed as little as possible. This is the reason that observers should follow some simple guidelines:

- You should leave the beach by 23.00. This way if the turtle does become disturbed, she has the chance to try again.
- Do not shine torchlight directly at turtles. It is better to walk quietly on the beach without lights and listen for the sound of flying sand. This will indicate that a nesting turtle is nearby.
- When you see a turtle, make sure you approach her from the rear. Do not crowd the turtle, make any sudden moves, talk loudly, or take flash photos. If the turtle becomes frightened, she may flee back to the sea.
- Watch only one turtle at a time. If you visit all the turtles, you are bound to disturb some.
- Once the turtle has started to lay, she can be observed from a shorter distance, but you should still move cautiously.
- Do not take photographs of the turtle until she is well into her egg-laying phase or returning to the sea, otherwise she may become distressed and abort her nesting attempt.

- Do not drive vehicles on the beaches or shine headlights on to the beach.
- Do not light fires on the beach.
- Do not make undue noise or play loud music on or near the beaches.

Birdwatching

On Boatswain Bird Island, a rock off the coast of Ascension, there are thousands of birds to be observed. If you wish to watch birds at a closer range, you can view the sooty terns on the Wideawake Fairs. During the breeding season, the place is awe-inspiring, and very noisy. In 2002, the breeding season will start in March, with peak hatching around mid-May.

There are a few guidelines that the visitor should follow in order not to disturb the birds or their nests:

- Always view the colonies from at least 40 yards (35m) away.
- Never go into the colonies when birds are present. They may desert their nest, or there is the possibility that one of the camouflaged chicks or eggs could be accidently stepped on.
- Never attempt to flush birds from their nests, as frigatebirds are always at the ready to swoop in and take unprotected tern chicks.

Fishing

Fishing goes on all around the island whether from the shore or on boats. There are several skippered boats (with fishing gear included) available to hire at very reasonable rates. The most common catches are grouper, silver fish, soldier fish and moray eel. Sometimes the fisherman gets lucky and lands a small shark! One of the safest spots to fish is the Pierhead in Georgetown. Because of the unpredictability of the waves, you must use extreme caution when fishing off the rocks, as there is a danger of being swept away. Before attempting any form of fishing on Ascension you would be best advised to seek the advice of an experienced fisherman.

Diving

Popular free-time activities are diving and snorkelling: Ascension is reputed to be one of the best places in the world for these activities.

Due to the wide array of fish contained in the waters around Ascension, it is a virtual paradise for snorkellers and divers. Bear in mind, however, that where the small tropical fish are, there will inevitably also be larger fish who feed on them, so you must always be cautious of where you are. The diving conditions are usually excellent, with clear warm water and a wide variety of marine life. Sea conditions are variable particularly from November to May. Large swells can build up which make diving impossible. There are no rescue or hyperbaric facilities on the island. Conservative dive profiles, safety stops and voluntary depth limits are enforced. This makes sense because the nearest decompression chamber is at least an eight-hour flight away.

There is a diving club on Ascension, with members trained under many different organisations. This club is British Sub Aqua Club (BSAC) affiliated.

They have a dive shack and compressor house near English Bay. They do not have any dive equipment for hire apart from a few weights and cylinders. Occasionally BSAC training courses are offered when there is a club instructor willing to run one. These are comparatively rare and generally only available to longer term residents, who would be in a position to put something back into the club.

Swimming

Sunbathing on the beach is a favourite activity. There are two beaches, English Bay and Comfortless Cove, which have specially roped off areas where it is safe to swim. These are the only two places which are deemed safe. Although the island is fringed with many sandy beaches, *swimming in the ocean elsewhere is not recommended* due to the strong underwater currents off much of the coast.

Ascension Island has three swimming pools that are all free to use and are open to the public. There is a saltwater pool in Georgetown. A freshwater pool can be found behind the Two Boats Club in Two Boats village. There is also a pool at Traveller's Hill, which is officially the emergency water supply for the island. This pool is only open if a lifeguard is present.

Gymnasiums

There are plenty of ways to keep in shape on Ascension. There are two gymnasiums, one at the American Base and one at RAF Traveller's Hill. Both are well equipped with cycling machines and a wide variety of weight lifting equipment. The gym at the America Base even has a sauna. There is a badminton court near the Pierhead at Georgetown and courts are also available at RAF Traveller's Hill gymnasium. There are two very good glass-backed squash courts available at RAF Traveller's Hill gymnasium. There are tennis courts at Georgetown, the American Base, Traveller's Hill and at Two Boats Village, which are all free to use.

Golf

Golf is a popular game on Ascension. The islanders' knowledge of the two courses make them difficult opponents to beat. There are competitions most weekends which, for a small fee, visitors are usually most welcome to join.

One Boat Golf Club is located about half way between Georgetown and Two Boats village and is the more serious of the island's two golf courses. This 18-hole golf course offers a unique environment to play golf. The greens are called browns and are made of crushed compacted lava smoothed flat with diesel oil. Around the edges of the fairways can be found large boulders of volcanic rock. This can make for a very interesting game. The cost of playing is relatively cheap compared to other parts of the world. After you have finished your game, you can get a well-deserved refreshing drink in the clubhouse, the 19th Hole.

Georgetown Golf Course is a nine-hole course with similar terrain to the One Boat Golf Club. It has the distinction of being the worst course in the world. There is no cost to play here, and no clubhouse, but the two Georgetown bars are nearby.

Part Three

Tristan da Cunha

TRISTAN DA CUNHA AT A GLANCE

Location South Atlantic Ocean, 1,519 miles (2,444km) west of Cape Town and about 1,326 miles (2,133km) southwest of St Helena

Size 38 square miles (98km^2)

Highest point 6,760ft (2,060m)

Status Dependency of St Helena

Capital Edinburgh of the Seven Seas

Currency Pound sterling

Population 285 (1998)

Language English

Religion Christian

Time GMT

Electricity 240V, 50Hz. The standard electrical socket is the 13-amp flat or round pin used in the UK.

International dialling code +2 897. Alternatives are INMARSAT satellite codes +874 or +871 ; these calls are extremely expensive.

Background Information

Tristan da Cunha has something of the air of a Scottish island in the middle of the South Atlantic. Viewed from the sea, it is dominated by the mountain, while its only settlement presents an attractive picture of freshly painted, colourful houses.

The current population of Tristan is about 300 people of mixed descent, and most of them related in some way. English is the only language spoken. The neighbouring islands of Inaccessible and Nightingale (and the small Stoltenhoff and Middle islands) are uninhabited. The more distant island of Gough, some 250 miles (400km) away, has an inhabited weather station. The islands have a very distinctive flora and fauna and are an important breeding ground for seabirds.

GEOGRAPHY AND CLIMATE

This small island of volcanic origin is in the South Atlantic, midway between South America and South Africa. It is located about 2,330km to the south of St Helena. Its shape is almost circular and covers 38 square miles (93km²) in area and just over 25 nautical miles around. The peak of the island rises 6,760ft (2,060m) from a plateau known as the Base, which rises steeply from the shore to 2,000ft (600m). A number of gullies, locally called gulches, lead down to sea-level from the Base.

The area around Edinburgh, the island's only settlement, and along the coast to the potato patches, is grassland where the animals graze. Being volcanic, the terrain is mainly rough on the majority of the island. There are, however, small plains which are used in a variety of ways by the islanders. Most of these areas are only accessible by sea.

Tristan da Cunha's climate is temperate with rapid weather changes and a wide temperature range of 40–85°F (4–26° C). The average rainfall is about 66 inches (168cm) per year.

NATURAL HISTORY AND CONSERVATION
Birds

The Tristan da Cunha group and Gough Island are extremely important for three albatross species. The endemic **Tristan albatross** *(Diomedea dabbenena)* breeds on Gough Island (about 1,580 pairs were known to exist in 1980) and Inaccessible Island (two or three pairs were known to exist in the late 1990s) within the Tristan da Cunha group. They are classified as endangered due to a very restricted breeding range, and limited potential for expansion within the known breeding range. The exact population is not really known but thought to be stable or possibly declining because of mortality from longline fishing and the ingestion of plastics.

The **yellow-nosed albatross** *(Diomedea chlororhynchos)* is a large, black-and-white seabird with long slim wings and a short, rounded tail. The back, upper wings and tail are blackish and the rest of body white. Some individuals have pale grey on their head and neck. The underwing is white with a narrow, dark trailing edge and a broader dark leading edge. The dark bill is slender and hooked, with thin yellow stripes on the culmen. The young bird has a black bill and no grey on the head. Their habitat is the open ocean and they are rarely seen from shore. They lay a single egg in a lopped mud cone placed on a cliff ledge, slope, or plateau. The nests are generally solitary but some birds also breed in colonies of hundreds of pairs. Yellow-nosed albatrosses feed mainly on squid and fish.

The **sooty albatross** *(Phoebetria fusca)* is a huge bird, with a wingspan of 80 inches (203cm). They are sooty-grey in colour and eat crustaceans, fish, squid, and the remains of petrels and penguins. They nest on steep coastal cliffs.

The vast majority of the world's **great shearwaters** *(Puffinus gravis)* breed within Tristan da Cunha. Conservative estimates are of more than five million breeding pairs. On Gough Island there are between 600,000 and three million pairs. There is an annual harvest of shearwaters on Nightingale Island. This bird has a dark cap contrasting with white lower cheeks, neck and breast. A narrow white collar separates the cap from the greyish hind neck and mantle. The greyish back is strongly patterned with a series of pale crescents or scaling, contrasting with the dark-brown upper wings. They have an arc of white on the rump or upper tail coverts. The underwing is mainly white with a dark trailing edge, an incomplete dark leading edge and other blotches which also extended on to otherwise white underparts.

In addition to the above, there is a good variety of other breeding seabirds, including the rockhopper penguin *(Eudyptes chrysocome moseleyi)*, Kerguelen petrel *(Pterodroma brevirostris)*, great-winged petrel *(Pterodroma macroptera gouldi)* Atlantic petrel *(Pterodroma incerta)*, soft-plumaged petrel *(Pterodroma mollis)*, broad-billed prion *(Pachyptila vittata)*, spectacled petrel *(Procellaria conspicillata)*, grey petrel *(Procellaria cinerea)*, little shearwater *(Puffinus assimilis elegans)*, grey-backed storm-petrel *(Garrodia nereis)*, white-faced storm-petrel *(Pelagodroma marina)*, black-bellied storm-petrel *(Fregata tropica melanoleuca)*, white-bellied storm petrel *(Fregetta grallaria leucogaster)*, common diving petrel *(Pelecanoides urinatrix dacunhae)* and the Antarctic tern *(Sterna vittata)*.

Sheep

Sheep are abundant on the island. Their wool is special and used to produce local handicrafts, like jumpers and socks.

Marine life

The waters around Tristan are rich in finfish, rock lobster (*Jasus tristani*) and octopus as well. Other species which can be found are fivefinger, bluefish, stumpnose, steambras, soldier and mackerel.

Fur seals, elephant seals, the rare Shepherd's beaked whale and the southern right whale all make visits to the island.

HISTORY
Discovery and settlement

Tristan da Cunha was discovered in 1506 by the Portuguese explorer Tristão da Cunha, who didn't actually set foot on the island, although he did name it after himself.

The island was first permanently settled in 1816 by the British government, anxious to prevent the French from using the island as a base from which to launch a rescue for Napoleon on St Helena. A couple of years later, common sense prevailed, and the garrison was withdrawn. However, one of the soldiers, Corporal William Glass from Scotland, was granted permission to remain on the island with his wife and children, and stores remaining from the garrison were made over to his family. Today, there are still direct descendants of Glass living on Tristan.

During the 19th century, the island served as a useful stopover for whalers in the South Atlantic. Sailing ships en route from Europe to Africa also found the island a useful staging post. As the sailors took advantage of the opportunity to restock with water, livestock and potatoes, the local community thrived. Prosperity was short-lived, however, and by the end of the century, with the demise of both whaling and the years of sail, the island returned to obscurity.

Early in the 20th century, before the advent of the South African union, the British government suggested that the island should be taken over by the government of Cape Colony. The offer was declined; but for this, Tristan da Cunha would now be under the jurisdiction of South Africa.

In 1938, Tristan became a dependency of St Helena. During World War II, in great secrecy but with the full co-operation of the Tristanians, a naval communications centre was maintained on the island. In 1949, on the establishment of a local fishing industry, the British government appointed a resident administrator.

Volcanic eruption of 1961

When the volcano erupted in 1961, all 264 islanders were evacuated to England. It was assumed that they would stay, but in 1963, when the eruption subsided, all but five wished to return to their home. The government arranged for the repatriation of the community. An administrator was reappointed and the post continues to this day.

In 1981, without any notification, the people's rights as British citizens were taken away from them. Although they may visit South Africa or the UK for recreation or study, they are not able to work there, and they do not even have a right of abode on St Helena. The situation is under review.

The hurricane of 2001

On May 21 2001, Tristan da Cunha was hit by hurricane-force winds. The storm ripped roofs from houses, severely damaging both the hospital and Prince Philip Hall, the island's community centre. Power cables were blown down and the inhabitants of Edinburgh had inches of water in their homes with only candles to light the darkness. Other people sought refuge in a neighbour's home. All lines of communication were cut off, so the island was totally isolated from the rest of the world.

Fortunately, no-one was seriously injured due to the storm. The following day, the islanders pulled together and began the cleaning up and repair efforts. Before dusk that night, the roofs of all the houses had been replaced. The village remained without electricity for six days, but thanks to the efficiency of the electricians on the island a temporary line was installed from the factory and the following day the administration office was back in operation. Unfortunately the heavy winds also damaged the potato patches. Many of the sheds holding next year's crop were blown away and the seed damaged; the effect on the 2002 potato crops could be disastrous. In addition, at least 30 cattle were lost and several sheep as well.

Donations to help the islanders came quickly from the islands of St Helena and the Falklands, and aid was also received from the British government and from as far away as the Netherlands and South Georgia.

GOVERNMENT AND LAW

The governor of St Helena has executive authority over the island and he makes his yearly visit to Tristan in January when the *RMS St Helena* makes her scheduled stop there. There is a resident island administrator, appointed by the British government. The government on the island is comprised of 11 different departments. The administrator is advised by the island council, led by the chief islander and comprising eight elected members (including at least one woman) and three appointed members. The councillor who receives the most votes in the election is appointed chief islander. Elections are held every three years.

Tristan has its own legislation but St Helena law applies to the extent that it doesn't conflict with local laws or circumstances. There is one full-time police officer and two special constables. The administrator is the magistrate, but crime is practically non-existent.

ECONOMY

Tristan is largely self-sufficient. Only large capital projects require funding from overseas. The economy relies mainly on the revenues of crayfishing and returns on investments. These finance government activities such as providing free health care and education. The main market for Tristan crayfish is the Far East, but recently the demand has decreased, so there is concern about a substantial deficit.

The sale of postage stamps also provides some income for the island. There have been talks about ideas for potential economic developments. Bilateral assistance is moderate and consists of the provision of medical care on the island and the continuing support of the Fisheries Management Project.

Tourism is not something that contributes a lot to the island's economy. There is a limited tourist industry based on the few ships which call here. The main employer on the island is the government which employs 146 people. The next largest employer is the crayfishing industry with 23 permanent positions working in the factory and casual employment for another 100 people working on 20 small island boats.

Because of the remoteness of Tristan da Cunha, regular imports of supplies is not possible. To some extent the islanders rely on their own stock, poultry and crops for their food. Each family is limited to two cows and seven sheep, in order to conserve grazing land. The island's main crop, potatoes, are grown at the Patches. The Agricultural Department grows other vegetables for the island. The Island Store imports a variety of food, household appliances and clothing.

THE PEOPLE

The people of Tristan are friendly, though a bit reserved. One can imagine that, living in a small isolated community of about 300 people, they are not used to many outsiders. The buildings are mainly white and visitors are reminded of the Scottish Hebrides and the green of the landscape also conjures up visions of Scotland.

About 35 children attend school on the island. The school was built in 1975 and is staffed by islanders, most of whom have received their teacher's training abroad, either on St Helena or in the UK. They attend school until the age of 15 and then a few go on to higher schooling on St Helena. Specialist training (nursing, fish management, policing and nature conservation), is gained mainly in the UK.

Visiting Tristan da Cunha

GETTING THERE

There is no airstrip on the island, and there is absolutely no possibility of air service being established here. Even though there hasn't been an eruption since 1961, the volcano is still considered to be active. Transport to and from Tristan da Cunha is provided by the *RMS St Helena*, an occasional cruise/passenger ship, crayfish concession vessels, and the South African research vessel *SA Agulhas*, all of which anchor offshore. *RMS St Helena* stops for two days with the passengers returning to the ship each night to sleep, but cruise ships usually stop for just one day. Due to the rough seas, the small harbour is only accessible 60–70 days a year. Improvements to the harbour are vital to Tristan's future.

The seas in the Roaring Forties are not always calm and it is at the discretion of the captain of the vessel whether he feels it is safe to let people go ashore. *This isn't always possible.* The ship anchors outside the harbour. If you arrive by the *RMS St Helena* you must climb down a rope ladder to get into the launch, which will take the passenger between two breakwaters into the harbour. Once you have entered the harbour you step ashore and then you walk up the slope into the island's only settlement, Edinburgh.

The **RMS St Helena** makes her annual call each January. Booking well in advance is advised. For details, contact Andrew Weir Shipping Ltd, Dexter House, 2 Royal Mint Court, London EC3N 4XX; tel: +44 020 7265 0808; fax: +44 020 7816 4835.

The **MV Hanseatic** makes her annual call in November on her way from the Canary Islands to the Falklands. For details, contact Hapag Lloyd Cruiseship Management, Ballindamm 25, D-20095 Hamburg, Germany; tel: +49 040 3001 4764; fax +49 040 3001 4761.

The **MV Explorer** currently makes her annual call in October, en route from the Canary Islands via Ascension Island and St Helena to The Falklands. For details, contact Explorer Shipping Company, 1520 Kensington Road, Oak Brook, Illinois, 60521, USA; tel: +1 630 954 2944; fax +1 630 572 1833.

The **Professor Molchanov**, a Russian expedition ship under Dutch charter, calls in April at Tristan da Cunha on her way from the Falkland Islands via South Georgia, before heading onwards to St Helena, Ascension and Europe. For details, contact Oceanwide Expeditions, Bellanypark 9, NL-4381 CG Vlissingen, Netherlands; tel: +31 118 410 410; fax: +31 118 410 417; email: expeditions@ocnwide.com.

For longer stays on the island, consider the following:

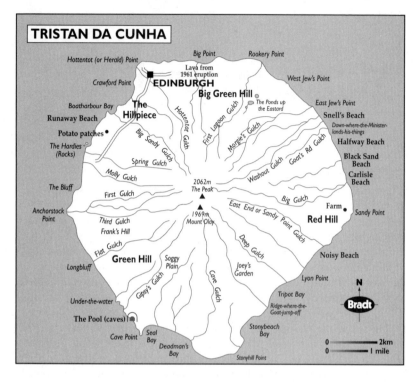

The **SA Agulhas** calls annually at the island in September/October sailing from Cape Town. The ship also acts as a supply ship, visiting the weather station on Gough Island to change personnel. She stays around Tristan for approximately three weeks, visiting on the way to and from Gough Island. To ensure landing in rough seas, the ship carries its own helicopter so is always able to get passengers ashore. This is the only regular and practical means by which visitors can spend two weeks on the island (with prior permission from the island council). For details, contact Table Bay Marine, PO Box 557, Maitland, 7405 Cape Town, South Africa; Tel: +27 0 21 531 4700; fax +27 0 21 531 4794

Two **lobster concession vessels** in the area, the *MFV Edinburgh* and the *MFV Kelso*, each make about three visits a year to Tristan, staying for about two or three months. Do be aware that both are small, and are working fishing vessels. For details, contact Premier Fishing, PO Box 3770, Cape Town 8000, South Africa; Tel: +27 0 21 419 0124; fax +27 0 21 419 0731.

RED TAPE

Permission is required, and normally granted, from the island council and the administrator to visit the island. When applying you are required to give the purpose of the visit and length of stay. All visitors must have:

• A valid passport
• A confirmed and fully paid return passage

SAILING TO TRISTAN DA CUNHA
Anchorage
Visiting yachts should anchor off Edinburgh settlement (advice may be obtained from the harbourmaster). The small harbour has a draught of only about 3ft (0.9m) and is completely unprotected. There is a constant heavy swell, at its worst in a northwesterly; yachts can rarely stay for long.

The harbour is closed to visiting vessels after 19.00 in the summer (October–March), and 17.00 in winter (April–September), though it may close earlier on fishing days or in the event of bad weather.

Landing is prohibited on Gough and Inaccessible islands. Landing on Nightingale, Middle or Stoltenhoff islands is allowed only if accompanied by a local guide, for a fee of £6. The guide must be picked up from Tristan and returned the same day before nightfall. In all cases the guide will be in charge of the party. For guide fees, see page 143.

Clearance
Radio Tristan will contact the yacht on VHF channel 16. The yacht will be boarded by immigration and medical officials, who then complete formalities ashore.

Crews should come ashore in their own dinghy. They may not normally use the government boat carrying the officials, although yachts without a dinghy may apply to the administrator for the use of a government boat, for a fee. In the event of a medical emergency a boat will be provided.

Yachts should maintain contact with Tristan Radio while at the anchorage, and inform them of their estimated time of departure and destination.

Fees
There is a landing fee of £15 per person. Overtime is charged by arrangement. Use of a government boat for transportation ashore costs £25. All fees are to be paid in cash or travellers' cheques at the Treasury Office in sterling, rand or US dollars. Yachts arriving at a weekend or public holiday should pay their fees to the immigration officer.

Repairs
The islanders may be able to help with repairs, as may the government workshop, but a yacht in serious trouble would have to await the arrival of RMS St Helena to be shipped out.

Fishing
Fishing for lobster is strictly prohibited. Yachtsmen wishing to catch finfish for their own consumption must ask the administrator for permission.

- Health insurance to include coverage for medical evacuation to Cape Town
- Sufficient funds to cover their visit. A combined passport and landing fee of £15 per person is charged.

For cruise-ship passengers and the cruise passengers on the *RMS St Helena*, permission from the island council is not required, but permission is required by the ship's agents before each visit.

No person may land at Nightingale, Middle, Stoltenhoff, Inaccessible or Gough islands without first clearing immigration at Tristan and then obtaining permission from the administrator

Journalists and film makers must inform the island ahead of time of the purpose of their visit. The island council normally grants only one permit per year to film makers. A fee of £5,000 is charged. The only restriction placed on such visits is that no intrusion is made into the islanders' private lives.

WHERE TO STAY

There are two guest cottages on the island, offering the possibility of self-catering, particularly for those on longer visits. Accommodation can also be provided in island homes at a cost of £20 per night for full board (includes three meals and laundry). There are no reductions for long-term stays. Camping is not permitted on Tristan da Cunha.

A visitor needs to obtain official permission from the island council in order to stay on the island. Unless you have personal connections on Tristan, you probably will not stay overnight, as visitors usually sleep on the vessel on which they came to the island.

WHAT TO SEE AND DO

Although the island is small, there are some interesting things to discover. Most people who visit the island are here only for a few hours at the most, depending on the duration of the visiting ship's call.

The settlement of Edinburgh

Nestled at the foot of the mountain, the settlement is just a small village. Interestingly, it is only possible to see the peak of the volcano from the sea.

One of the island's major employers, the **crayfish-processing factory**, is located just above the harbour. Here the products are packed and frozen for shipment to Cape Town, from there being shipped further to France, the United States and Japan.

The **Government Building**, which houses the administrator's office, the treasury, the police station and the video library, is worth a look inside to view the council chamber. Going further up the same road we come to the **hospital**, which was built in 1972. There is a resident doctor and two nurses, with occasional visits from a dentist and an optician.

There are two churches located on Tristan da Cunha. The **Catholic church**, St Joseph's, is the one most visible. The **Anglican church**, St Mary the Virgin, is tucked away at the back of the settlement. Next door to St

Joseph's is Jane's Café, which is open for light refreshments each weekday evening. On the other side of this is a **swimming pool**, built in1986 because of the dangers of swimming in the harbour and the surrounding waters. It is in use for about six months of the year.

Prince Philip Hall, which was seriously damaged in the hurricane of 2001, is the social centre of the island. A weekly dance is held here as well as indoor sporting events. There is an adjoining pub, as well.

There is a little **museum** with a craft shop. The museum has nicely presented displays which tell the history of the island. The craft shop also carries a few souvenirs, such as socks knitted from Tristan wool, and models of the traditional island longboats. Nearby is the **post office** with an assortment of stamps and first-day covers.

The **supermarket** is quite small. In addition to foodstuffs, it carries clothing, cosmetics, cigarettes, alcohol, souvenirs and local crafts. The **radio station** is located close by and maintains regular telecommunications services with the outside world via Cape Town. Radio Tristan broadcasts four days a week and transmits the BBC World Service News.

Scattered around the settlement and the lower hillsides is the allotted livestock owned by the island's inhabitants. To the east of the settlement lies the mass of solidified lava from the eruption in 1961.

The potato patches

The centre of the island is where the volcano is located, leaving very limited flat land for roads and walking areas. There are about three miles (5km) of road on the island, and an estimated 60 vehicles. A minibus – the only scheduled public transport on the three South Atlantic islands – runs from the settlement to the potato patches. Here, all the families on the island cultivate their annual supply of potatoes, an important staple food of the islanders.

The volcano

An excursion can be made by the longer-term visitor to the volcano. The Base is about 2,000ft (610m) up and then it is another steep climb of 5,000ft (1,524m) to reach the top, but it is unusual for the two-day visitor to have the opportunity to reach even the Base. Anyone wishing to walk on the volcano must be accompanied by a local guide – eight people maximum per guide. Do remember, though, that the weather may not be in your favour, and guides also have other commitments so may not always be available.

Guide fees

A fee of £10 is payable to the guide or, where there are only two walkers, £17. Fees are payable in cash (sterling, rand or US dollars) or travellers' cheques.

The outlying islands

Coming from or going to Tristan from South Africa, you pass the outlying islands belonging to the Tristan Group. No ship has scheduled stops at these islands, so they are just passing sights of interest.

Inaccessible Island is, as its name says, not accessible. It has been a nature reserve since 1994, and a management plan for the reserve is to be published shortly. **Nightingale Island** has a few huts for occasional stays by islanders. Visits to Nightingale, Middle or Stoltenhoff Islands are allowed only if accompanied by a local guide. The guide must be picked up from Tristan and returned the same day, before nightfall. There is a charge for guides; for details, see *The volcano*, page 143. Part of this fee goes to the island's conservation fund.

Gough Island, 250 miles (400km) from Tristan, is a World Heritage site and has a rather hostile environment. The weather station on the island is manned by South African personnel. The island has a Wildlife Management Plan to protect its unique environmental status. The *RMS St Helena* does pass by Gough Island on her return voyage from Tristan da Cunha to Cape Town.

The declaration of Gough Island as a World Heritage site and of Inaccessible as a nature reserve means that 40% of Tristan da Cunha's land area is under protection.

Appendix 1

ENDEMIC FLORA OF ST HELENA

with David Sayers

Babies' toes, *Hydrodea cryptantha* (Aizoaceae), grow in large numbers, mostly in barren, arid and rocky areas such as Sandy Bay, Stone Cap, Turks Cap and Prosperous Bay Plain. Sometimes these plants can be found right up to the sea's edge. This is a small plant adapted to growing in very dry conditions. It stores water within its tissues, giving the stems and leaves a fleshy appearance. It is a distant relative of the more common creeper. The young plants first appear after the winter rains from May to June. They are bright green in colour, turning yellow with age and finally drying up around November to December as the weather becomes hotter. Small flowers appear around August to September. They are much like those of the ice plant, also a distant relative and very common species of the Crown Wastes. A single plant seldom spreads more than 15in (38cm) in diameter, and only reaches 1–2in (2–5cm) in height. The plant is so succulent that it will not support its own weight, so it spreads across the ground in a compact mass.

There are four main populations in the wild. Like the other dryland endemic species (scrubwoods, salad plant, bone seed and also the indigenous samphire), they have been recovering naturally since the removal of goats from the Crown Wastes and now exist in their thousands. Although there is no immediate threat to the plant, conservation measures include the collection of seed for 'safekeeping' and the distribution of seed to increase the areas already covered by this species.

Bastard gumwood *Commidendrum rotundifolium* This tree is very similar to the gumwood *(Commidendrum robustum)*, but is smaller in height. None of the trees known today are taller than 10ft (3m) and all have weak growth. The leaves are of a mid-green colour and are about 2–3in (50–70mm) in length. Flowering begins in March or April and continues through to May and June. The flowering heads form in clusters between the leaves near to the ends of the branches. They are whitish, turning brown with age.

A single bastard gumwood was known to have grown at Black Field, Longwood in 1868. After the death of this tree, the species was thought to have become extinct. In 1982, however, another single tree was discovered by Stedson Stroud, growing out of a cliff close to Horse Pasture; it was identified by George Benjamin, the resident botany expert on the island. The tree died in August 1986, but not before a cutting and seedlings had been raised at the Endemic Nursery. Only a single cutting of the tree was successful and, although this, too, died, seedlings raised from the tree were successfully planted in Pounceys, representing all that is left of the whole species. The bastard gumwood is extinct in the wild. Today, research is being carried out to determine why attempts to germinate seed and root cuttings have so far failed.

Black cabbage tree *Melanodendron integrifolium* (Compositae) The black cabbage is a spreading tree with a dark trunk permanently moist and usually supporting a dense growth of mosses, lichens and ferns, giving it a dark appearance. Once it grew possibly to 26ft (8m) tall, but present generations are 13ft (4m) at most. The smooth dark green leaves are thick and fleshy and crowded towards the end of the branches, having an appearance similar to cabbages. During October and November, daisy-like flowers about a half-inch (12mm) across are borne in clusters on the ends of the branches, surrounded by the leaves. The seeds germinate well on the tree ferns in the moist habitat of the peaks. As the cabbage tree grows, it is supported by the ferns; although its weight eventually causes the ferns to fall over, both continue to grow, demonstrating their interdependence.

The black cabbage once grew in great abundance amongst the tree-fern thicket, *Dicksonia arborescens* of the island's Central Ridge, and spanned the ridges from the Depot to Green Hill, at altitudes between 2,300 and 2,690ft (700–820m) above sea level. Numbers have declined considerably as a result of clearance of natural vegetation and the invasion of alien plant species, in particular flax. The most common of all cabbage trees, the black cabbage can today be found scattered across Diana's Peak National Park, where there are approximately 800 specimens. Fewer numbers can be found at High Peak, and one or two grow at the Depot. There is an ongoing programme to clear away invasive exotic plants from the Peaks both to encourage natural regeneration and to restock populations with nursery raised seedlings. Cuttings will be used for a seed orchard at High Peak. This will not only allow easy access to the trees but will mean that seed for replanting programmes can be taken without putting pressure on the natural populations. Long-term storage of seed does not appear possible because the seeds remain viable for only a short period of time.

Boneseed, *Osteospermum sanctae-helenae*, is a rough hairy herb with thin straggling stems that creep along the ground and long narrow grey-green leaves. The flowers are yellow, about a half-inch (1.2cm) in diameter and daisy-like. The fruit is star-shaped. The seeds are less than one tenth of an inch (2mm) long, and are hard, angular and sticky due to the short hairs which cover them. It grows in the very dry outer parts of the island between 98 and 656ft (30-200m) above sea level, appearing after the onset of the winter rain in July and August. It grows quickly to produce flowers and then seed before dying back in the summer.

Little is known about the history of this species, which was described as 'not uncommon' by Meliss in 1875, and 'very rare' by Kerr in 1970. Small populations of boneseed can be found around the Sandy Bay area stretching from the road leading to the White Sands by the old lime kiln towards Lot's Wife ponds. Other sightings are recorded in Turk's Cap Valley, near Flagstaff, Frightus, Bencoolen, near Prosperous Bay Plain, the Asses Ears, and South West Cliffs. The plants spread down the slopes, often down small, steep 'guts'. It grows alongside a mixture of native species – babies' toes, french grass, salad plant and samphire – and exotic species, including ice plant, creeper, venus rose and atriplex. Although it appears to be recovering well since goats were removed from the Crown Wastes, it is still classified as endangered.

Boxwood *Melissia begonfolia* The native boxwood, until recently thought to be extinct, once grew on the southeastern side of the island, at Long Range and Stone Top. In early 1999, a single boxwood was found growing among the boulders below Lot's Wife. Although about 400 seeds were collected before the shrub appeared to die, germination has yet to be successful. Nevertheless, half the seeds remain in storage, to be used once successful germinating techniques have been established.

The St Helena boxwood grows to a height of about 8ft (2.5m). The stems of this shrub are crooked and branching, seldom exceeding 2in (5cm) in thickness. In October, pretty white blossoms appear under the leaves and are barely visible without lifting them up. A species of snail *(Succinea)* feeds upon the plant. The dried branches were once used by St Helenians for firewood.

Dogwood *Nesohedyotis arborea* (Rubiacea) The dogwood is a species of the tree-fern thicket and can be found growing at the highest elevations on the island, alongside tree ferns, black cabbage trees, whitewoods and ferns. It is a small, often multi-stemmed,

tree up to 10ft (3m) tall with upright branches and leaves with a down-turned drip-tip. It forms a dense, spreading canopy that is able to catch the mist quite often surrounding the Peaks, which then drips from the leaf tips on to the ground. On the steep slopes of the Peaks, dogwoods are often found, which have partly collapsed. An attached branch continues to grow below it and is easily mistaken for a second individual. The leaves are lance-shaped, smooth and have a glossy green colour. The flower-cluster is found at the tips of the branches and made up of many small bunches of greenish-white flowers measuring only about a tenth of an inch (2–4mm) across. These trees either bear male or female flowers and hence the dogwood is dioecious.

Flowering takes place from December through to March. The fruit is a small dark brown capsule. Like many of the St Helena endemic plants, the dogwood was named for its resemblance to a common European species, in this case the European dogwood, but it is not in any way related to it,.

The dogwood is the second most common tree species left on the Peaks after the black cabbage. Despite this, there are probably less than 150 individuals remaining. Of these Dr. Quentin Cronk has determined that 69 are female, with 17 'undetermined'. The largest populations can be found growing within Diana's Peak National Park, while others are to be found between Coles Rock and Rose Cottage, and at High Peak and the Depot. During the last few years, as many dogwood seeds and cuttings as possible have been collected. Germination rates are high, and the resultant seedlings have been replanted on the Peaks, as part of the park management programme, while rooted cuttings are to be planted out in a seed orchard within Diana's Peak National Park. It is hoped that by growing a representative sample of trees of each species in one place, cross-pollination will be encouraged, thus maximising the future variation of the species. Variation is vitally important to the future survival of the species.

Dwarf jellico *Sium burchellii* The dwarf jellico is an umbelliferous plant which grows to a height of approximately 24in (60cm). It has thick, fleshy, green stems which are hollow, and compound leaves up to 12in (30cm) long. The flower bears 'umbels' of white flowers which produce small green fruit in December. Seeds are fertile and sometimes fall on to the tree ferns, where they germinate freely.

This plant was recorded as being 'very rare' in 1875, but there are scattered populations still growing in the wild at High Peak, the Depot, Diana's Peak and Sandy Bay Ridge overlooking Rose Cottage. Measures have been taken to save this endangered species by collecting seed and cuttings, and some seedlings have already been planted at Diana's Peak to increase population.

Ebony *Trochetiopsis ebenus* (Sterculiaceae) According to historical records, the ebony was once an abundant tree that grew on the southwestern parts of St Helena. Its decline was a result of the introduction of goats around the 16th century. Its former distribution can

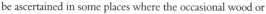

be ascertained in some places where the occasional wood or roots may still be found washed out of the soil by periodic rains. Occasionally, a piece of the once-prized wood, known for its rarity, may still be found washed up on the southwestern shores of the island. The destruction of the ebony was so immense that dead stumps were soon all that remained in some places. These were then used for the burning of lime, which prompted the name 'Lime Kilns' at Sandy Bay. The tree was finally assumed to be extinct by 1850. In November 1980, however, two small bushes were re-discovered by Quentin

Cronk and George Benjamin on the cliff between Lot's Wife and the Asses Ears. Cuttings were successfully rooted and from these over 4,000 plants now thrive on St Helena, at Pounceys, High Peak and Ebony Plain.

Records show that the ebony once grew to a height of up to 15ft (5m), but currently it grows more in the style of a low-spreading shrub, with horizontal stems. The leaves are heart-shaped, longer than broad, with brown hairs on the underside. The flowers are large, 3in (8cm) when open, bell-shaped, white with a dark purple centre and spreading widely from the stem. They appear throughout the year, peaking from June to August. As the flower ages, it turns pink before forming a seed pod.

False gumwood *Commidendrum spurium* The false gumwood was once a common species of moist gumwood woodland, growing at altitudes of about 1,500–2,000ft (500–650m) above sea level. A small tree, growing to a height of 10ft (3m), it has a branching pattern like that of the other gumwood species. The leaves, which are light green and slightly hairy, form clusters at the ends of the branches and are toothed. The flowerhead is densely packed with tiny petals (ray florets) and a yellow-green centre (disc florets). Flowering occurs from December through to March or April.

By 1875 the false gumwood was recorded as 'very rare' by Meliss, and only about ten trees now survive in the wild, in three isolated populations: at Mount Vesey, Coles Rock and on pastureland at Oaklands. The false gumwood appears to have few practical uses, so its rarity is probably due to loss of habitat. Fortunately, the tree does not appear to have reproductive problems – over 2,000 seedlings have been raised to date! These seedlings will be planted out at Mount Vesey and Coles Rock close to existing trees.

Gumwood *Commidendrum robustum* (Compositae) Gumwood woodland once stretched across approximately a third of the island, along the mid-altitude zone from 1,200ft to 1,800ft (400–600m). Like all the original woodland trees, the gumwood, at 26ft (8m), was once much taller than it grows now. It has a branching structure, forking low and producing an umbrella-like canopy. Its gnarled and crooked stems and domed crown makes this a distinctive and picturesque tree, popular for sketching. The leaves are 3–4in (7–10cm) long and vary from grey-green to dark green on the top, with a white cottony appearance below. They are thick and hairy, giving a wrinkled appearance, and are borne in tight whorls. Flowerheads are off-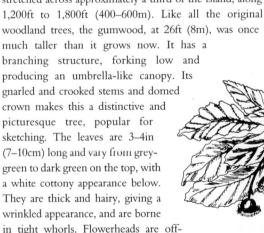white, on a long drooping stalk from the ends of the branches, and are usually borne during winter and spring. Seeds germinate freely to produce a carpet of seedlings under the canopy of the parent plants.

Almost all the original gumwood woods have been destroyed through grazing and collection of firewood. The awkward location of most of the remaining trees, growing close to or actually out of the cliffs, has probably contributed to their survival. In 1991 the Peak Dale gumwoods were attacked by the jacaranda bug, *Orthezia insignis,* which swept through the population, killing hundreds of trees. The jacaranda, which looks a little like a whitefly, is a sucking insect that takes the sap from the tree. A black sooty mould covers the branches, attracted by the honey dew produced by the bugs. Fortunately, a ladybird, *Hyperaspis pantherina,* introduced from Kenya, brought the infestation under control, although it has not been eliminated altogether. The Millennium Gumwood Forest Project was launched to ensure that this tree once again flourishes and covers the island (see page 158). The gumwood was adopted as the national tree of St Helena in 1977.

He cabbage *Pladaroxylon leucadendron* (Compositae) The he cabbage is a small, spreading tree growing to a height of 10–13ft (3–4m) with a characteristic di- or trichotamous branching habit from its bark. The bark is grey-green in colour. The leaves are longer than they are wide and are clustered towards the end of each branch and vary greatly in size, growing up to about 12in (30cm) in length. They are pale green and rougher than those of the black cabbage, and have slightly toothed edges with very prominent veins. The white composite flowers, appearing from June to August, form terminal clusters on the branches, resembling the head of a cauliflower.

The he cabbage was once abundant amongst the cabbage tree woodland, growing alongside whitewoods and she cabbages, but is now considered to be very rare. The few trees which survive today can be found growing at High Peak and within Diana's Peak National Park. There is very little evidence of natural regeneration, although the largest population of 35 individuals does have a mixture of age ranges including young seedlings. Under the National Park Management Plan, he cabbages raised from seed are being planted in several locations across the Peaks.

Large bellflower *Wahlenbergia linifolia* There were once four species of bellflowers endemic to St Helena, of which two are now extinct; of the two that remain, the large bellflower is endangered. The large bellflower has a habit of spreading and can reach a height of about 20in (50cm). It has long narrow leaves up to 2in (50mm) in length that are slightly edged with notched, toothlike projections. The flowers are white, bell-shaped and a little less than an inch (20mm) in diameter. Flowering occurs all year round with the main flowering period in the months of July and August. The bellflowers naturally grow out of the live trunks of tree ferns and cabbage trees, but are also found growing on exposed cliff sites.

At present, the large bellflower can only be found at High Peak, although it once grew commonly amongst the tree ferns of the Peaks. In the mid 1800s Meliss records the large bellflower as being quite common on the Sandy Bay side of the ridges, and even commented on how well the white flowers of the bellflower contrasted with the red flowers of the fuchsia, a species which had escaped from people's gardens after being introduced to the island. Today, instead of large bellflowers growing out from the trunks of the tree ferns and cabbage trees, the fuchsia grows in great profusion and has become a serious weed on the Peaks. The Environmental Conservation Section (ECS) has begun a study of the large bellflower from four cuttings which have been taken from plants in the wild. Eventually, a seed orchard will be established to provide seed and seedlings to restock the populations at High Peak and to reintroduce the bellflower to Diana's Peak National Park.

Large jellico *Sium helenianum* This is a beautiful umbelliferous plant which grows to a height of 6–9ft (2–3m). It has thick, fleshy green stems that are hollow, and spreading compound leaves about 3ft (1m) long with many spike-edged leaves. The flowers are borne at the tops of the plant in a large spreading umbel of many hundreds of small white flowers which produce small green fruit. Flowering usually occurs in December but, depending on weather conditions, it may flower at different periods.

The large jellico can be found in several 'guts' on the Peaks, and is often the dominant vegetation type where it is present. These stalk-like plants most probably once grew abundantly, but have declined due to the invasive growth of flax and bilberry on Diana's Peak and High Peak and along the Central Ridge. The stems of this plant were once eaten raw by the islanders and could be bought at the local market. Areas where large jellico are heavily invaded with alien species are to be cleared in line with the Peaks Management Plan.

Old father live forever *Pelargonium cotyledonis* (Geraniaceae) This plant was given the name of 'old father live forever' by St Helenians because of its ability to stay alive for months without either soil or water. It is related to the garden geranium. This perennial grows up to 12in (30cm) with gnarled, chocolate-brown, fleshy rough-barked, often prostrate stems, and roundish, heart-shaped leaves clustered at the branch tips. It is sometimes difficult to distinguish it from the rock upon which it grows. The plants can be leafless for much of the year. White flowers, up to three-quarters of an inch (2cm) across, first appear after the summer rains, about May or June, when the stems are still leafless. The leaves are light green, rounded and thick, sometimes hairy underneath. The leaves die away so that for much of the year they resemble a knotted mass of old fir tree roots. Old father live forever produces pointed fruit and small seeds which disperse in the wind.

The old father live forever occurs naturally in the dry outer parts of the island, often in the most inaccessible places where little or no other vegetation grows. Other endemic species with which it is associated are the tea plant, plantain, salad plant, scrubwood and the indigenous hair grass. There are a number of patches of old father live forever growing on the rocky cliffs at South West Point, Distant Cottage, Asses Ears, Frightus, Gregory's Battery and Turk's Cap. The plant is regenerating naturally in small, scattered populations and, since the removal of goats from the Crown wastes, numbers appear to be recovering. The ECS monitors the numbers and regeneration of the different populations as part of their rare plant surveys.

Redwood *Trochetiopsis erythroxylon* When the island was first discovered, redwoods were found growing in large numbers in the upland areas below the tree fern thicket. They grew with a straight trunk resulting in a medium-sized tree of about 20ft (6m) tall. Today the redwood only grows to about 10ft (3m). Some trees still grow with a straight trunk but others are considerably dwarfed and misshapen. The leaves are pale green, about 3in (75mm) long and about 2in (50mm) wide. Older leaves quickly turn yellow and speckled and fall to the ground. Although flowers can be produced throughout the year, the main flowering season is in November. They are about 3in (75mm) long and open up to 2in (50mm) in diameter and hang down from the tree. At first they are pure white, turning pink with age, until eventually the dying flower turns a deep red.

The redwood was the most valuable endemic tree to settlers on the island because it produced a fine hard grain timber and the bark of the tree was used for tanning the hides of cattle. Very quickly, nearly all the trees were cut down or stripped of bark, which resulted in near extinction as early at 1718. Since then, redwoods have remained very rare, only being recorded near Diana's Peak and High Peak. By the 20th century, there was a single redwood tree found growing near High Peak, and today the tree is extinct in the wild. In April 1997 the first ever cross-pollinated redwood seedlings were planted out in a seed orchard within Diana's Peak National Park, in an attempt to improve the genetic base of the plant.

Scrubwood *Commidendrum rugosum* (Compositae) The scrubwood is a long-surviving shrub that can tolerate both the semi-desert climate and the saline soils of the Crown Wastes. It is able to capture moisture from the sea mist, enabling it to grow out from the sheer cliffs that surround the island. The leaves that fall under

the protective branched canopy provide a mulch that helps to develop the scrubwood's own pocket of soil. A low-spreading shrub, it grows to about 3ft (1m) in height and is often wider than it is tall. The branches are dark brown in colour and are scattered with leaf scars left after older leaves have fallen. The toothed leaves are somewhat sticky and grow up to 2in (50mm) long in tight rosettes. Large, greenish-yellow, daisy-like flowers, about 1in (25mm) in diameter, are borne at the tips of the branches almost throughout the year. With age they become tinged with red.

In earlier days, scrubwoods would have survived in large numbers throughout the dry outer parts of the island, growing among the ebonies, tea plants, old father live forever, plantain and salad plant. Today only fragments of the larger populations survive, at Distant Cottage, Man and Horse, and Great Stone Top, still growing beside other endemics with the exception of the ebonies. The scrubwood has been the most successful of all endemic plants to recover in numbers. Several populations are naturally regenerating, from Flagstaff to South West Cliffs, and they are also being cultivated at Pouncey's, George Benjamin Arboretum and Scotland.

She cabbage *Lachanodes arborea* The she cabbage is a fast-growing, quickly maturing tree species with a slender, upright habit. Within ten years it can grow up to a height of 24ft (7.5m). It has a single, unbranched stem up to 9ft (3m) tall with very large leaves clustered on the top, much like a cabbage. As the tree ages it begins to branch.

Before 1977, the she cabbage was considered quite rare, or possibly even extinct in the wild. In 1977, however, a group of mature trees was discovered at Osbornes, surviving within a hedge line of thorn trees *(Erythrina caffra)*. Surrounded by pastureland, the trees are growing in grass, along with a number of exotic trees and scrubs, instead of surrounded by other endemics (tree ferns, redwoods and false gumwoods) in a moist rich organic soil. In 1993, 89 individual specimens were recorded at Osbornes, but today only 19 remain, and these are suffering from attack by the Lepidopteran moth larvae. It is not yet clear whether this is the primary cause of death in the trees, as it is possible that they are initially attacked by a fungus or bacteria. While research continues, a seed orchard has been established at Scotland, and it is hoped that healthy seed will be produced from this planting to restock the wild populations and reintroduce seedlings to areas where they have been lost. Cultivated populations can be found at Pounceys, the George Benjamin Arboretum, the Clifford Arboretum, Hardings Spring, Napoleon's Tomb, Taylor's and Mount Pleasant.

Small bellflower: *Wahlenbergia angustifolia* (Campanulaceae) In the mid 1800s, Meliss described the small bellflower as 'quite rare', but today it grows abundantly in many different areas on the island, usually at altitudes of 1,800–2,400ft (600–800m). A small creeping plant, it can be seen growing in rock crevices and along grass verges at the roadside. It is similar to the large bellflower except that it is much more spreading in habit. The narrow leaves are a little less than an inch (25mm) in length and can also be slightly serrated. The small, white, bell-shaped flowers are 4in (10cm) in diameter and can appear almost all year round, although the main flowering months are July to August. The small bellflower can be found growing at Man and Horse Cliffs, Frenches Gut, Peak Dale, Coles Rock, Mount Vesey, Deep Valley, Rock Rose and many other sites around the island. There appear to be no real threats to the survival of this species, although the ECS continues to monitor the situation.

St Helena lobelia *Trimeris scaevolifolia* (Campanulaceae) The St Helena lobelia is a fleshy-stemmed shrub. The conspicuously scarred leaves are about 3in (75mm) long and thin, and both the leaves and the stem are a bright light-green colour. Flowers are white with a yellow centre and are about 4in (10cm) in diameter. They are usually borne in twos, appearing between August and November.

In 1875, there was an abundance of this plant on the Central Ridge from High Peak to Diana's Peak, but numbers have considerably declined and today the lobelia is found only in small scattered patches on the Peaks. Although the species is relatively rare, and seed is collected, there is no recovery programme in place at present.

St Helena lobelia

St Helena olive *Nesiota elliptica* The St Helena olive is a native tree of the tree-fern thicket and cabbage tree woodland, but is now extinct in the wild. It is a fairly large, spreading tree, with dark-coloured, hard and very useful wood. The leaves, 2–3in (50–70mm) in length, are thick, rounded, curling outwards at the edges, hairy underneath and borne in opposite pairs. The flowers are small, less than a half inch (10mm) in diameter, pink and borne in clusters. The main flowering months are June and July, but flowering often continues throughout the year. Seed capsules develop slowly and usually contain three ovules. Today, when fertilisation is successful, only one seed is usually viable. The olive is normally self-incompatible, meaning that pollen from flowers on the same tree is rejected.

In the 1850s there were between 12 and 15 trees growing on the northern side of Diana's Peak, but in 1977, George Benjamin discovered a single plant, possibly the last survivor from the population described by Meliss over a hundred years earlier. The tree he found had collapsed, but was about 16ft (5m) tall with a trunk diameter of about 16in (40cm). It died in 1994. Cuttings were taken to try and propagate it, but only one survived, and from this just three seedlings have been raised. A fungal infestation means that the last surviving tree is dying from the roots up. Research is continuing into the plant, and work to study the incompatibility mechanism will be carried out using money donated by the WWF as part of the endemic plants rescue programme.

St Helena plantain *Plantago robusta* (Plantaginaceae) This plant is related to the ground plantain (*Plantago major*), a common weed on the island) and is considered the largest among plantains. Its size is quite variable, ranging from 6in (15cm) to over 3ft (1m) long. The plant forms a rosette with long, narrow, strap-like leaves up to 16in (40cm) in length. It flowers in July and August. When the flower stalk rises from the centre of the rosette, it resembles a thick rat's tail, clustered with many small, insignificant, green flowers. Small, round fruit are produced containing minute, flat seeds. It grows in the drier parts of the island, mainly in the far southwestern corners, in loose soil, on rocky outcrops and in crevices, and is associated with plants such as the tea plant and scrubwood. With the removal of goats from the Crown Wastes there is no longer any major threat to the plant, but the ECS continues to monitor the species annually.

St Helena rosemary *Phylicia polifolia* The St Helena rosemary resembles the UK herb from where it takes its name. The rosemary forms a straggling or upright herb. The leaves are bright green on the upper part, and have dense white hairs on the lower surface giving a silvery appearance to the underside of the leaves. The flowers appear in the month of

October and they are small, green and inconspicuous. Round green fruit, about the size of a pea, are formed which then turns black when mature. The fruit contains viable seeds.

The St Helena rosemary is one of the island's most endangered plants. It has been recorded growing wild amongst wild mango, scrubwood and *Phlebodium aureum* at Lot, and other bushes grow at High Hill Cliffs amongst the fir trees *(Pinus pinaster)*, gobblegheer, wild coffee, wild carrot, cow grass, bilberry, small bellflower, hair grass and ferns. As part of the WWF funding project, counting is in hand for all sites and cuttings are being taken for a seed orchard at Scotland.

St Helena salad plant *(Hypertelis acida)* The salad plant is a small, low-growing plant, also known as the Longwood samphire. It survives in the hot dry conditions of the coastal zone, and is associated with the scrubwoods, tea plant, creeper, ice plant and wild coffee. Its succulent leaves have a salty acid flavour and have been used in salads. A small, upright, bushy plant, it grows to about 8in (20cm) tall, but can grow up to 3ft (1m) in diameter. The succulent, slightly swollen leaves are about 2in (5cm) long and bluish grey-green in colour. Pure white flowers with yellow centres are borne in groups of two to three at the top of the 3–4in (7–10cm) flower stem. The salad plant flowers in the months of July to September.

There are a few scattered populations of these plants growing on the cliffs from Distant Cottage through Asses Ears, Nags Head to Lot's Wife's Ponds and Great Stone Top and Bencoolen. Although there is no immediate threats to the plants, their habitat, in rocky inaccessible places, makes them vulnerable to natural events like rockfalls and landslides.

St Helena tea plant *Frankenia portulacaefolia* There are no records of this plant ever having been used as a substitute for tea. Possibly its name is derived from its small leaves which, when dry, resemble dried tea. A small-leaved, crooked, wiry-stemmed plant, it is brittle with branching stems. It grows to a height of 3–5ft (1–1.5m). The wood is hard when dried and mahogany in colour. It has tiny round leaves that turn brown when they age and fall to the ground looking like dried tea leaves (hence the local name). Small white flowers often cover the bush and produce minute seeds.

Small populations grow in the wild at The Barn, Gregory's Battery, Turk's Cap and Prosperous Bay, as well as along the cliffs of Man and Horse and Old Joan Point, where they are supported by hair grass and scrubwoods. Like other dry-land species, the plant is regenerating naturally, although the the small size of these isolated populations and the low rate of seed germination poses a threat to their future survival. The ECS continues to monitor all populations as part of the rare-plants survey.

Tree fern *Dicksonia arborescens* The tree fern is very easy to recognise as it is the only fern on the island with a distinct trunk, from the top of which grow fronds, giving a rather palm-like appearance. The trunk, which is covered with hairlike roots, is 6–8in (15–20cm) in diameter and grows 16–20ft (4–6m) in height. The fronds are dark green and over 3ft (1m) long. When young, the plant is hairy and looks like a monkey's tail. Fallen tree-fern trunks can sprout along their length to form new growth.

Tree ferns were once numerous on Diana's Peak, forming a thicket covering St Helena's highest peaks, up to 2,700ft (823m) above sea level. Small pockets and isolated tree ferns can still be seen along the roadside, particular along the ridges of Sandy Bay and Cason's area. Although the plant is not threatened, in 1995 it was estimated that the tree-fern thicket was being lost at a rate of 5½yds (5m) a year, mainly because of the invasion of flax, wild fuchsia and bilberry. A five-year management plan has been put together to clear the invasive plants in order to stop this loss and to help rehabilitate the tree fern thicket growing within the national park.

Whitewood *Petrobium arboretum* (Compositae) This is the smallest of the cabbage trees, growing up to 10–13ft (3–4m). This tree is more upright and less spreading than the black cabbage tree; the leaves are smaller, and are borne in opposite pairs. Each leaf is about 3in (75mm) long, broadly oval in shape and with a slightly serrated edge. The young leaves appear bronze in colour. The flowerheads are borne at the ends of the branches in groups of six to eight, with male and female flowers on different individual trees. The flowers, each about a third of an inch (8mm) across, have a composite structure composed of ten to twelve white florets. Flowering occurs from March to June.

The whitewood is mainly restricted to remaining areas of high-altitude vegetation such as Diana's Peak National Park and High Peak, growing among tree ferns, cabbage trees and dogwoods. A widely scattered species, like the dogwood, it is primarily threatened by the fragmentation and degradation of its original habitat. Specimen trees have also been planted in the George Benjamin Arboretum. Since 1995, whitewood seeds and cuttings have been taken, although seed viability is very low.

Appendix

CONSERVATION ON ST HELENA

There are place names on the island which give a strong indication of the once plentiful forests of which the gumwood was the dominant species: Deadwood, Longwood, Bottom Woods, Levelwood, Woody Ridge, Woody Point, Woodlands, Gumwoods, Half Tree Hollow and Thompson's Wood. Before the attempt at reforestation was undertaken, there were only three ancient gumwoods remaining. They were probably planted sometime in the early 20th century. In the mid 1980s, 65 acres of gumwood trees were successfully reintroduced on Horse Point Plain between Bottom Woods and Bryan's Rock. Additionally, in 1995 and 1998, there were some gumwood plantings undertaken, taking St Helena a step further towards regaining its once widespread gumwood forests.

St Helena boasts at least 40 species of plants unknown anywhere else in the world. Even though there were once many more species, some plants have survived and can still be found on the island. Most of these are found within Diana's Peak National Park. Those who walk on the Peaks will see various species of endemic flora including tree ferns *(Dicksonia arborescens)*, black cabbage tree *(Melanodendrum integrifolium)*, he cabbage tree *(Pladaroxylon leucadendron)* and the she cabbage tree *(Lachanodes arborea)* along with ferns, mosses, grass and other rare endemics. Diana's Peak is also the site of three disappearing species: St Helena olive *(Nesiota eliiptica)*, stringwood *(Acalypha rubra)* and Roxburgh's bellflower *(Wahlenbergia roxburghii)*.

There are 22 endemic species found only on Prosperous Bay Plain, the potential site of the airport/airstrip. Of these, only five are sole members of an endemic genera; the mineral salts present in the earth, gypsum and calcium sulphate, limit the types of species that can grow in the area. The area is dominated by the indigenous shrub *Suaedia fruticosa*, the herbaceous *Atriplex semibaccata*, the mat-forming creeper *Carpobrotus edulis*, the annual endemic *Hydrodea cryptanha*, the endemic *Euphorbia sanctaehelenae* and the indigenous *Portulaca olecea*. The area marked for the airstrip is not protected under any legislation, although the area immediately surrounding the plain is protected under the Forestry Ordinance of 1954.

Although many species of endemic flora have disappeared over the years, the occasional variety of these 'extinct' plants will be found, sometimes quite unexpectedly. The St Helena olive was found in 1977, and the endemic flowering shrub, the St Helena ebony, believed to have been extinct for over a century, was 'rediscovered' in 1980. As recently as 1999 came the rediscovery of the boxwood, *Melissia begonfolia*.

Conservation programmes
Millennium Gumwood Forest
This is a project supported by the St Helena Government to celebrate the Millennium. It involves the planting and reforestation of the gumwood, *Commidendrum robustum*, which is the national tree of St Helena. The project is meant to symbolise growth and life on the island and to convert the wasteland where the planting took place. The area was once part of the Greatwood.

One of the main aims of the project is to support conservation of the endemic gumwood tree. Through many years of felling for timber, fodder and fuel, a very large portion of the forest on the island disappeared. When the forest dwindled, this contributed to some serious soil erosion. Through the planting of these trees, it is expected that the damage which has been done can be stopped and hopefully reversed. Along with the reforestation, it is anticipated that this area can once again support other species of plants, birds and insects. At the beginning of the island's history, it was covered in lush green vegetation. Through this project the intention is to cover the barren brown area with the bright green of the trees, adding some much-needed vegetation to the landscape. The forest is intended to become a recreation and amenity site. There is a gatehouse with a small information centre that stands at the entrance to the forest. Inside are noticeboards providing information about the project and the names of those people who planted a tree or had one planted on their behalf.

The project had purposes other than environmental ones. It was hoped that this would give all the people of St Helena, young and old alike, a chance to participate in something together as a people. The original goal was to have 5,000 trees planted, one for each resident of the island.

People overseas were invited to buy a tree and either plant it themselves, if they were visiting the island, or have someone plant it on their behalf. The project symbolises a local interest in the environment and should show visitors to St Helena that the inhabitants care about the environmental future of their island. It was hoped that the public would get involved not only in the planting of the trees but also in caring for them; happily, people are already returning to look at the progress of their trees and to enjoy the forest.

The project is currently managed by a Steering Committee, consisting of representatives of government departments that have a direct stake in the project. Funding for the project has come from the Foreign and Commonwealth Office Overseas Territories Environment Fund, the (St Helena) Governor's Discretionary Fund, the (UK) Eden Project and donations from other persons and organisations both on the island and overseas.

Once the National Trust is established it is hoped that the management of the Millennium Forest will come under the umbrella of the National Trust.

Endemic plants
In 1997 the UK branch of the Worldwide Fund for Nature (WWF) funded a two-year project to support the recovery of the following five endemic species of flowering plants and to try to prevent their extinction:

Bastard gumwood *Commidendrum rotundifolium* 54 seedlings have been germinated and a seed orchard has been established.

She cabbage *Lachanodes arborea* Seed viability and productivity are low. Two seed orchards have been established. Seven previously unknown species have been discovered in two places. The population is decreasing due to many plants dying, but clones and seedlings are continuing to thrive in seed orchards.

St Helena olive *Nesiota elliptica* It has continued to decline despite all efforts. Only two plants are known to exist.

St Helena rosemary *Phylica polifolia* Attempts were made to get the plant to grow from rooted cuttings but the efforts have repeatedly failed following transplantation. Two seed orchards have been established. Seed production and viability are both good.

Large bellflower *Wahlenbergia linifolia* Cuttings have failed repeatedly. A seed orchard has been established and seed viability is good.

St Helena Nature Conservation Group

In 1993, the St Helena Nature Conservation Group (PO Box 48, St Helena Island STHL 1ZZ, South Atlantic Ocean; tel: 4419; fax: 4978) was established for the purpose of fostering awareness and conservation of flora and fauna both on land and in the water.

The group is primarily involved with trail and path restoration, awareness raising and species conservation work. Work has begun on two projects. The first project is the production of a guide to the trees of Jamestown; the second is a guide to the flora of St Helena.

A litter campaign, managed in collaboration with the St Helena Conservation Group, has been started on St Helena to combat the growing problem of litter. One may think of St Helena as an island in the middle of the ocean with clean air, land and water; unfortunately, this is no longer the case. With the development of tourism, the islanders are working to restore this idyllic image.

The aim of the campaign is to change people's attitudes and encourage them to see the importance of a clean environment. The campaign involves the school children, as well as adults. The litter issue will be brought to everyone's attention through the radio, the newspaper, poster campaigns, teachers including litter/waste themes in their lessons, and a recycling workshop to show how certain items can be re-used.

Environmental centre

Sandy Bay First School, which was closed in August 1987, has now been developed into an Environmental Centre, which was formally opened in February 1998. The goal of the centre is to educate pupils and teachers about the environment and ecology. The centre is open year-round and has displays about the history, geology and natural history of the island. Endemic plants are found in the grounds. The centre is one of the stopping points on organised tours of the island.

Appendix

GIVING SOMETHING BACK

After or during a visit to St Helena, Ascension, or Tristan da Cunha, many people feel the need to give something back in return for the island and the islanders' hospitality. There are several organisations, both on and off the islands, through which those of us who have been captivated by these islands can remain in contact and indeed, give positive help from time to time. If you are keen to give something back to the island which has given you so much pleasure and interest, and you feel you have a personal contribution to make to the organisation described, and would like to learn more about it, the people to contact are listed at the end of the individual descriptions.

As mentioned earlier, donating books that you no longer wish to read or transport back home will help keep the library supplied, as well as offering access to books that the library might otherwise not have been able to get. Visitors may also like to make a small donation to the guides or scouts. These are worthwhile organisations and give young people a lot of opportunities. They always welcome some support. Those planning to stay on the island for a longer period of time, would perhaps consider volunteering some time at one of the schools or the archives. Both of these places are very grateful for help and it adds a new dimension to the visit, making you feel a part of the life on the island, not to mention the good feeling it gives to do something beneficial for the island and her people.

On St Helena

There are numerous opportunities to get involved on St Helena itself:

Millennium Gumwood Forest Project

Planting thousands of gumwood trees on a plain near Horse Point (see page 158). There you have the chance to support one of the endemic species and return a little part of the island to the way it was many, many moons ago. Contact: Millennium Gumwood Forest Project Committee, 1 Main Street, Jamestown, St Helena Island STL 1ZZ; tel/fax: (+290) 2105; email: isabel@sainthelena.gov.sh

Diana's Peak National Park

The island's national park is named after the highest point on the island – Diana's Peak, at 2,700ft. Much of the original vegetation had already been destroyed in the 19th century with the import of plants and animals and made worse by the cultivation of New Zealand flax, whose fibres were used to make linen, exported for clothing until the mid 1960s. In 1995, a project was begun to cut back the flax, in the hope of encouraging the regeneration of the island's 45 endemic species such as the tree fern (which can grow up to 20ft tall), the black cabbage tree, he cabbage tree, she cabbage tree, whitewood and dogwood. Help is always needed in maintaining and upgrading the access paths within the Peaks. For further details, contact: Endemic Section of the Agriculture and Forestry Department St Helena STL 1ZZ; tel: (+290) 4724; fax: (+290) 4603. For other projects currently running or in the planning stages, contact Isabel Peters, Agricultural Environmental Coordinator, Environment Planning and Development Section, 1 Main Street, Jamestown, St Helena STHL 1ZZ; tel/fax: (+290) 2105.

St Helena National Trust
The St Helena National Trust is dedicated to the preservation of the islands' heritage. It is a newly formed organisation which covers a lot of areas like heritage, conservation, art and crafts, etc. Contact: Lynette Bloomfield, St Helena National Trust, St Helena STHL 1ZZ; tel: (+290) 4552; email: STYLES.HOME@helanta.sh.

St James' Church
St James' Church is the oldest Anglican foundation in the southern hemisphere, built on or close to the site of earlier churches dating back to the early 1500s. It has a fascinating history and is still a centre of worship and a focal point for both the town and visitors to the island. Currently, the St James' Church Restoration Action Group is fundraising to undertake a major restoration project – the roof needs replacing as does the plasterwork, designed to protect the walls of locally quarried soft red-stone, which has separated from the stone. The funding of this project estimated to cost £120,000 is far beyond local resources and any assistance from overseas will be appreciated. Contact: Mrs Ivy Ellik, tel/fax: (+290) 4733; email: poppins@helanta.sh. Donations can be sent to The Government Savings Bank Jamestown, St Helena. The account for the St James' Church Restoration Action Group is 20851. Alternatively, donations can be sent directly to St James' Church Restoration Action Group, c/o Fr Fred George, The Vicarage, Jamestown, St Helena STHL

On Ascension Island
On Ascension, there are currently two environmental projects running.

Green Turtle project
The aim of the Green Turtle project is to set up a dedicated natural history and conservation centre in Georgetown which will include a permanent exhibition on the green turtle. Contact: mtn@mtrg.u.net.com(Dr Godley) or RRR.FRAU@atlantis.co.ac (Robert Frauenstein).

Royal Society for the Protection of Birds
This project to restore the seabird colonies to Ascension Island is being managed by the Royal Society for the Protection of Birds. (web:www.rspb.org.uk).

Ascension Island Heritage Society
The society was founded in 1966. It is an entirely voluntary body whose aims are to awaken public concern in, and appreciation of, the geography, history, natural history

and architecture of Ascension Island, and to secure the preservation of features of historic or public interest. The society relies on public donations and small profits from the sale of pamphlets for survival. Contact: Ascension Island Heritage Society, Ascension Island, South Atlantic Ocean ASCN 1ZZ; email: StephenFowler@heritage.org.ac.

Organisations in the UK

The following organisations meet in the United Kingdom. They ensure that people in the outside world can keep close contact with certain aspects of island life. An important point to note here is that all these organisations exist to respond to the islands' requests and needs, and not in any way impose their view or authority on the islands.

The Society of the Friends of St Helena

The Society of the Friends of St Helena comprises people who have had some connection with St Helena, possibly through working on the island or visiting in an advisory capacity, or purely as interested tourists. The Friends meet officially twice a year in order to share news of the island, to listen to a speaker on some topical matter of importance to the island, and to gather with fellow enthusiasts. The Friends are in close touch with the St Helena Heritage Society and, over several years, have been working hard to give support to the appeal to set up a new museum in Jamestown, to help to ensure that the unique history of the island is preserved. The Society has also helped in a number of philanthropic ways by providing much-needed items for the island, eg: books, an invalid chair etc. Members are frequently called upon to give illustrated talks about St Helena to organisations in the UK and abroad. This is very important indeed, in terms of making other people aware of this unique place. The Friends also produce their own publication, *The Wirebird* which is published twice a year. It contains articles, notes and correspondence from people interested in St Helena. Contact: Friends of St Helena, Chair: Mr Mure Smith, 3 Charlecote Mews, Zetland Road, Malvern, Worcs WR14 2JJ; tel: 01684 893258; Secretary: Dr Dorothy Evans, 3 Barns Hay, Old Marston, Oxford OX3 OPN; tel/fax: 01865 24209; email: devans@barnshay.freeserve.co.uk; Editor of *Wirebird*: Dr Alexander Schulenburg, 41 Coneyburrow Road, Tunbridge Wells, Kent TN2 3NB; tel: 01892 531324

The Link Committee

The Link Committee, based at the Cheltenham and Gloucester College of Higher Education, has played a very important role in educational terms for many years. It was formed in the late 1950s as an official body working in conjunction with the St Helena Education Department, the Department for International Development (DFID), the British Council and the Foreign and Commonwealth Office (FCO). The Link has served three major purposes:

- to respond to the educational needs of the island
- to receive island students and teachers into the United Kingdom to enable them to participate in whatever courses, qualifications, school attachments or experiences they need
- on invitation, to visit the island in an advisory capacity, to give in-service training or whatever training/ advice is required.

The members of the Link are principally people who have had some experience on the island in a teaching or advisory capacity, and any Saints who are currently in the UK through the Link are encouraged to join all meetings in order to give firsthand feedback to the Link on the progress of their programme. Contact: Dr Tony Charlton (Chair), Cheltenham and Gloucester College of Higher Education, PO Box 220, The Park Campus, The Park, Cheltenham, Glos GL50 2QF; Mrs Angela Hodgkinson (Secretary), (address as above); tel/fax: 01242 532746; email: AHodgkinson@chelt.ac.uk.

The St Helena Diocesan Association

The St Helena Diocesan Association exists in order to give whatever support is needed to the Anglican Bishop of St Helena and his ministry team on the island. There are also close relationships with people of other Christian denominations on the island such as the Baptists, Salvation Army and Roman Catholics. The Association comprises members, both clergy and lay, who have a particular enthusiasm to maintain their links with the people and the churches and their ministry on the island. There are eleven churches in the Diocese, some very small, in four parishes. The particular task of the Association is to provide help with fares for clergy travelling to and from the island and to find resources and materials from this country and to share news, ideas and prayer. Contact: Reverend Canon Derek Brown (Chair), Christchurch Centre Bungalow, Rowan Road, Havant, Hants PO9 2XA; tel: 02392 481730; Dr Dorothy Evans (Secretary), 3 Barns Hay, Old Marston, Oxford OX3 OPN; tel/fax: 01865 24209; email: devans@barnshay.freeserve.co.uk.

South Atlantic Working Group

The South Atlantic Working Group (SAWG) is a component part of the United Kingdom Overseas Territories Conservation Forum. Its members are all people who have particular skill or experience in environmental matters related to St Helena, Tristan da Cunha, Ascension Island or the Falklands. At each of its meetings, the SAWG receives current environmental news from each of the islands and seeks to respond in terms of giving support, often of a specialist nature, to help the islanders to face the challenges of preserving their unique environmental heritage. The SAWG works in close co-operation with other environmental organisations such as the RSPB and the WWF. Contact: Mr David Taylor (Chair), 53 Lillian Road, Barnes, London SW13 9JF; tel: 0208 7480202; email: Dta2530440@aol.com; Mrs Frances Marks (Secretary), Forum Co-ordinator, 15 Insall Road, Chipping Norton OX7 5LF: tel: 01608 644425; email: fmarks@ukotcf.

Island Commission on Citizenship

The UK Branch of the Island Commission on Citizenship (ICC) was established in 1992 by Bishop John Rushton, the Bishop on St Helena at the time. The commission is confident that their aim will soon be fulfilled, namely that St Helena and its dependencies (Ascension and Tristan da Cunha) will have their full British citizenship restored to them. Contact: Reverend Canon Nicholas Turner (Chair), The Rectory, Broughton, Skipton, N Yorks BD23 3AN; tel: 01282 842332; email: the.wanderer@virgin.net; Mr Jeff Cant (Secretary), 53 Bringewood Rise, Ludlow, Shropshire SY8 2ND; tel: 01584 872105; email: jeff.cant@talk21. com.

St Helena Association

The St Helena Association brings together many St Helenians who now live in the United Kingdom, but who keep a strong link with their relatives and friends on the island, and with each other in the UK. Non-St Helenians are welcomed to their activities, which include sports and dances. Over the years, the Association has given considerable help, financial and otherwise, for specific causes on the island, and to individuals. Contact: Mrs Jenny Pattenden (Chair), 24 Queen's Close, Shipton-under-Wychwood, OX7 6BU; tel. 01993 831421; Mrs Audrey Leo (Secretary), 24 Somerville Road, Poulner, Ringwood, Hants BH24 1XJ; tel/fax: 01425 475254.

Tristan da Cunha Association

The Tristan da Cunha Association has a strong membership, both on and off the island. They maintain an enthusiasm for the island and a desire to keep in touch with the people and their activities, and also respond to any requests. The committee comprises people with firsthand knowledge or experience of Tristan da Cunha. They receive news regularly from the administrator of the island, and the annual general meeting of the Association is always enthusiastically attended by many members. Opportunity is given through firsthand reports, speakers, island videos, and other media to maintain these close links. Contact: Mr Michael Swales (Secretary/Treasurer), Humble Bee Bank, Alton, Stoke-on-Trent ST10 4BT; tel: 01538 703322; Mr John Woolley FRGS (Editor of *TdaC Magazine*), The Garden Flat, 2 Upgang Lane, Whitby, N Yorks YO21 3EA; tel/fax: 01947 604505.

Appendix 4

FURTHER INFORMATION

The majority of the titles listed below and many more can be supplied by **Miles Apart** (Ian Mathieson), 5 Harraton House, Exning, Newmarket, Suffolk CB8 7HF, UK; tel: (+44) 01638 577627; fax: (+44) 01638577874; email: imathieson2000@yahoo.co.uk.

St Helena
History

The first full history of the island was published in 1808 by the then Government Secretary Thomas Brooke as *A History of the Island of St Helena from its Discovery by the Portuguese to the Year 1806*. A second edition, published in 1824, extended the coverage to 1823 and included the period of Napoleon's captivity.

This work remained the standard reference for the next 100 years although some notable additions were produced during the period. The island born governor Hudson Janisch appreciated the value of the government archives and published his *Extracts from the St Helena Records and Chronicles of Cape Commanders* in 1885. A revised second edition was published in 1908 and this was subsequently reprinted by W A Thorpe and Sons in 1981. Melliss' *St Helena* (see under *Natural history* below) also includes a good historical section.

E L Jackson's *St Helena* appeared in 1903 and is described by Day as 'one of the corner stones of St Helena historiography ... although its seven chronological and thematic chapters sometimes lack cohesion'. Its lack of index diminishes its value as a reference but it is an interesting and well-illustrated read.

It took another government secretary, G C Kitching, to really lay the foundations for an updated history of St Helena in the 1930s. His *Handbook and Gazetteer of the Island of St Helena Including a Short History of the Island Under the Crown 1834-1902* was never published although a re-typed version of the 1937 manuscript is still available. Kitching effectively documented the remainder of the 19th century following on from Brooke and provided inspiration and guidance for what remains the standard reference, Philip Gosse's *St Helena 1502-1938,* published in 1938 and re-published with a new introduction by Trevor Hearl in 1990.

Although Dorothy Evans' *Schooling in the South Atlantic 1661-1992*, 1994, and Edward Cannan's *Churches of the South Atlantic 1502-1991,* 1992, provide subject matter histories, the island is in need of an updated history, not only to re-interpret the events of the early years, but also to place on record much of St Helena's 20th-century history. Two amateur historians, Trevor Hearl and Percy Teale, have separately produced material on a range of historical items over the last 20 years which provide a valuable source for the next chronicler of island's history. A geographer, Stephen Royle, has also published extensively on St Helena in scientific journals during the last 15 years.

General descriptions and guides

The earliest general descriptions of St Helena dates from the early 19th century and include *A Description of the Island of St Helena; Containing Observations on its Singular Structure and Formation; An Account of its Climate, Natural History and Inhabitants* published anonymously in 1805, *A Geographical and Historical Account of the Island of St Helena* also published anonymously in 1812 and *A Tour Through the Island of St Helena* by Captain John Barnes published in 1817.

Napoleon's captivity caused a minor publishing boom for about ten years from 1815. Virtually all the works produced during this period were aquatint prints, often by earlier visitors to the island attempting to cash in on the great national interest that was suddenly aroused; the best known are by Bellasis and Pocock (both 1815) and Wathen in 1824. Throughout the 19th century numerous travellers, mainly on their way back from the East, called at St Helena and provided a descriptive chapter on the island supported by a print or two in works otherwise concerned with India and the Orient. One of the earliest of these types of works, and one of the best, was the description in *Viscount George Valentia's Voyages and Travels to India, Ceylon and the Red Sea, Abyssinia and Egypt in 1802-1806*, reprinted in 1994.

The first tourist guide was Benjamin Grant's *A Few Notes on St Helena and Descriptive Guide*, to which is added some remarks on the island as a health resort, published in 1883. This was followed in about 1900 by a *Souvenir of St Helena* by E L Jackson. This guide was taken up, modified and issued in a variety of forms over the next 40 years by E J Warren. A good description of the island was produced in Findlay's *A Sailing Directory for the Ethiopic or South Atlantic Ocean* in 1874 and this maritime descriptive process has been continued to the present in the *Admiralty Pilot for the South Atlantic*. More detailed but informal accounts of the island were produced by Oswald Blakeston in *The Isle of St Helena* in 1957 and by Margaret Stewart Taylor in *Ocean Roadhouse* in 1969. It was not until 1980 that a proper descriptive book of the island was produced by Tony Cross – *St Helena Including Ascension and Tristan da Cunha*. The book formed part of the David and Charles island series. A number of pamphlet-type guides started to appear during the 1980s and 1990s and a detailed guide *Exploring St Helena a Walkers Guide* was produced by Ian Mathieson and Laurence Carter in 1992. Kenneth Bain's 1993 *St Helena the Island, her People and their Ship* was a return to the more informal type of travel account. The first, and to date only, modern style guide is Nick Phillips's *St Helena a Traveller's Handbook* published in 1998, while Lady Field's *History of Plantation House*, 1998, gives a good account of one of the island's main buildings.

The 19th-century sailing boat travellers have been replaced by yachstmen in the 20th century and there are a number of yachting books which have a chapter or two on St Helena. The genre was started by one of the best known, Joshua Slocum, whose *Sailing Alone Around the World* was published in 1900 and included details of a talk given by him on the island. Other writer-travellers passing through have included Gavin Young (*Slow Boats Home,* 1985) and Simon Winchester (*Outposts,* 1985). Also of interest are the works of South African travel writer Lawrence Green who managed to weave references to St

Helena or Tristan into virtually all his 33 books. The best of his island work is collected in *Islands Time Forgot*, 1962.

Insights into current island life are provided by several government publications notably the *Annual Statistical Review*.

Natural history

The first descriptions of St Helena's flora were provided by the early navigators such as Linschoten and Cavendish. Accounts by these authors are commercially available in reprinted form but as part of much larger works.

During the 19th century the awareness of St Helena's unique flora and fauna gradually increased. Early writings included observations by Joseph Banks, the naturalist on Cook's first voyage, William Burchell and Alexander Beatson's *Tracts Relative to the Island of St Helena* (1816) which was essentially an account of the introduction of new agricultural methods to the island but also covered much about the island's natural history including William Roxburgh's listing of plants.

In 1875 John Charles Melliss published *St Helena, a Physical, Historical and Topographical Description of the Island* (Reeve, London). This probably remains the single most important book about St Helena. The island's history is briefly dealt with before the unique flora and fauna is covered in great detail supported by a dazzling array of colour prints. The book has remained a standard reference work for over 100 years and has only been superseded by the joint publication in 2000 of *St Helena and Ascension Island: A Natural History* by Philip and Myrtle Ashmole and Quentin Cronk's *The Endemic Flora of St Helena*. Both these books were published by Anthony Nelson of Oswestry who has faithfully produced small print runs of books on St Helena over the last 15 years.

Prior to the production of the Ashmoles' more general description, detailed accounts of fish and birds were produced by Alasdair Edwards in *Fish and Fisheries of Saint Helena Island*, 1990 and *The Birds of St Helena* by Beau Rowlands et al in 1998. Both these books range well beyond the subject prescribed by their titles. Barry Weaver's *Guide to the Geology of St Helena*, 1990, gives a good account of the latest thinking about the formation of St Helena. A scholarly overview of the influence of St Helena's experience on the development of environmental thinking is provided by Richard Grove in *Green Imperialism: Colonial Expansion, Tropical Island Edens and the Origins of Environmentalism 1600-1860*, 1995.

Scientific expeditions

St Helena has been visited by numerous scientific expeditions and the majority of these have left descriptions and illustrations in works principally devoted to other subjects. Halley, Maskelyne, Cook (and Forster), Bligh, J C Ross, Darwin and Hooker are probably the big names with publications generally still in print in some form or other. Two 20th-century Antarctic expeditions include quite detailed accounts of St Helena – the Scottish National Antarctic Expedition and the Quest expedition which visited, after its leader Shackleton had died on South Georgia. Compared to Tristan however St Helena has always attracted much less scientific attention.

Longer stays and more detailed accounts are provided by some of the less well-known expeditions such as Prior's *Voyage Along the Eastern Coast of Africa to Mocambique,*

Johanna and Quiloa to St Helena (1819) and Webster's *Narrative of a Voyage to the South Atlantic Ocean in the Years 1828, 29, 30 performed in H M Sloop Chanticleer* which was reprinted in 1970.

Napoleon

The literature examining Napoleon's captivity on St Helena is vast. Many of the works contain good incidental descriptions and illustrations of the island but the majority are derived from principal works written by eyewitnesses. Of the contemporary accounts Barry O'Meara's *Napoleon in Exile* published in various editions between 1822 and 1880 is probably the most enjoyable. Gilbert Martineau's *Napoleon's St Helena,* 1968 and *Napoleon's Last Journey,* 1976 are still easily available and provide good introductions to the facts if a somewhat out of date interpretation. Arnold Chaplin's *St Helena Who's Who,* 1918 describes both major and minor players in the Napoleonic drama and Mabel Brookes provides a very readable account in *St Helena Story,* 1960. The whole approach to the study of Napoleon on St Helena has been radically altered by the very recent general acceptance that Napoleon was poisoned by a combination of arsenic and camomile. Two books are central to understanding this – S Forshufvud's *Who Killed Napoleon?* 1962 and B Weider and S Forshufvud's *Assassination at St Helena Revisited,* 1995. A recent account by a former Lebanese hostage John-Paul Kaufmann *The Black Room at Longwood: Napoleon's Exile on St Helena,* 1999 provides an interesting perspective on the mind of a captive. A children's book *My Napoleon,* 1997, by Catherine Brighton focuses on Napoleon's life on St Helena.

Fiction

St Helena has hardly featured in fiction at all. What exists is mainly concerned with the period of Napoleon's captivity and none of it can be particularly recommended. Probably the only mainstream author to have written a novel in which St Helena plays a prominent part is Thomas Pynchon in his 1997 *Mason and Dixon.* Duncan Watt wrote a South Atlantic Trilogy for children, the central book of which *Skulduggery in the South Atlantic,* 1995, is set on St Helena. Short stories have been produced by Bobby Robertson in *The Stowaways and Other Stories from St Helena,* 1996, and *Seasoned Tales* by Geoffrey Stamp, 1993.

Picture books

St Helena has a particularly rich inheritance of 19th century prints which has yet to be formally studied (see above under General Descriptions). Robin Castell's *St Helena Illustrated,* 1998 provides a glimpse of what has been produced. His earlier book *St Helena,* 1979 is still available and provides illustrations of many island homes – a more authoritative and well illustrated account of the island's architecture is provided by Hugh Crallan's *Island of St Helena: Listing and Preservation of Buildings of Architectural and Historic Interest,* 1997, although this is in report format.

H and A Schulenburg's *St Helena South Atlantic Ocean,* 1997, provides a large range of black and white photographs mainly of architecture and natural heritage but a long term favourite remains the inexpensive *Doctors Thoughts on St Helena* by S Wooltorton (1988) which provides good colour photos with a medical text.

Philately and coins

The first publication on St Helena's stamps was a booklet produced by Fred Melville in 1912. This is still sought after by collectors but the definitive work is Edward Hibbert's *St Helena Postal History and Stamps*, 1979. In 1985 Bernard Mabbett produced *St Helena, the Philately of the Camps for the Boer Prisoners of War 1900-1902* and in 1988 Stanley Gibbons published the *St Helena and Dependencies: Commonwealth Two Reign Stamp Catalogue*.

The only publication dealing with coins is David Vice's *The Coinage of British West Africa and St Helena 1684-1958*. Although this was published in 1983 the book is still available.

Maps and videos

The 1990 Ordnance Survey map in colour at 1:25,000 known as 'the tourist map' is the best map for visitors. The island is also fully covered at 1:10,000 and in parts at 1:2,500. A smaller map at 1:125,000 provides a nice image on an A4 sheet. In addition to Ordnance Survey publications there are charts published at various scales by both the English and French Admiralties.

A number of films have been produced about St Helena over the last 30 years but only two videos are commercially available (apart from a video drama about Napoleon's captivity). Charles and Julia Frater's *Saint Helena South Atlantic Ocean*, 1992, and *Island of Saint Helena*, 1962, is available as a single tape while Darrin Henry's *St Helena Island*, 1997, provides an islander's view of his home.

Bibliographies

Readers requiring a more detailed survey of St Helena literature should consult Alan Day's *St Helena, Ascension and Tristan da Cunha* 1997, Volume 197 in the World Bibliographical series.

Websites

Due to the nature of the internet, some of the addresses below may not be active by the time you try them or the content may change considerably. On the other hand many new sites are put on the net every day. If you look for information not found on these pages, check out the links on a working website or try a search engine.

Tourism

www.sthelenatourism.com This is the official homepage of the St Helena Tourist Office. It contains many helpful tips and a slide presentation. This is certainly a good starting point for anyone wanting to visit the island

www.rms-st-helena.com This website concerns the *RMS St Helena*, the link from the island to the outside world.

www-sthelena2002.com All about the planned celebrations for the 2002 quincentenary of the island's discovery.

www.sthelena.se This was one of the first websites set up about St Helena. It was established by two gentlemen from Sweden who are ham radio operators. The site is very informative, as they have visited the island twice and have some very nice photographs posted. There is information about the flora and fauna and a section about stamps. There are links to some helpful sites and there is even a mailing list for those wanting to discuss St Helena with others sharing the same interest.

Government/news/research

www.sainthelena.gov.sh This is the official homepage of the St Helena Government.
www.shda.helanta.sh The St Helena Development Agency was established in 1995 and is a quasi-autonomous non-governmental organisation that promotes and facilitates commercial development on the Island of St Helena. It has information about ongoing projects which they are helping to sponsor. This site includes business listings, information about politics, demography, as well as other items associated with the SHDA.
www.news.co.sh This is the website of the island's newspaper, the *St Helena Herald* which is published once a week. There are also daily news items posted and summaries of the local news which is broadcast on Radio St Helena.
www.shlcatalogue.net A news and services promotional site based in the UK. It is recommended for reading about current headline issues on St Helena.
www.fosh.org.uk/ The Society of Friends of St Helena aims to promote public education about the island of St Helena, including its history, culture and environment, and also to support practical projects of benefit to the Islanders.
www.st-helena.org This is the home page of the St Helena Institute. There one can find plenty of background information about various aspects of St Helena. There is a section for those working on their family history, and links to other informative sites. It includes a small online book shop, a historiography and a bibliography
www.telepath.com/bweaver/sh-lib.htm The purpose of this site is to provide electronic versions of literature related to St. Helena and also maps and views of St Helena. The emphasis is on the older, more scarce, St. Helena material (books published prior to 1900; maps and views published prior to 1800).

General

www.sthelenaonline.com This is a central port site which has been set up. It will point visitors to everything and anything on the Internet having to do with St Helena.
www.st-helena-island.net This website contains a comprehensive directory with subject areas of interest listed by category.
www.moors-clingham.net/SHBC_Homepage.htm This site relates the story of the fight of the Saints to regain British citizenship and to have the mistake of 1981 rectified. It begins when Lord Iveagh was preparing in early 1997 to steer the British Nationality (St Helena) Bill through the House of Lords. Under the 'News' section, there are updates on the current status on the return of British citizenship.
geowww.ou.edu/~bweaver/Ascension/sh.htm This is a privately owned website with informative sections on St Helena, Ascension and Tristan da Cunha. Useful for background information.
www.atlanticislands.org This is the official home page of the St Helena, Ascension, and Tristan da Cunha Philatelic Society.
www.thegovoernorscup.com The Governor's Cup Yacht Race is held every two years from Cape Town to St Helena and is one of the most unusual and 'newest' races in the international yachting calendar.

www.noonsite.com/countries This site gives all the necessary information for the skipper of a yacht calling at St Helena, Ascension or Tristan da Cunha.

www.scouts.st-helena-island.net This is the homepage of the 1st Jamestown Scout Group.

www.south-atlantic.net Free website hosting for residents of St Helena, Ascension and Tristan da Cunha as well as individuals and non-profit-organisations dedicating websites to these islands.

www.nic.sh/ This is where you can get your own .sh domain name.

Education

www.chelt.ac.uk/ess/st-helena/ This is the Cheltenham and Gloucester College of Higher Education, where some St Helena students attend. It gives good background information on St Helena, the education system, the island's environment, and photographs of various views of St Helena.

www.princeandrew.edu.sh This is the homepage of the only secondary school on St Helena.

Businesses

www.cams-stores.sh This is one of the few sites hosted by a local business on St Helena. Among its varied contents, you can find news about some current events (for example, the airport project and the citizenship issue), local recipes, and shipping news. They also offer online shopping for people wishing to purchase St Helena coffee and island souvenirs.

www.helanta.sh This is the official website of Cable and Wireless on St Helena. Here you can find an online telephone, fax and email directory. It lists by no means all the fax and email addresses, but it is a good place to find contact information for government offices.

wellington-house.st-helena-island.net This is the homepage of the Wellington House Hotel in Jamestown. There is some background information about the hotel as well as a current list of services and tariffs.

www.thorpes.sh This is a local company on St Helena which imports and sells groceries and hardware for sale to both retail and wholesale customers. There is a list of their products on their website.

www.st-helena-coffee.sh The Island of St Helena Coffee Company was founded in 1994. The St Helena coffee is unique, as it is not just a pure arabica coffee, but a single type of arabica bean known as Green Tipped Bourbon arabica. Due to the small harvest of this bean, it is a rarely found coffee. There is a link for secure ordering on the site.

www.richard-james.co.uk One of the largest freight-forwarding agents. They have been dealing with St Helena for many years and in the last ten years have expanded their services to include Ascension and the Falklands.

www.capricorn-video.com A privately owned website promoting the Island of St Helena. Souvenir videos of the islands of St Helena and Ascension are available for order online.

www.aws-co.uk Homepage from Andrew Weir Shipping, the current passenger and freight agents for the *RMS St Helena*.

www.shelco.sh The website of the St Helena company, who have submitted the current proposal to build an airstrip and tourist facilities on the island.

Ascension
History
Bartlett, L S *Ascension Island, 1960s*. 44pp. Author was the resident magistrate on Ascension Island from 1934 to 1936.

Keilor, John *Memories of Ascension 1929–1931*, Miles Apart, 1997. 42pp, 16 photos. Two years on Ascension by Cable & Wireless Telegraph Officer.

General descriptions and guides
Hart-Davis, Duff *Ascension: The Story of a South Atlantic Island*, 1972.

Ascension Today: An Islander Souvenir Guide, The Islander, 1996. A locally produced and sold guide with helpful information for the first-time visitor.

MacFall, Neil *Ascension Island Walks* Ascension Island Heritage Society, 1998.

Describing the Ascension Island Letterbox Walks with every walk ranked according to difficulty, giving the hiker a good idea of what to expect. Includes maps for every walk.

Natural history
Ashmole, Philip & Myrtle *St Helena and Ascension: A Natural History*, Nelson, 2000. 478pp. Compares the development of flora and fauna on the two islands. Great detail with photos, maps, diagrams and line drawings.

Huxley, R C *Ascension Island and Turtles: A Monograph*, Ascension Heritage Society, 1997. Contains new material from government archives.

Packer, J E and L *Contributions Towards A Flora of Ascension Island*, 1997. 67pp, ringbound with illustrations. Contains plant history and description with checklist.

Fiction
Stamp, G *Seasoned Tales*, 1993. 153pp. Short stories from Ascension Island and St Helena.

Philately and coins
Attwood, J H *Ascension: The Stamps and Postal History*, 1981, 71pp, illustrated.

Maps and videos
Map, 1:25000, single sheet, Edition 4, OS 1992, colour, 84 x 87 cm

A3 poster, *Ascension Island: What's So Special?* RSPB, 1997. Colour front with map and photos. B&w reverse with natural and historical information.

Video *Ascension Island*, Henry, D and Fowler S, 1995. Approximately 3 hours, includes 'Living on the Rock' and 1½ hours on history and natural history.

Websites
Tourism/government/news
www.aiwsa.co.ac Want to visit Ascension? Find out what to do here and book your accommodation online.

www.ascension-island.gov.ac This site gives a lot of information about Ascension Island: tips and information for visitors, about the administrator, the savings bank, police station and the post office (including Ascension Island postage stamps). It is very informative and has links to many local sites.

www.the-islander.org.ac This is the online version of the weekly Ascension newspaper, the *Islander*.

Fauna

www.seaturtle.org/mtrg This is the homepage of the Marine Turtle Research Group (MTRG) – a group of professional scientists and student volunteers dedicated to undertaking fundamental and applied research on marine turtles worldwide. The major aims of this project include assessing the current size of the Ascension Island green turtle population, the reproductive output of individual turtles, the sex ratio of hatchlings and identification of the feeding grounds of the turtles through the use of satellite transmitters.

www.turtles.org/atlgrnd.htm This site is devoted to the green turtle, which come to Ascension's shores each year to breed.

www.turtle.ky/scientific/ascension-island.htm This site contains information from the scientific papers of the green sea turtle nesting 1973–74.

www.users.zetnet.co.ok/johnfirth/ascension.html Here is a webpage by bird enthusiast John Firth about the birds of Ascension Island.

General

www.heritage.org.ac This is the official website of the Ascension Island Historical Society. It gives superb historical information broken down into several categories.

www.cwhistory.com/history/html/Ascension.html A website detailing the history of Cable and Wireless on Ascension and the history of the island in general. It displays several excellent photographs.

freepages.genealogy.rootsweb.com/%7Eagene/aschome.html This is a website containing many photographs of life on the island in the 1960s, created by ex-Ascensionite Mike Simpson

www.ascension-island.gov.ac/postoffice.htm This is the webpage of the Ascension Island post office. There is a link to the Philatelic Bureau where stamps, maps, postcards, coinage and paper currency from St Helena and Ascension Island can be ordered online.

eclipse.span.ch/live.htm Olivier Staiger is an astronomer and visited Ascension Island April 19–25 1998 to witness and report on the double occultation of Jupiter and Venus by the moon (a very rare event). He has documented his stay and created a very readable and interesting diary of his visit.

www.uksmg.org/ascension-1.htm Here is an excellent, information and photo-packed site by radio amateur Chris Gare chronicling his visit to the island in November 2000. It is highly recommended for anyone interested in the island.

www.atlantis.co.ac Cable and Wireless is the domestic and international telecommunications provider on Ascension Island. Ascension Island and St Helena phonecards are available for viewing and/or purchase online.

www.ais.co.ac/school/ Two Boats School is run by Ascension Island Services. It is the only school on Ascension Island and caters for all children on the island between the ages of 5 and 15.

www.scouts.org.ac This is the homepage of the 1st Ascension Island Scout Group.

www.the-islander.org.ac/webcam This site offers a live view of the Pierhead,

Georgetown. See real-time views of the weather, sea, fishermen, diving expeditions, ships and boats at anchor.

www.wunderground.com/global/stations/61902.html If you are interested in the current weather on Ascension Island, this is the website to view. It gives the current conditions at Wideawake field as well as the weather prediction for the next two days. It is partly in the Swiss German language, but not too difficult to figure out what is meant because there are illustrations along with the forecast. Temperatures are given in Celsius as well as Fahrenheit.

www.nic.ac This is the site to visit to obtain your own .ac domain name.

Tristan da Cunha
History
Mackay, Margaret *Angry Island: The Story of Tristan da Cunha* (1506–1963), 1963. 288pp, illustrated.

General
Barrow, K M *Three Years in Tristan da Cunha*, 1910. 280pp, illustrated.

Booy, D M *Rock of Exile – A Narrative of Tristan da Cunha*, London 1957, 196pp. Regarded by many as the most sensitive account of the island community.

Carmichael, Capt D *Description of the Island of Tristan da Cunha*, 1817

Crawford, Allan *Penguin, Potatoes and Postage Stamps*, Nelson, 2000. A personal chronical of a lifetime's involvement with the stamps, history and people of Tristan da Cunha.

Crawford, Allan *Tristan da Cunha and the Roaring Forties*, Edinburgh 1982, 256pp, fully illustrated. The standard account by the doyen of Tristan writers.

Falk Ronne, A *Back to Tristan*, 1967. 153pp. The story of the re-settlement of the island after the volcanic eruption of 1961.

Helyer, Patrick and Swales, Michael *Bibliography of Tristan da Cunha*, Nelson 1998. Entries on every avaialble topic, sourcing over 1,500 books, articles, films, etc.

Lajolo, Anna and Lombardi, Guido *Tristan da Cunha, the legendary island/L'isola leggendaria*, Genoa 1999, with parallel text in Italian and English. Outstandingly illustrated.

Munch, Peter *Crisis in Utopia*, 1971. 324pp, 28 photos. Effects of the evacuation on the community.

Natural history
Van Ryssen W, *The Birds of the Tristan da Cunha Group and Gough Island*, Capetown University, 1976, 31pp, illustrated, A5 card covers

Scientific expeditions
Denstone Expedition to Tristan da Cunha, Denstone College, 1993. 32pp, illustrated. Account of the 1993 expedition

Fiction
Harris, Zinnie *Further than the Furthest Thing*, Faber, 2000. A play about the 1961 eruption performed in London during 2000.

Watt, Duncan *Trouble on Tristan*, Tynron, 1991. 216pp, illustrated. Fictional adventure for children based on Inaccessible and the RMS.

Philately

Crabb, George *The History and Postal History of Tristan da Cunha*, 1980. 347pp, illustrated. Vast detail.

Maps and videos

Map, 1:30,000, Edition 1, OS 1971. Update of 1962 edition, black and white, 60 x 61cm
Video *Tristan da Cunha: The Island at the Top of the World*, Lombardi G & Lajolo A, 1992 Approximately 45 minutes. A film of unique charm.
Video, Allan Crawford's *Tristan da Cunha*, Frater C, 2001. Tristan in another age filmed mainly during the war with Crawford's later commentary added. Unique footage of island life. 80 minutes.

Websites
General

website.lineone.net/~sthelena/tristaninfo.htm This is the official website of the administrator of Tristan da Cunha. It gives a lot of useful information about the formalities of visiting the island as well as providing potential visitors with practical information before they go.

www.sartma.com Here you can find links to headlines from the island's newspaper, the *Tristan Times*.

home.ican.net/~noe/views_of_tristan.htm This website contains some very nice pictures of the island. The site was created by a small group studying the incidence of asthma on Tristan da Cunha. There is some general information about the island as well as a report about the inheritance of the gene that causes asthma.

website.lineone.net/~sthelena/tristan.htm This is the Tristan da Cunha information section from the St Helena Institute's website.

www.sthelena.se/tristan/tdca.htm This is a link to the Tristan da Cunha Association of England. It contains information about the annual general meeting in the UK, as well as the contact address for the editor of the newsletter.

MEASUREMENTS AND CONVERSIONS

To convert	Multiply by
Inches to centimetres	2.54
Centimetres to inches	0.3937
Feet to metres	0.3048
Metres to feet	3.281
Yards to metres	0.9144
Metres to yards	1.094
Miles to kilometres	1.609
Kilometres to miles	0.6214
Acres to hectares	0.4047
Hectares to acres	2.471
Imperial gallons to litres	4.546
Litres to imperial gallons	0.22
US gallons to litres	3.785
Litres to US gallons	0.264
Ounces to grams	28.35
Grams to ounces	0.03527
Pounds to grams	453.6
Grams to pounds	0.002205
Pounds to kilograms	0.4536
Kilograms to pounds	2.205
British tons to kilograms	1016.0
Kilograms to British tons	0.0009812
US tons to kilograms	907.0
Kilograms to US tons	0.000907

5 imperial gallons are equal to 6 US gallons
A British ton is 2,240 lbs. A US ton is 2,000 lbs.

Temperature conversion table
The bold figures in the central columns can be read as either centigrade or fahrenheit.

°C		°F	°C		°F
−18	0	32	10	50	122
−15	5	41	13	55	131
−12	10	50	16	60	140
−9	15	59	18	65	149
−7	20	68	21	70	158
−4	25	77	24	75	167
−1	30	86	27	80	176
2	35	95	32	90	194
4	40	104	38	100	212
7	45	113	40	104	219

NOTES

Index

Page references in bold indicate main entries; those in italics indicate maps
ASC = Ascension; TdC = Tristan da Cunha